Music in American Life

A list of volumes in the series Music in American Life
appears at the end of this book.

THAT
HALF-BARBARIC
TWANG

THAT
HALF-BARBARIC
TWANG

The Banjo in American Popular Culture

K A R E N   L I N N

UNIVERSITY OF ILLINOIS PRESS
Urbana and Chicago

Illini Books edition, 1994
© 1991 by the Board of Trustees of the University of Illinois
Manufactured in the United States of America
P 5 4 3 2 1

This book is printed on acid-free paper.

Library of Congress Cataloging-in-Publication Data

Linn, Karen, 1957–
That half-barbaric twang : the banjo in American popular culture /
Karen Linn.
    p.   cm. — (Music in American life)
    Includes bibliographical references and index.
    ISBN 0-252-06433-X (alk. paper)
    1. Banjo. 2. Musical instruments—United States. 3. Popular
music—United States—History and criticism. 4. Popular culture.
I. Title. II. Series.
ML1015.B3L5   1991
787.8'80973—dc20   90-44638
                                                   CIP
                                                     MN

Previously published in a cloth edition
by the University of Illinois Press: ISBN 0-252-01780-3.

On the other hand, the banjo has a
positive musical charm in the country.
Here we can see that it fits the
surroundings. Its half barbaric twang
is in harmony with the unmechanical
melodies of the birds.

— *Philadelphia Music and
Drama*, 1891

Contents

Preface

THIS IS AN INTERPRETATION of the changing and conflicting images of a musical instrument as found in the national, commercial culture of the United States. A musical instrument is more than wood, wires, and glue; the essence of the object lies in the meanings the culture has assigned to it. In this study I neither chart chronologies, nor search for musicological laws, nor see as my goal the presentation of collected data. Rather, I view the data of instrument construction, decoration, and performance practices here as signs whose interpretation depends upon an understanding of the changing life of these signs within American culture.

The cultural context for this study is a difficult one: American popular culture. I use "popular culture," certainly a problematic concept, to indicate shared behaviors and understandings that exist beyond the local level, often at the national level, and shared messages that are usually transmitted through commercial or official institutions (such as the popular music industry or school systems). Partially, I use "popular culture" to emphasize that this is not a folk music study. Because of the prevalent idea of the banjo in the late twentieth century, many people assume that any study of the banjo is a study of folk music. Regional and non-commercial traditions are studied here only when they intersect with the national popular culture.

The most difficult aspect of this cultural context—American popular culture—is diversity. When dealing with a pluralistic industrialized society, questions about power relations become central to the discussion. As a result, I try throughout to return to issues of race, class, gender, and region in the attempt to avoid misleading depictions of uniformity within American popular culture. Additionally, these relations create meaning for the musical occasion: for example, we cannot understand the late nineteenth-century banjo fad among the Northern white bourgeoisie without acknowledging that they recognized the banjo as a Southern black instrument. Musical meaning occurred within this curious framework of metaphorical power relations. Given the diversity of American culture, a consensus could not form about the meaning of the banjo; each idea of the banjo that I explore stands separate yet implicitly linked to the other ideas of the banjo.

The following four chapters do not progress in a neat chronology; they overlap and intertwine, each presenting a different, and ultimately unresolvable, idea of the banjo. I have concentrated on the 1880s to the middle of the twentieth century because in that span the idea of the banjo was most contested, and it is the working out of these various challenges that interests me most. This explains why I place "The Southern Black Banjo" after the chapter on "The Elevation of the Banjo": I wanted to present the ideas surrounding the Southern Black Banjo as an ideological construct that could be challenged, rather than as an inevitable idea that would simply be accepted. Furthermore, the time frame of chapter 2 extends into the mid-twentieth century, well beyond the turn-of-the-century ending for chapter 1.

I have benefitted from the help and encouragement of many people and institutions. I first thank both Jeff Todd Titon and Archie Green for their always-perceptive comments on my various drafts and their genuine enthusiasm for the topic.

I am thankful to the Smithsonian Institution's Fellowship program; the financial support, access to the collections and archives, and the help, advice, and intellectual interactions with the staff and Fellows of the American History Museum have all been very important to my work. I am especially grateful to John Hasse, curator in the Division of Musical History.

During my fieldwork in the summer of 1985, I was graciously received and aided by Andy Cahan and by Kip Lornell of the Blue Ridge Institute and I am indebted to Elias Kaufman and the members of the American Banjo Fraternity for generously sharing their knowledge and allowing access to personal collections. I thank David Reed and Rebecca Zurier, who, in the course of doing their own research, kept me in mind and found important illustrations and articles for me. Joe Hickerson of the Library of Congress Archive of Folk Culture deserves a special thanks. Ellen Cooke's equestrian advice was helpful, as were my discussions about authenticity with Christine Hoepfner. I gratefully received comments on parts or all of the manuscript from the following people: James Baker, Judith McCulloh, Ron Radano, Neil Rosenberg, Wayne Shirley, Nina Silber, Susan Smulyan, and Julie Weiss. I owe a special thanks to Charles McGovern, for his careful reading of drafts, his banjo discoveries in the Ayer Collection and the *Saturday Evening Post*, and, most important, for giving me the confidence to be more bold in my writing. I thank Dick Gilman for giving me my first banjo lesson — in a way, this is all his fault. Finally, I thank Nick Femia for his support, companionship, and proof-reading skills.

THAT
HALF-BARBARIC
TWANG

Introduction:
The Banjo before the Civil War

The instrument proper to them is the Banjar, which
they brought hither from Africa
— Thomas Jefferson,
Notes on the State of Virginia

THE NORTH AMERICAN BANJO developed from an African
prototype.[1] The early banjo was made from a gourd with a slice
taken out of it and then covered with a skin head, fitted with a
neck, and strung with several strings (often four). Evidence
supports the theory that the short thumb string was of African
(or at least African-American) origin. Dena Epstein, in the
many accounts that she found from Africa, the North American continent, and the West Indies, discovered that the banjo
carried many names; by far, most names related linguistically to
"banjo" ("banza," "banjil," "banjer," "banshaw," etc.). These
early reports by European and Euro-American observers always
acknowledged the banjo as an African instrument.
Although most early accounts of the banjo include a description of the
instrument, after about 1810, authors generally gave their readers no description,
"as if it were too well known to require detailed reports."[2] Robert Winans, in
his survey of eighteenth-century runaway slave advertisements,[3] finds that,
even in that century, the banjo was rarely described. Presumably, the white
population already knew the instrument well and the banjo no longer needed
explanation. Winans's research also suggests a regional tradition for the banjo
in the eighteenth century among African Americans living in the Chesapeake
Bay area. By the early nineteenth century the tradition had spread. Out in

western Kentucky in the early 1820s, composer Anthony Philip Heinrich listened to black banjo players, composed a piano piece entitled "The Banjo" (some thirty years before Gottschalk's piece of the same name), and used a cover illustration of an African-American man with a gourd banjo for one of his compositions.[4]

Before the American Revolution, white actors with burnt cork smeared on their faces created black stage characters for the popular entertainment of other white Americans.[5] By the late 1820s, blackface acts had become a popular part of circuses and as a skit presented between the acts of plays. In the 1830s, some performers, most notably Joel Walker Sweeney (who claimed to have learned to play from a black slave in Virginia),[6] used a banjo in their blackface act. By the early 1800s, Americans had become familiar with the idea—though not necessarily with the reality—of the banjo as an instrument of black culture, and so it seemed a natural addition to the "Ethiopian Delineator's" bag of tricks. The banjo, as an African instrument for an early nineteenth-century audience, bestowed authenticity upon the cork-faced musician, even in its new form: a wooden hoop to replace the gourd and a standardized five-string setup. A comparison of American and European banjos of the 1840s shows that the banjo had achieved a stable artifactual tradition in the United States but not in Europe.[7] With its African percussiveness and short sustain on stopped strings, the banjo was ill suited for the slow legato melodies of much European music, and so seemed, by European aesthetic standards, to be emotionally limited and incapable of musical profundity. The banjo was thus a fitting instrument for the minstrelman's creation of the image of the slow-witted but happy slave, and the banjo has been called a "happy" instrument ever since.

A great deal of ink has been spilled in the banjo world over the controversy of the fifth string. Through the years, most banjoists have credited Joel Walker Sweeney with the invention of the fifth string. Presumably this happened sometime during the late 1820s. The new string generally was assumed to be the short thumb string. Evidence suggests that if Sweeney did "invent" the fifth string, it was probably the bass string, not the thumb string. Perhaps the most convincing evidence is the painting "The Old Plantation" (painted sometime between 1777 and 1800) in which an African-American banjoist plays a gourd banjo that clearly has a tuning peg placed halfway up the neck.[8]

The first full-length blackface minstrel show, presented by the "Virginia Minstrels," played in New York City in 1843. The troupe included two banjo players, Dan Emmett and Billy Whitlock. The show enjoyed tremendous success and within a few years many minstrel troupes toured throughout the country and western Europe playing in large cities and small towns. It became the most popular commercial entertainment form for much of the nineteenth century. Along with the blackface minstrel show, the banjo also enjoyed a related popularity in Anglo-American culture. It was the newest thing in popular music—for men. Travelers carried the banjo west, sailors brought it to sea, lumbermen to the lumber camps, and some soldiers managed to tote their banjos along during the Civil War. Not only popular, the banjo was also portable.

The minstrel theater was not the only place to hear banjo music in the city. Although current literature only mentions this context, banjoists frequently played in barrooms and various "out-of-the-way places." One reader wrote to a journal about groups of banjo players gathering at the race track to play tunes.[9] Charles Morrell, banjo maker and player from San Francisco, described a banjo tournament that he attended in New York City on 19 October 1857.[10] They held the contest at the Old Chinese Assembly Rooms, at 539 Broadway. Morrell lists twenty contestants, primarily recognized professionals; I do not know if all of the players were white, but all of the contestants were male.[11]

By eight o'clock, the hall already held three thousand people, and by the time the contest started at eight-thirty, more people had crowded into the back of the theater. The audience, both "ladies and gentlemen," sat in distinct sections dictated by neighborhood loyalties. Each contestant came from a different neighborhood—Washington Market, the Bowery, a place called "the Hook" located uptown on the East Side, two players from Brooklyn, etc.—and each contestant had his own neighborhood gang there to cheer for him, gangs that for many contestants numbered in the several hundreds. When the master of ceremonies announced each banjoist, his section commenced to make as much noise as possible. The two best players, Charles Plummer and Picayune Butler, were saved for last. The two men drew lots, and it fell to Picayune Butler to go next:

> And when he made his appearance you should have heard the reception he got. I thought the roof would fall off, but it was plainly seen that he was a little under the influence of liquor; so much so, that he broke two strings during his trial . . . [which] weakened his turn considerably.
>
> When Charles Plummer was announced, his reception was still greater, if possible, than all the others. He played his five tunes as a medley, running one tune into another [a waltz, schottische, polka, reel, and jig required from all players], until he finished his five tunes without stopping. The judges commenced there and then to figure up, and . . . announced . . . that Charles Plummer was entitled to the one hundred dollar prize banjo, and the champion banjoist of America.

The 1857 contest illustrates that urban players, even those who traveled a great deal with theater groups, were part of a strong community (their neighborhoods), and that the banjo had secured a place in white working-class culture beyond the confines of the minstrel theater.

In 1890 Morrell sent his memory of the New York banjo tournament to S. S. Stewart in Philadelphia, and Stewart published it with reluctance in his banjo journal. Stewart had little respect for the playing of these old-timers, and did not want the banjo to be associated with drunken performers and neighborhood friends who stomped their feet and screamed indelicately. Stewart had other ideas about what should be done with the banjo. Thus he published the story of the 1857 banjo contest with a disclaimer: "Historical reminesinces [sic] are always more or less interesting, even when they chronicle the 'pugilistic' banjo age, which is now a thing of the past." By 1890, a new idea of the banjo had challenged the old.

Notes

1. Dena J. Epstein, "The Folk Banjo: A Documentary History," *Ethnomusicology* v. 19, n. 3 (September 1975): pp. 347–71. This material is integrated into her 1977 book *Sinful Tunes and Spirituals: Black Folk Music to the Civil War*.

2. Epstein, "The Folk Banjo: A Documentary History," p. 355.

3. This information is from a paper Winans delivered at the thirteenth annual meeting of the Sonneck Society for American Music in Pittsburgh, Pa., 2–5 April 1987.

4. Gilbert Chase, *America's Music: From the Pilgrims to the Present* (rev. 3d ed.), pp. 272–75. The cover illustration is reproduced on p. 275.

5. On the beginnings of minstrelsy see Hans Nathan, *Dan Emmett and the Rise of Early Negro Minstrelsy* and Robert C. Toll, *Blacking Up: The Minstrel Show in Nineteenth-Century America*.

6. A. Woodward, "Joel Sweeney and the First Banjo," *Los Angeles County Museum Quarterly* v. 2, n. 3 (1949): pp. 7–11.

7. Akira Tsumura, *Banjos: The Tsumura Collection*, devotes pp. 130–38 to color photographs of "Minstrel-Age Banjos" (both European and American) from the collection of Mr. Reuben Reuben.

8. This painting has been reproduced many times; for example, see the entry for "banjo" in the *Grove Dictionary of Music*, or p. 37 in *Sinful Tunes and Spirituals* by Dena J. Epstein.

9. Charles H. Day, "Merry Banjoists," *Stewart's Banjo and Guitar Journal* v. 9, n. 5 (December 1892–January 1893): p. 2. — a reminiscence of old times.

10. Charles Morrell, "The First Banjo Tournament in America," *Stewart's Banjo and Guitar Journal* v. 7, n. 2 (June–July 1890): pp. 1–2.

11. S. S. Stewart, "The Banjo Tournament in New York," *Stewart's Banjo and Guitar Journal* v. 2, n. 1 (May 1883): p. 2. An 1883 contest in New York City was integrated; however, if any of the 1857 contestants had been African-American, it probably would have received special comment, as it did in 1883.

1

The "Elevation" of the Banjo in the Late Nineteenth Century

A soiree musicale was given on Friday evening, January 6th, [1888] at the residence of Mrs. Dundas Lippincott, No. 509 South Broad street [sic], Philadelphia. The affair was given for the benefit of the Cooking School, and five hundred tickets were sold at two dollars each. The entertainment included Mr. D. C. Everest's violin solos, and banjo selections by the lady pupils of Mr. T. J. Armstrong.[1]

AT THE SOIREE MUSICALE in the spacious home of Mrs. Lippincott, we find the banjo in the heart of late nineteenth-century bourgeois society. The various journals for banjo, guitar, and mandolin players, such as S. S. *Stewart's Banjo and Guitar Journal* (Philadelphia), *Gatcomb's Musical Gazette* (Boston), and *The Cadenza* (Kansas City, Mo.) always filled several pages of each issue with short notices like this telling of various performances, recitals, or the formation of new clubs. As performance and social contexts, these were a great change from the typical settings of earlier in the century: the morally suspect worlds of the theater, medicine show, and barroom.

Early nineteenth-century banjo music and minstrel shows presented the first commercial use of African-American musical culture by white entertainers. This beginning of the white use of black music was accompanied by the mandatory blacking of the white man's face. With the late nineteenth-century banjo fad, white culture incorporated a recognized symbol of African-American music without the theatrical metamorphosis of burnt cork. Beginning in the late 1860s and reaching its highpoint in the 1890s, a group of players and makers of the banjo proposed a new set of ideas about what the banjo should be. The banjo needed "elevation," they believed, to a higher class of musical practice and a better class of people. The five Dobson brothers, all banjoists, and a young Californian actress named Lotta Crabtree, popularized the instrument with the society women of New York City starting in the late 1860s.[2] By the 1880s, the banjo was a fad among young women from the upper classes in many parts of the country. In the 1890s many communities and colleges had banjo clubs that performed orchestra-fashion, generally combining banjos with guitars and/or mandolins. Professional players began to find acceptance on the variety stage without the blackened face, big shoes, and comic gags that had been the tradition of the theater banjo since its inception, although most continued to work with the still-popular minstrel show. Some banjoists managed to make a career of giving private lessons and recitals, and directing local banjo clubs, thus completely breaking with the old-time banjo tradition.

What follows is an examination of the ideas and values connected to the effort to elevate the banjo as evidenced in publications, advertisements, design and decoration of the instruments, and performance practices. Although the missionaries of the elevated banjo believed they could bring the banjo into consonance with official Victorian culture, a look at the images and ideas found in the popular culture reveals that though the surface manifestations changed, on a deeper level there was continuity in society's idea of the banjo.

The occasional writer who makes mention of this era and banjo style usually refers to it as "classical banjo," or "parlor banjo,"[3] but these terms, although occasionally used at the time, mislead the reader today. The adjective "parlor" is best understood as meaning "high quality," and not necessarily as indicating the physical locale. The term "classical banjo" is also misleading; twentieth-century readers, who are accustomed to a bifurcated culture of low- and high-brow art, read it as meaning that banjo repertory consisted of "classical" music rather than "popular" music. Existing photographs reinforce that image by showing stylishly dressed banjoists in clothing that now appears terribly staid, their typically unsmiling faces forever frozen in black and white. It must be remembered that in the late nineteenth century, the strong split between classical and popular art had not fully formed.[4] "Classical" banjo music was decidedly popular; performing unpopular music would have been unthinkable.[5] Although a few performers played Mendelssohn and Chopin on the banjo in the 1890s and in the twentieth century, the repertory of most banjoists was composed of light dance tunes, sentimental ballads, "old-time banjo songs," and "characteristic" melodies (black-influenced or -derived music, often syncopated, which was seen as being "characteristic" of blacks).

The term that many banjoists frequently used to describe their goal was "elevation," and for that reason I use it here. Victorian Americans used this term often in connection with the arts, and it has a particular resonance with the didacticism of the times: the arts should elevate the soul, i.e., improve the individual both intellectually and spiritually. "Elevation" demanded the intellectual and moral reform of the banjo. In the twentieth century, many writers have assumed that an "elevation" of the banjo implied a musical shift from "popular" to "classical" literature, but examination of the actual repertory does not justify this dichotomy. Parlor, concert hall, and minstrel banjoists all were broadening their repertory beyond the banjo songs and traditional dance tunes commonly associated with the banjo. The "elevated" banjoists still played popular music, but in a very different context. The journey from barroom to parlor and minstrel stage to recital hall implies a change of class orientation and social values.

In his book *No Place of Grace*, Jackson Lears suggests that the central doctrine of modern American culture has always been the faith in the beneficence of material progress.[6] Around this central tenet clustered a set of values that can be posited as being part of the "official" culture of late nineteenth-century America; these ideas formed the publicly accepted values of bourgeois society well into the twentieth century, and still find a voice today. The official culture of the United States was wedded to technological progress and modernization, self-discipline, and rationalism.

Yet even in the outwardly self-confident times of the late nineteenth century, there lingered doubt about an emerging technologically dominated society dedicated to change, and the ability of humans to live life fully and sanely within it. These concerns were not limited to only the intellectual class. Middle- and working-class people surely had their doubts as they left farm for factory, home for the unknown west, or saw their town transformed into an urban-industrial center. Their doubts about the official values of modern America appear in popular culture expressions, minstrel shows, song texts, and popular illustrations. In the voicing of doubt (always a minority position) artists, writers, and musicians articulated a set of values in opposition, perhaps better described as complementary, to the official values of the late nineteenth century. By placing the articulation of such sentiments in the symbolic language of artistic behavior, society had a sanctioned method for expressing these feelings without having to view them as real alternatives to the official values of American culture. This second set of values we will call "sentimental," though the term is meant to include emotions and ideas of greater force than those usually described as "sentimental." The longing for home, sweet home, the fear of over-civilization, pastoral visions of premodern life, medievalism, primitivism, and an antimodernist aesthetic all help to form the sentimental values of American culture. The official values were loudly proclaimed in formal writings and civic speeches, but the sentimental values were more often whispered in artistic expressions.

Perhaps it will add clarity if I compare my terminology to the works of several other writers. Jackson Lears[7] contrasts "official" culture with "antimodernism." For Lears, antimodernism includes such diverse, though related, sentiments as the arts and crafts movement, the martial ethos, and the fascination with oriental culture. John Kasson[8] also calls the nineteenth-century genteel culture the "official" culture. He is interested in the breakdown of "official" culture hegemony around the turn of the century by the forces of a nascent mass/consumer culture, but he uses no particular term for what lay at the roots of this new cultural style. W. J. Rorabaugh[9] describes this valual split as rational/hard/masculine versus emotional/soft/feminine. Rodney D. Olsen[10] expressed the contrasting sets of values as the "head" versus the "heart"—the heart being the "sentimental idiom." Ann Douglas defined sentimentalism in a particularly apt manner for this work: "Sentimentalism is a complex phenomenon. It asserts that the values a society's activity denies are precisely the ones it cherishes."[11]

In the respectable world of "classical music," the darker sentiments of Victorian values appeared. The incestuous-mythological world of Wagner enjoyed popularity, as did the sex and violence of Italian *Verismo* opera. But once the curtain closed and the house lights were lit, the audience could feel proper, progressive, and upwardly mobile for being patrons of the fine arts. The musicians were the exponents of the European elite tradition. They had achieved their position through years of rational study and diligent practice. Whatever ideas the performance offered, after the artistic experience, the role of the musician and his musical practice could be presented as consonant with the official values of society. Furthermore, this music, as an institution of elite culture, conferred status on its patrons.

In contrast, the banjo, in the popular mind, existed completely outside of official values. As an instrument with acknowledged African and African-American roots, it served as a symbol of musical primitivism. Most white Americans believed that blacks were emotional, not very rational, instinctively artistic souls (in a simple way) whose natural habitat was the plantation South, where life slipped lazily by like the Mississippi river, in complete ignorance of the stresses of modern industrial life. The idea of the banjo was so overwhelmingly Southern black that inevitably a transference of meaning occurred. Though the "Ethiopian harp" was pleasant in its own way, its value to bourgeois society lay in its expression of the sentimental side of Victorian-American values.

The dramatic change proposed by the proponents of the elevated banjo was not really so much a new repertory or even playing style as it was a shift in cultural values. They wanted to bring their instrument out of the sentimental shadows and into the bright light of official culture.

The major manufacturers of the banjo in the late nineteenth century were located primarily in the urban North: New York City (Buckbee, Dobson), Philadelphia (S. S. Stewart, Weymann & Son), Boston (A. C. Fairbanks, Cole, J. C. Haynes), and Chicago (Lyon and Healy, J. B. Schall).[12] Samuel Swain Stewart of Philadelphia was an important figure, not only for the high standards of quality that he set for the industry, but also for his abundant publishing dedicated to the missionary work of elevating the banjo. Though he was certainly not above profit seeking, his personal mission was more than financial; his zeal was immense.

Stewart became wholly committed to uplifting the image of the banjo and made no secret of it in his journal, even if he insulted potential customers. Stewart demonstrated his willingness to risk losing customers for the sake of his missionary work during his mid-1880s crusade against the "ham." Today the term has a generalized theatrical meaning, but at the time it referred to minstrel theater actors and musicians—they used hamfat with burnt cork to create the blackface makeup. A "ham" on the banjo played the old-time way: by ear. Stewart wrote the following response to the complaints he had received:

> There are some few who seemed to have objected to our advertising the famous "Ham Cures" in the *Journal*. But there are people who would object to everything if they only had the chance. . . .
> Our constant allusions to the "ham" has been purely a humanitarian act. We saw, long ago, that unless something was done to save the banjo from the "ham," that the "ham fever" would become contagious, and the rise of the banjo impeded for another generation. . . . [13]

Stewart and others attempted to create a product both modern and acceptable in middle- and upper-class social contexts. The name of an instrument could reflect a modernist aesthetic, for example the A. C. Fairbanks "Electric Banjo," which was not electrified. By using a high-technology word for a product name, manufacturers hoped to transfer a modernist image onto their product. There was also an "Electric" soap being sold in the 1890s: "Only be careful not to get an imitation. There are a great many Electrics and Magnetics, all intended to deceive the public."[14] However, rather than a high-technology image, names for banjos generally conveyed an elitist image, such as the "Imperial" or the "Thoroughbred."

Unlike violin manufacturers, who stressed a centuries-old craft, banjo makers wanted to distance themselves from what they considered to be the instrument's "degraded origins." Manufacturers considered the African origin of the banjo a real image problem and they addressed the issue directly. One catalogue advertisement included a blurb to educate prospective customers about why they should invest in a high-quality instrument: "It [the banjo] is no longer considered only 'a Nigger instrument'; it is now being used by the most intelligent gentlemen and ladies."[15]

Promoters of the banjo at times tried to Europeanize the instrument: the Waldo Manufacturing Company respelled banjos to "banjeaux."[16] A Fairbanks and Cole advertising card (figure 1) pictures a Spanish serenade with the young señor playing the banjo. The substitution of the banjo for the expected guitar is humorous. Nonetheless, it also relocates the exotic roots of the banjo in a region then popular in fine art music as a source of romantic inspiration. But the association of Southern blacks to the instrument was too strong in American culture to be erased by French spellings or Spanish serenades. Therefore, the normal tactic was to stress the banjo as a bit of Americana—the only true American instrument—and one more truly American by being the reformed product of Yankee ingenuity (see figure 2).

Banjo manufacturers often presented themselves as inventors rather than craftsmen. They likened constant innovation to evolution, and in their advertisements they made frequent use of Darwinian evolutionary metaphors to convince the public of the contemporary banjo's distance from its degraded origins. About 1890, S. S. Stewart published an eleven-page poem (excerpt given below), with illustrations and advertisements interspersed, entitled *The Rise of the Banjo*. In it, Stewart extended the evolutionary model beyond the biological world, a typical analytic device of the times. Figure 3 is an illustration from the booklet showing the humble gourd banjo being left behind by the well-dressed modern banjos.

> [The banjo]
> Evolved from a cheese box—
> (Such may have been the case),
> But from less than a cheese box,
> Came the human race.[17]

An 1890 introduction to George C. Dobson's method book combines the idea of mechanical evolution with a presentation of the author as inventor. "From the rude, unformed gourd of Jo Sweeny, step by step he [Dobson] has elaborated the four stringed gourd of the Virginia canal boat, until to-day, it appears in the 'Victor' Banjo of the concert stage, and parlor, a triumphant demonstration of the principle of mechanical evolution."[18]

During this era of rapid industrialization and devotion to technological advancement, it is not surprising that the banjo looked increasingly mechanical. "Stewart's **$125 'Presentation Banjo'** is a piece of **musical mechanism** fit to occupy a place in the music-room or parlor of a Prince."[19] Modernizing the banjo to late nineteenth-century taste meant increasing its mechanical qualities. The amount of metal used in a banjo increased greatly, rims were covered with spun "German silver" (an alloy of copper, nickel, and zinc), "bell" metal (another alloy, purported to have special acoustic properties), or nickel (on the cheaper instruments). The number of brackets (the screws used to tighten the

COMPLIMENTS of FAIRBANKS AND COLE

Fig. 1: Warshaw Collection, Archives Center, NMAH, Smithsonian Institution.

Fig. 2: Illustration used in advertisements for Alfred Farland in *Stewart's Banjo and Guitar Journal*, 1896.

head) went from about six (or none) to a norm of twenty-four to thirty, sometimes as many as thirty-eight or even forty-eight. Figure 4 is from a musical instrument catalogue of around 1891. The comparison of the two banjos, the 1880 model and the 1891 model, demonstrates what changes many banjo makers had made during those years. The "Monarch" (note the elitist name) was a low-quality instrument, so typically the number of brackets on the 1891 (thirty-eight) was far more than what was functional: the high-quality instrument makers did not indulge in purely gratuitous brackets. Machine-like parts became aesthetic: "30 Highly Ornamental Brackets." The Monarch banjo changed from a nickel-plated band around the hoop to a full nickel rim, with added raised frets (the 1880 model's fret markings are flush with the neck). Many banjo makers experimented with the inside of the musical mechanism, and they patented and produced a myriad of metal tone ring designs.

In the tradition of a true inventor—the modern man of the 1890s—many manufacturers eagerly sought and then advertised new patents for the banjo. The 1883 J. C. Haynes and Co. musical instruments catalogue contained the following about the Dobson banjos: "THE PATENT SILVER BELL BANJOS, are the fruit of a life-long study and experiment, by the only real inventor among the many self-called banjo inventors of the present age."[20] Advertisements offered prospective customers rational and presumably scientific reasons for the superiority of their musical engineering. Banjo manufacturers were wedded to the American belief in technological progress coupled with an entrepreneurial spirit. This resulted in a host of offspring: mandolin banjos, piccolo banjos, bass and cello banjos, guitar banjos, banjeurines, ladies' banjos, even banjos with harp attachments. Invention ran wild.

During the nineteenth century, the decoration of banjos changed significantly.

" The Banjo may have grown up from a three-string gourd."

Fig. 3: Warshaw Collection, Archives Center, NMAH, Smithsonian Institution.

Pre–Civil War American banjos were quite plain. A scrolled peg head was normal, the front and back of the instrument were typically plain wooden surfaces (rare examples had inlaid wood patterns along the fingerboard), sometimes with position markers etched into the wood in such a way as to be unnoticeable from a distance. The head was either tacked on or held on with typically from six to eight brackets. The instrument might get a splash of color or some small amount of ornamentation, but would receive nothing approaching the ornamentation of the top-of-the-line instruments of the late nineteenth century. If the banjo were to become an instrument of a higher class of music, the object itself needed to be transformed into art, thus making it a worthy object for the parlor of a prince. In the book *High Victorian Design*, the author Simon Jervis explains that decoration was, for many, synonymous with art. "A plain object could be rendered artistic by the addition of decoration," or, as John Kouwenhoven explains, a vernacular object received the veneer of "cultivated taste" with the addition of ornamentation.[21] In the Victorian aesthetic, plain surfaces were inartistic. If the banjo were to be more than an object of use, its plain surfaces should be enriched with decoration. The more "artistic"

A $12. IMPROVED MONARCH STAGE BANJO,
FOR ONLY $8.00.

30 Highly Ornamental Brackets.   For Concert or Parlor Entertainments

A GREAT SUCCESS.

Sent C. O. D. to any part of the UNITED STATES with Privilege of Examination,

As remodeled Aug. 10th, 1880.

We desire to call particular attention to the new improved Monarch Stage Banjo. The success of the "Monarch" has led to still greater improvements from the hands of a skillful Banjoist now in my employ. His thorough knowledge of the instrument has led to several practical improvements that will be fully appreciated by those understanding the instrument. The Rim is of Ebonized Ash, encircled by a broad full nickel-plated band, to which 30 highly ornamented Brackets are attached, and are also connected with a burnished metallic hoop that secures the head in place in a most scientific manner, and prevents all danger of the head tearing, as is too often the case with low grade instruments. The Arm is of Black Walnut finely finished. The appearance of the Banjo is at once striking and novel.

STILL GREATER IMPROVEMENTS.

As remodeled Jan. 1st, 1891

The enormous demand for the Monarch Stage Banjo will enable me to make some very important changes and improvements. The profit on each banjo was small, but as the demand was on such an extensive scale they netted me a handsome sum and assured me that a first-class low priced banjo was a popular want. To meet the demand I propose to give a greater return for the money. The banjo as now improved has a full nickel rim. 38 nickel safety brackets take place of the old style; an immense improvement. 18 raised frets take the place of inlaid strips. Ebony fingerboard with pearl position dots is an entirely new addition. A new style tail-piece completes the list of 8 great improvements. The Monarch Stage Banjo as now improved is in every way equal to a banjo I sold for $17 in 1880.

I know it seems improbable to give so much for so little money, but by building 1000 at once the cost of producing is reduced to the lowest point. I claim that for $8 I can furnish not only the handsomest but the best banjo ever offered for so small a sum. The best proof I can offer is the banjo itself.

As I wish to verify every statement made, and that the banjo can be seen before buying, I will, on receipt of $2 as a guarantee, send Banjo to any part of the United States, with privilege of examination before buying; then if perfectly satisfied with instrument, the balance can be sent me; if not, banjo can be returned and deposit refunded. When full amount is remitted, we will send a printed agreement that if not satisfied you can return it, and the money will be refunded.

Remember you will not be obliged to keep Banjo unless perfectly satisfied.

Fig. 4: Warshaw Collection, Archives Center, NMAH, Smithsonian Institution.

of the late nineteenth-century banjos had elaborate mother-of-pearl inlay work along the ebony fingerboard, intricate wood carving on the back of the high-grade hardwood neck, and sometimes etching on the spun-metal cover for the wooden hoop (see figure 5). The instruments that received the full ornamentation were the top-of-the-line instruments; the more affordable instruments remained quite plain. The top-of-the-line instruments represented the ideal, something that most customers would look lovingly at in the front of the catalogue before turning back to the section within their price range.

Banjoists of the period often congratulated themselves for their technological and artistic innovations, which they believed brought the banjo to a level of near perfection. Banjo reformers often referred to the older style of instrument as a "crude plantation device" or as an "old tub." These earlier banjos had been larger in size, lower in pitch, darker timbred, with short sustained tones on stopped strings, which gave the instrument a percussive quality (a more African quality). Late nineteenth-century banjo manufacturers followed the general trend of Western art music: gravitation to higher pitch, brighter timbre, and longer sustain tones. Banjoists slowly accepted raised frets during the 1870s and 1880s. By the end of the century, the pitch of the instrument had risen by a minor third, from A to C, adding brightness to the tone. A high-quality banjo of the 1890s sounded remarkably different from that of an 1840s banjo, but it also sounded very different from a twentieth-century bluegrass banjo with its metal strings and resonator (gut or silk strings were used throughout the nineteenth century, and banjoists today who play this repertory use nylon strings). It is important to keep in mind that changes in tonal quality, though always presented as improvements in advertisements, were not essentially improvements, but changes.

For those who wished to uplift the banjo, it was important to learn, to play, and to teach "by note." Musical notation was not only the accepted method of musical transmission for the musical establishment, it was also rational, and it standardized musical performances. Playing by ear or tablature was for the "ham"—i.e., the old-timers of the minstrel stage—and not for the "elite banjoist" (the title of a short-lived journal). Notation also allowed musical learning in the privacy of the home, a less intimidating situation for many than spending large amounts of time in places where banjoists congregated to share tunes and techniques. Method books by the early minstrel banjoists taught and used notation, but it was not part of the actual performance tradition of the "old-timers," as they were sometimes referred to. The old-timers were ear players, singers, and comedians, but were not musically erudite.

In addition to playing from notation, proper banjo students needed to discipline themselves with technical exercises and the practice of scales. Many banjo teachers wrote *Stewart's Banjo and Guitar Journal* complaining about students who took up the instrument because they had thought that it would

Fig. 5: Stewart's Instrument Catalogue of 1896, p. 7.

be easier than the piano or violin. If the banjo were to be socially uplifted, it was an insult to think that it was any less difficult than its more socially reputable cousins.

Instrumental technique also changed dramatically in the wake of the effort to uplift the banjo. The older technique of "stroke" playing (or "banjo style") apparently came from Africa. The basic action for causing the string to sound differs from European string techniques: the performer strikes the string in a downward motion with the back of the finger using either a thimble or the fingernail to actually hit the string (a thimble is a small metal pick worn on the index finger covering the fingernail). Theatrical players usually used a thimble: it was louder than just the fingernail alone. Both the index finger and the thumb sounded the notes. The basics of this technique survive in the Southern banjo tradition, but it is called either "clawhammer," "frailing," "knocking," or "rap." The term "stroke" is no longer used.

In 1865 Frank Converse wrote *New and Complete Method for the Banjo, with or without Master,*[22] probably the first banjo method book that taught the "guitar style" (as well as "stroke"). As the name suggests, it adapted nineteenth-century guitar technique to the banjo, a two-finger plus thumb up-picking (European) style. Frank Converse may have been the first to use guitar style; banjoists often referred to him as the "Father of the Banjo" because of his role in popularizing the new banjo style.

Guitar style was well suited for playing the types of popular music then being performed in the parlor, a music quite different from the more rhythmic and monophonic early nineteenth-century minstrel banjo style. By the late nineteenth century, inlaid fret markings, later raised frets, guided the performer in the upper positions, allowing the performance of a more harmonically based music with full upper-position chords, and enabled the banjoist to play in any key without returning. This can be done in stroke style as well, but the mechanics of stroke call for the regular sounding of the short fifth string. This string is never stopped and acts as an upper drone. In guitar style, the performer only plays the fifth string when melodically or harmonically called for; the string no longer serves a rhythmic function. With the loss of functional (rhythm and drone) power for the fifth string, the banjo is more suited for Euro-American popular music: modulations, slow ballads with arpeggiated accompaniments, and incursions into remote harmonic areas pose less of a problem. Most of the promoters of the elevated banjo believed guitar style to be more artistic than stroke, and certainly more suited for the parlor than the overly noisy stroke style. Banjo clubs and orchestras always used guitar style; however, many of the "old-timers" thought guitar style amateurish and effeminate.[23]

The first experiments with raised frets were in the 1860s, but banjoists only hesitatingly accepted them during the 1870s and 1880s. Some resisted the addition of frets to the fingerboard; they thought it not only looked inartistic but also led to inartistic playing, and some argued that with frets, if the neck should warp, the player could not compensate for the resultant intonation problems. Raised frets finally won because they aided the speed of execution, and, providing that the neck stayed straight, they helped most people to play in tune. But it would be a mistake to assume that, with the introduction of frets, a completely new chordal style of banjo music suddenly arose. The flush frets and position markers had already made chordal and upper-position playing possible.

Playing the banjo "by note" depended on the availability of notated banjo music. It was not until the early 1880s that banjo music was commonly published; at the same time the banjo caught on as a society fad. Before that time, buying banjo music took time and money. Albert Baur, a well-known player and early promoter of the banjo's new image, bought some music through the mail in 1869 from Frank B. Converse. The music was not published, but rather entirely hand written, making the cost exorbitant. His variations on "Home Sweet Home" cost six dollars (which would be about fifty dollars today), the "Last Rose of Summer" and the "Mocking Bird" variations each cost five dollars. Unidentified clogs and hornpipes were a bargain at only one dollar apiece.[24] By the 1890s, publishers sold much of their popular music in arrangements for a variety of instruments including those ubiquitous banjo, mandolin, and guitar arrangements, either for solos or in different ensemble combinations.

The bulk of the published music for the banjo was popular dance music (reels, waltzes, polkas, schottiches, marches, etc.), sentimental ballads (an accompaniment for a vocalist, a banjo genre that declined in popularity by the end of the century), "old time banjo songs" (in "negro dialect"), and "characteristic" music (generally syncopated melodies such as cakewalks and ragtime, seen as "characteristic" of blacks). Musically, the style was fairly simple, chordal, and mainstream. Reels, clogs, jigs, and hornpipes tended to be monophonic. Many tunes that are today considered folk tunes from oral tradition were published for banjoists (as well as for other instrumentalists), such as *Arkansas Traveler, Devil's Dream Hornpipe,* and *Irish Washerwoman Reel.*

Geographically, efforts to elevate the banjo did not spread evenly over the country. Interest centered in the mid-Atlantic states and New England, with Pennsylvania and New York taking the lead. Even so, banjo clubs and teachers could be found in almost every state; large cities and small towns from Omaha, Nebraska, to San Diego, California, could boast of their banjo orchestras. Banjo clubs also appeared in England, Australia, Canada, and even South Africa. One area noticeably missing is the South. In Frank Woodrow's 1895 and 1896 listings of *Banjo, Guitar, and Mandolin Artists, Teachers and Composers of the United States and Canada,* the author lists no banjoists for the states of Alabama, Mississippi, Tennessee, North Carolina, South Carolina, or Florida. Stewart printed in his *Journal* a letter from Natchez, Mississippi, in 1891.[25] Mr. Baker announced that a small banjo club had been organized there, and that he believed it to be the only one in all of the South. The Southern middle and upper classes apparently did not share in the fascination with this originally African-American instrument.

In the 1890s and early twentieth century, banjo music went in two seemingly opposite directions, indicative of the growing gulf in the United States between the socially sanctioned fine-art music and the mass appeal of African-American–influenced music. "Characteristic" music grew to be tremendously popular, and not just in the banjo world. The syncopated melodies of cakewalks, walkarounds, "coon songs," and ragtime all found a natural home in the banjo repertory. Banjoists Vess Ossman and Fred Van Eps had successful recording and performing careers with this repertory. They made commercial recordings during the industry's infancy, and through this new mass media, they pioneered a growing nongenteel popular music directed toward the middle class. Chapter 3 will discuss the careers of early twentieth-century ragtime banjoists.

"Characteristic" music never ceased to be an important part of the repertory of nineteenth-century banjoists, elevated or not. This was not seen as contrary to the spirit of banjo reform until the mid-1890s and Alfred Farland's opening of the high road to elite music. In the 1880s, when the Boston Ideal Club gave a performance, members took turns at solo or duet spots. Typically the guitar and mandolin played something characteristically Mediterranean, such as the overture to Bizet's *Carmen*, and George Lansing, the star banjoist of the Boston Ideals, played something characteristic for the American banjo, such as his composition *Darkey's Dream*. Titles and song texts that appear today as crudely racist were not viewed in the late nineteenth century as being in poor taste: they were part of a widely accepted white belief system. Although Farland preferred to play Chopin and Liszt (and he saw this as the future of the banjo), in order to please his audience he generally inserted a Stephen Foster song or an arrangement of a popular "coon song" — something "characteristic." A 1913 *How to Enter Vaudeville* booklet advises banjoists always to "include a few characteristic southern tunes . . . they are invariably well taken by the audience."[26] The college banjo clubs always included characteristic music in their performances. The persistence of this part of the repertory reveals the indelible mark of the sentimental idea of the banjo: the romanticized blackness of the banjo had a positive value in the Northern white popular imagination.

The other direction that banjo music took was what we may now call the "classical" banjo, and this musical direction most expressed the desire to elevate the banjo. In the mid-1890s, Alfred A. Farland caused a stir in the banjo world. He appeared, seemingly out of nowhere (actually Pittsburgh), playing music that no one else had ever tried before, or thought possible or advisable. Farland's repertory consisted primarily of transcriptions of European art music such as Mendelssohn's Violin Concerto, Beethoven sonatas, and Rossini's *William Tell Overture*. Farland was billed as "the Progressive Banjoist," or as the "Scientific Banjoist of Pittsburgh, Pa." Both of these professional nicknames placed Farland squarely on the side of the official values of late nineteenth-century America, and clearly opposed to the sentimental values that the popular culture traditionally assigned to the banjo.

Stewart, who came to see Farland as the ideal banjoist, graphically depicted the dichotomy between Farland and the old-timers.[27] Figure 6 depicts the idea of the banjo—a blackface minstrel with a plain fretless banjo—as formed by the reader's grandfather. But turn the page (figure 7), and we have now "A Chaste Picture," free of the degraded touch of the black man, the immoralities of the theater, and free of any antiprogressive values. Farland: the virtuous virtuoso who performs high-class music for a higher class of people. The message is certainly clear.

In the written materials of the period, awareness of social class is an omnipresent anxiety, a generalized concern in the late nineteenth century with its labor unrest, plutocrats, and an ever-widening social class system. Americans jockeyed for position. Banjo teachers bragged in notices to the journal: "Most of his pupils belong to the upper classes of society" or he has "a good class of pupils of the best society people."[28] These statements are from the early 1880s and resonate with many banjoists' unexpected delight at being accepted into "proper society." If being accepted by upper-class women and Ivy League schools wasn't enough, the banjo-playing habits of the European aristocracy provided the ultimate argument for respectability. It was a source of pride that Albert, Prince of Wales (later King Edward VII), played the banjo.[29] Stewart proudly announced in 1885 that the banjo was catching on in England with leading aristocrats, in France it was being introduced, and "In Russia, the banjo only awaits competent teachers to introduce it to the nobility."[30] Albert Baur had suggestions on how the banjo's image could be elevated:

> In a former letter I spoke of "elevating" the banjo. In expressing it in that way I did not intend to impress upon the reader that it was necessary to play a high or difficult grade of music. There is a far better way of elevating an instrument than to play difficult music on it. Take it into good company, and keep it there. The more refined and intellectual the company the better it will be, and the longer and firmer hold it will take. The advance of the banjo began when it was taken up by the ladies, and by them introduced into the home circle. Before that it was heard most frequently in bar-rooms and out of the way places, with an occasional glimpse of it on the minstrel stage, coupled with a grotesque impersonation of a plantation negro. In that age of the banjo it was never heard in the drawing room or around the fireside. . . . I was in New York four years and a half and gave lessons to hundreds of pupils, most of them among the wealthiest and most fashionable families in the city.[31]

Of course Albert Baur, like most banjoists of the time, did not learn in such delicate surroundings. His first remembrance of a banjo was at a minstrel show at the Bowery Theater, and he learned to play from some old-timers who met in an upstairs room on Fulton Street. Baur was a ten-year-old runaway working in a bookbindery at the time.[32] In another column he reminisces about playing in barrooms with Lew Brimmer, a talented old-timer whose barroom visita-

S. S. STEWART'S BANJO AND GUITAR JOURNAL.

── THE BANJO AS IT USED TO BE IN THE
LAST GENERATION

Should you say

"Banjo Concert"

to your

Grand-Father, he

might have

this picture in his

mind's eye

If so,

call the old

gentleman's attention

to the next

page

THE BANJO WAS ONCE MONOPOLIZED BY THE NEGRO MINSTREL PERFORMERS, AND HENCE IT BECAME ASSOCIATED WITH THE BLACK FACE, AND WAS SOME TIMES CALLED THE "NEGRO INSTRUMENT." THE BANJO OF TO-DAY IS ALTOGTHER ANOTHER INSTRUMENT.

YOU WILL NOT ──

see any thing like the above at the great Banjo Concert, at the Academy of Music, Philadelphia, on Saturday Evening, January 13th, 1894.

Fig. 6: *Stewart's Banjo and Guitar Journal,* December 1893, p. 14. From the collection of Elias and Madeleine Kaufman.

tions led to an early alcoholic death. Baur goes on to warn young teachers that "the patrons of the banjo to-day are [of] the most refined and select circles of society, who would not for a moment tolerate the aroma of a grog shop in their presence. By catering to the tastes of the most enlightened people in his community and winning their approbation, he advances the banjo."[33]

A Chaste Picture—
—The Banjo of 1894

The Farlands, Alfred A. Farland, Banjo Virtuoso

The greatest soloist of the age, whose performances of high class music on the **Stewart Banjo** have astonished musicians all over the Country, assisted by Miss Annie Farland, Pianiste, will positively appear at the Grand Banjo Concert and Banjo, Mandolin and Guitar Club Tournament, at the Academy of Music, Philadelphia, Saturday evening, January 13th, 1894.

SECURE SEATS IN ADVANCE

Fig. 7: *Stewart's Banjo and Guitar Journal*, December 1893, p. 15. From the collection of Elias and Madeleine Kaufman.

References to old-time banjo players and alcohol consumption are not unusual. The Introduction included the story of how Picayune Butler lost the 1857 New York City banjo tournament due to his state of intoxication. Old-time professional banjo players were a mobile, rootless group that wandered in and out of minstrel theater troupes and medicine shows, and if work could not be found, playing in the grogshop could bring in a little cash, at least enough to pay for drinks. By the second part of the nineteenth century, the temperance movement had greatly affected the drinking behavior of most Americans,[34] but the socially liminal old-time banjo player remained unreformed, and became an embarrassment to the new generation of banjo players. In the desire to truly uplift their favorite instrument, some banjoists eschewed the roving life of the stage and settled down to a more respectable lifestyle as teachers of the banjo and local recitalists.

By the 1890s, a new generation of professional players had come up who had never been part of the old-time social context, but the players and the teachers, who were the pioneers for a higher-class banjo in the 1880s, seemed never to have been fully reformed. They had to remind one another not to arrive at the homes of their new-found patrons with the smell of the grogshop on their breath, and they still traded stories about old times in theater troupes, medicine shows, and barrooms through the pages of the 1880s banjo journals. Even S. S. Stewart took a break from his banjo reform work to write a dime novel (a genre associated with the working class) about a young banjoist who plays in medicine and minstrel shows.[35] Banjoists wanting to elevate their instrument not only had to fight the stereotyped image of the black man; one senses that they had to wrestle with themselves.

In the 1880s the picture is one of male banjo teachers, secretly tugging on their starched collars, and female students, young "society ladies" who liked to tie ribbons on their banjos, learning to play passably well some of the popular tunes of the day. Serious-minded banjoists acknowledged their debt to upper-class women for allowing them into refined circles, while at the same time complaining that these same women did not really take their studies very seriously.

Although banjoists feared that society women had the power to ultimately hurt the public image of the banjo by not taking their studies seriously, the banjo business worked for their continued patronage. They advertised banjos as being more appropriate than guitars for ladies, claiming that guitar playing caused women to sit in an unfeminine position, and banjo strings were less likely to hurt delicate fingers than guitar strings. Most manufacturers made smaller-scale "ladies' banjos." Alfred Farland, in his recital programs, advertised ladies' banjos. After enumerating his many reasons about why the banjo is the most suitable of all instruments for women, Farland exposes some concern about the feminization of the instrument's image when he finishes with this statement: "From the foregoing it may be concluded that the banjo is not only the best of all instruments for women, but also for men — *manly men*."[36]

In the 1890s banjo clubs (a performance ensemble) became popular. Following the example of the "Boston Ideals" (formed in 1883), almost all of the banjo clubs had a mixture of banjos with guitars and/or mandolins. The size of the groups varied greatly, from quartettes to an 1893 Philadelphia orchestra numbering 125 banjoists, mandolinists, and guitarists. Ten to fifteen players was a typical size. The creation of different-sized banjos, such as the piccolo banjo and the banjeaurine, allowed for an orchestral scoring of popular tunes and light classical numbers. If a club did not have these specialized instruments, regular banjos would do, and they commonly used guitars for the low-pitched parts. Many cities and towns had banjo clubs or orchestras, many undoubtedly formed by teachers for their pupils. A closer look at the amateur clubs gives a middle-ground view of contemporary ideas of the banjo, somewhere between the idea of the professional players and that of the general public.

Banjo clubs enjoyed great popularity in American universities and colleges in the 1890s. The clubs were associated with the glee and mandolin clubs, and the whole group frequently spent university vacations on the road together, giving performances, meeting alumni, often raising funds, and certainly having a good time. There were banjo clubs at all of the Ivy League schools, as well as at MIT, Georgetown, University of Wisconsin, Trinity College (Canada), Amherst College, St. Lawrence University, Johns Hopkins University, Wesleyan College, Barnard, Smith, Pembroke, and many others.

The banjo clubs of Georgetown and Brown universities will serve as examples of the men's college club (see photographs in figures 8 and 9).[37] The Georgetown University Glee Club Organization was formed in 1892. The club's goal was stated in the 1893–94 college catalogue as "the advancement of musical talent among the students of the several departments of the University. It is composed of a Glee, Banjo, and Mandolin Club, and numbers some fifty members." The organization is listed among other student groups such as the debating society, the dramatic club, and the athletic association. Students usually served as the leaders of the banjo and mandolin clubs; sometimes a lower-level faculty member helped with the organization (probably more as an adviser and chaperone than as a musician). Georgetown contracted a banjo, mandolin, and guitar teacher (one teacher for all three instruments was typical) for the students and they paid an extra fifteen dollars per quarter for lessons. Lawrence Callan, the teacher, usually played with the clubs, but a student directed the group. Concerts consisted of a succession of light, popular music, each group only playing one piece at a time (a sample program from Brown is provided in figure 10). The constant switching during performances between the banjo club, the mandolin club, and the glee club was interrupted by an occasional baritone solo or a comic reading, and the program always finished with a combined performance of the Georgetown Alma Mater.

The Brown University Banjo Club started a few years earlier than the Georgetown club, in 1887. Brown's club closely resembled Georgetown's: it was always connected with the Glee Club, and later with the Mandolin Club (formed in 1890), a teacher was contracted for lessons (Mr. J. H. Jennings), but a student always directed the club. Programs were very similar to Georgetown's in structure and content (with the addition of whistling and yodeling solos), and the clubs toured often to advertise the merits of Brown University to the public. Both the Georgetown and the Brown organizations occasionally played benefit concerts for athletic clubs. Several Brown programs included baseball schedules for the coming season.

It should not be thought that music departments in the 1890s accepted the banjo. At Georgetown and Brown, like most places, there was barely any music department. Georgetown did not offer its first course in music until 1895, the same year that English and American literature were able to get through the academic doors of Georgetown. Dr. Anton Gloetzner was the professor of music and his course concentrated on harmony, counterpoint, and composition—with a dash of history. Learning to actually play music, even if it was the violin or piano rather than the banjo or mandolin, was something done outside of the music department. Brown University also offered its first music course in 1895, and the department focused on theoretical study, allowing applied music to continue as a student-organized activity. A 1917 article by J. Lawrence Erb in the *Musical Quarterly* advises that university music departments start involving themselves with the various student music-making clubs such as the glee clubs, orchestras, and mandolin clubs to help them reach a higher order of music. If he had written this fifteen years earlier he undoubtedly would have mentioned banjo clubs. "These are now too often without definite connection with or intelligent supervision by the university, though owing their existence entirely to it and regarded to a great extent as representative of its musical taste, culture, and activities."[38] The glee, banjo, and mandolin clubs were not so much a part of American universities as they were a part of student life. Even so, the clubs served as the musical representatives of their university, and went on tours to recruit and to better alumni relations. When browsing through university archives, it is clear that the glee, banjo, and mandolin clubs were the most popular and busy musical organizations on campus.

The women's colleges also sported banjo clubs, but they received little notice by the banjo journals. They seem to have only occasionally toured and rarely ventured far beyond their local communities. Mount Holyoke, until the mid-1890s, had always strictly scheduled their students' time, filling the nonacademic hours with periods for introspection, devotion, and manual labor. When the college finally released them from these demands, the students quickly formed the social organizations typical of 1890s collegiate life, including a banjo club. An 1896 photograph of the Pembroke banjo quartette[39] shows the young women smiling and arranged in a theatrical pose expressing remarkable informality for a late nineteenth-century group photograph. The picture certainly indicates a lighthearted atmosphere, such as was

Fig. 8: Georgetown Club of 1897. Special Collections Division: Georgetown University Archives.

Fig. 9: Brown University Club of 1891. Brown University Library.

◄▷──Programme──◁►

PART I.

1. BROWN MEDLEY.................................*Arr. Llewellyn, '93*
        QUARTETTE.
2. SPANISH MARCH—"Roumania,"............................*Granado*
        MANDOLIN CLUB.
3. SCRUB...*Arr. Webb, '92*
        QUARTETTE.
4. GUARDMOUNT......................................*Eilenberg*
        BANJO CLUB.
5. WHISTLING SOLO—"Open Thy Lattice,"........................*Greg*
        MR. TAYLOR.
6. WANG SELECTION.....................................*Boettger*
        MANDOLIN CLUB.
7. SCHNEIDER'S BAND....................*Arr. Mason, Harvard, '86*
        QUARTETTE.

PART II.

8. COCOANUT DANCES..................................*Arr. Cady, '95*
        BANJO CLUB.
9. { a. SPIN, SPIN.......................................*Jungst*
   { b. MY PRETTY MAID................................*Neidlinger*
        QUARTETTE.
10. VALSE ESPANOLE—"Andaulsia,"..........................*Le Thiere*
        MANDOLIN CLUB.
11. YODLE—"Matin Bell,".................................. * * *
        MR. LLEWELLYN AND QUARTETTE.
12. MEDLEY—"On the Levee,"........................*Arr. Norton, '92*
        BANJO CLUB.
13. BON SOIR—"De Golden Wedding,".......................*Bland*
        QUARTETTE AND BANJO CLUB.

PRESS COMMENTS.

We would respectfully call your attention to the following Press Notices, as indicative of the manner in which the BROWN UNIVERSITY MUSICAL CLUBS have been received in the past seasons.

The tour this summer includes Connecticut, New Jersey, Long Island, Rhode Island, Massachusetts, Maine, the White Mountains, Lakes Champlain and George, and Saratoga.

Please address all correspondence to the Advance Agent,

H. H. RICE, 153 Weybosset Street, Providence, R. I.

Boston Herald—Special Dispatch.
"Captivating the Pier."—"The pretty Casino was packed. The audience did not let a single number go without an encore. The boys are meeting with a remarkable ovation."

The Boston Times.
"Certain of their renderings had beauty of so exquisite force and feeling as to make one realize much of the truest capabilities of the mandolin."

The Worcester Spy.
"The various selections were in great measure of the refined sort that appeal to cultivated tastes."

The Wellesley Prelude.
"The program was a varied one; each club showed good training, and there were no attempts at that kind of poor fun which glee club concerts in general are seldom free from. * * * In short, the concert was a remarkably good one."

The Hartford Times.
"The playing of the Mandolin Club was a revelation to most of the audience. The violin lent a strong and rich tone color to the harmony, and where it rose into an obligato was most effective."

Worcester Gazette.
The voices are excellently trained and the instrumental performers played with precision and expression. A whistling solo called forth much applause.

Fig. 10: Brown University Glee, Banjo, and Mandolin Club Summer Tour of 1892. Brown University Library.

cultivated by the men's collegiate banjo clubs. Some of the spirit of reform apparently affected the Smith College Banjo Club; a newspaper article of 1892 reported that "during the long winter evenings the club has frequently visited a local mill boarding-house and has delighted less favored sisters with a genuine old-fashioned serenade."[40]

The music of the collegiate banjo clubs should not be viewed as a music aspiring to be fine art, but rather as light social music, jauntily adolescent in an upper-class context. At Harvard and Yale, it became a tradition to have a joint concert of the instrumental and glee clubs the night before the annual Harvard-Yale football game.[41] Henry Seidel Canby in *American Memoir*[41] writes an evocative description of college life at the elite men's schools of the 1890s and 1900s. The arrogant unrespectability in the men's colleges provided an adolescent escape from hometown proprieties. What mattered most to these students was neither grades nor course work but activities like the college paper, athletics, fraternities, and music clubs. A strenuous "college life" expressed loyalty to the segregated society of their school. And the waggish boys of the glee, banjo, and mandolin clubs served their schools with distinction. A reporter for the *Baltimore Sun* gave a sentimental account of an 1897 concert in Baltimore by the Georgetown Glee, Banjo, and Mandolin clubs: "All the rollicking and merry songs common to student days and student life were rendered with a reverberant effort which charmed the audience. The quickness of the college lad to seize upon the ludicrous side of things was more than apparent, and the large audience in attendance was alternately pleased and softened by a recurrent medley of airs popular and yet consistent with the demands of good musicians."[43]

When comparing the Georgetown program cover in figure 11 (a design that they used for several years) with a similar picture from a banjo catalogue (figure 12), it is apparent that the amateurs of the Georgetown club and the professionals who worked so hard for the elevation of their instrument presented differing images and ideas to the public. Although both images are of a solitary white male banjo player, the casual clothing (high boots, shirt-sleeves) and relaxed posture of the Georgetown musician create quite a contrast to the rather decorous image of George Gregory, a classical banjoist of the Farland type. Unlike the "elevated" image of banjoist Gregory, the Georgetown illustration creates a leisurely image of banjo playing. The banjo, for the boys of Georgetown, was not part of the official values of work, progress, and rationalism, but a respite from them.

The banjo journals and catalogues presented the banjo as masculine more often than feminine, as a piece of musical technology, as an object now endowed with the values of an elite art, and as an instrument now worthy of serious and prolonged study. And what were the reactions to Farland's concerts? For most, hearing Farland was a "revelation" of the technical possibilities of the instrument and his mastery of it, but he remained a novelty. Even fellow banjoists, who recognized his superior technical skills, expressed some doubt about the proposition that they needed to adopt the European "classical" music repertory to legitimize the banjo. An 1894 columnist for *The Cadenza* wrote: "But as it is, the banjo is an American instrument, and I can enjoy a Southern darkey's music as well as Mr. Farland's, that is when he can play, and put his whole soul in the few pieces that he does play."[44]

The banjo was clearly very popular in the late nineteenth century, but its popularity, despite the efforts of people like Farland and Stewart, was not based on the musical values of the old genteel order. For most of the nineteenth century, as Lawrence Levine has demonstrated,[45] cultural categories were more fluid than the strict hierarchies of twentieth-century America. These late nineteenth-century banjoists, sensing the widening split in the arts between the elite and the popular, thought that they knew how to manipulate the signs of respectability. Yet they did not fully comprehend the exclusionary principles of the increasingly rigid elite culture. Nor did they understand the beginnings of "mass culture." The middle and upper classes, particularly the young, had begun to be drawn to a popular culture rooted in the lower classes, and it was this impulse that had led many to play the banjo.[46] For the true believers of Victorian culture, the eccentricities and bad taste shown by some

Fig. 12: George Gregory from Stewart's Instrument Catalogue of 1896, p. 38.

Fig. 11: Program Cover of 1900. Special Collections Division: Georgetown University Archives.

members of the "better classes" was a shock. The following passage is taken from an 1888 article in a Springfield, Massachusetts, newspaper: "How in the name of common sense, an instrument with such an unmusical quality of tone, and which was never intended for anything more than a barbaric sort of an accompaniment, for the weird and wild songs and dances of the uncultivated Negro race, could have ever taken such a hold on people who are supposed to be cultured, is a mystery."[47]

Even though the banjo, for many Americans, could never represent refined musical taste, it could still have a positive value, but that positive value did not come from the official values or elite arts. Banjo imagery found in popular magazines, literature, paintings, and illustrations differed significantly from the masculine, technological, and elitist image offered by the banjo journals and catalogues. The few white masculine images that appeared in popular sources tended to be of a comic nature (showing inappropriate Victorian male behavior), youthful (not yet adult), or connected to collegiate playing. For example a 1905 article on cartoonist Richard F. Outcault, creator of "Hogan's Alley" and "Buster Brown," includes in the description: "To this day, in his hours of ease, when not drawing Buster Browns or royalties therefrom, he dons his cap [an art student's beret] and jacket and strums student songs on the banjo."[48]

In contrast to the masculine and technological view offered in the banjo journals and catalogues, the rest of society tended to see the then-fashionable banjo more through the eyes of the young society ladies than through their teachers' eyes. And though the popularity of the elevated banjo spread in the 1890s, the young-feminine image remained the strongest in the popular culture.

Mary Cassatt, the well-known American impressionist artist, created two pastels entitled "The Banjo Lesson"; the one of 1894 (figure 13) is clearly a reworking of the 1893 work. Cassatt has an elegantly dressed woman playing the banjo while a young girl watches intently. Cassatt also included a woman playing the banjo, in the outdoors, in her 1893 mural "Modern Woman," which she created for the World's Columbian Exposition in Chicago.

Figure 14 is from an 1888 *Harper's Magazine*.[49] The illustration accompanies a story about White Sulphur Springs, a resort in Greenbrier County, West Virginia. The people in the picture are a young honeymoon couple. The attractive woman lounging in the hammock with banjo in hand and her music tossed carelessly on the floor is hardly the picture of serious musicianship. Rather than Farland's "chaste picture" that appeared in the banjo journal, *Harper's* gave the general public a picture of upper-class privilege, with a hint of feminine decadence.

Why did young women choose to play an instrument long associated with working-class barrooms and Southern black plantation workers? At this point, it would be illuminating to back up in time and look at the theatrical career of Lotta. The Californian actress Carlotta Crabtree, who was known professionally as simply "Lotta," made her New York theatrical debut in 1864. But it was not until 1867 that she became one of the favorites of the New York stage, a position she enjoyed for about fifteen years. A *New York Times* reviewer of 1867 described her as "a specimen of life, light and beauty" and a "spirit of mischief" who "plays a banjo solo like a prize negro minstrel."[50] Lotta was generally showcased in productions that allowed her to indulge in vivacious stage antics and, of course, some banjo playing—and she was apparently quite a good banjo player. George Odell wrote that "Lotta could not act, but she could hold us by sheer power of her magnetic personality. There was always a wonder as to what rule she would break next."[51] Lotta was a rule breaker and a boundary crosser. She was an adult woman who behaved like a child, and who even had the "eccentric" audacity to play a man's role for a week in 1870.[52] She was accused by the 1867 *Times* critic of forgetting "her sex to imitate a very far gone state of tipsiness." Her California origins indicated to the New York audience that she came from a land that was free of the constraints of settled society, so Lotta was free to act out new feminine behaviors. The banjo, which she played like a "prize negro minstrel," was one more symbol of her boundary crossing.

During the late 1860s and 1870s, when Lotta was a hit in the New York

Fig. 13: "The Banjo Lesson" by Mary Cassatt, 1894. Virginia Museum of Fine Arts, Museum Purchase: The Adolph D. and Wilkins C. Williams Fund.

theaters, many young society women of New York took up the "Negro instrument," and by the 1880s, the fad had spread through the urban North. The choice speaks of a desire to cross old boundaries and to redefine upper- and middle-class feminine behavior. Figure 15 is an 1889 drawing from *Collier's*, and it illustrates that the "Sirens of Today" were no longer confined to roles of domesticity and as upholders of the genteel culture. Both tennis and the

Fig. 14: "A reminiscence of the White Sulphur Springs," *Harper's Magazine,* 4 August 1888, p. 576.

banjo, presented here as graphic twins, represent new freedoms. And here, as in the other examples, feminine banjo playing is connected to depictions of nature and its implicit wildness.

Julian Hawthorne has an upper-class young woman play the banjo in his 1890 story "Millicent and Rosalind." Hawthorne takes time to explain to his readers that "there are such things as good banjoes," i.e., well-made instruments played in properly genteel fashion. Though Hawthorne mentions that men also play the banjo, he has chosen a sexually alluring young woman to be his banjoist:

> Rosalind sat down, and, holding the head of the banjo against her thigh, and the handle [neck] across her breast, she tried and tuned the strings for a few moments, and then began a prelude, very light and low, but eloquently modulated. By and by her voice came, as the storm swells and rises after the first mutterings afar off.... The song Rosalind sang was one of the North Country, entitled "Caller Herrin.'" It was well suited to her voice; and the accompaniment she played to it seemed to be resonant with the calling of the waves of the German Sea. There was a free, semi-barbaric quality in it—in its musical aspect, at least...."53

Although Rosalind was playing a finely made banjo, an artifact of the elevated-banjo trend, and was undoubtedly playing in a genteel guitar style, Julian

Fig. 15: "The Sirens of To-day." The 15 June 1889 issue of *Collier's Magazine* (then called *Once a Week*).

Hawthorne does not paint a particularly "chaste" picture. The passage is sexually provocative, filled with antimodern sentiment indulging in a semi-barbaric Teutonicism. And here, as in the other examples, the description of feminine banjo playing is connected to descriptions of nature and its implicit wildness.

In 1910, *Collier's* ran the short story "Banjo Nell" by James Hopper. The opening illustration shows a young, attractive Nell with her banjo, surrounded by admiring men on board a ship bound for the Philippines.

> She sat up there in a long white chair set upon the white deck, her gown a touch of color in the circle of white uniforms; and, her feet drawn up in the attitude of a child eating something good, her head inclined like a bird's, with her slender fingers she pinched the strings [of the banjo] into little fusillades of puerile sound. The big ship slid onward gravely, with a deaf and absorbed air, and incessantly the tinkling notes, released in handfuls, flew over the bulwarks to strew like flights of impalpable butterflies the impassive sea. Sometimes she sang as she strummed — light songs that fluttered like ribbons; . . . But always she tinkled, sang, or fluttered; never was she silent, never was she still; and always there emanated from her a sort of turbulent and empty joy — which had the faculty of making us sad.[54]

Their sadness is a foreshadowing of Banjo Nell's fate in the tropics. She is on her way to the Philippines to marry a missionary who turns out to be somber and austere. He objects to the frivolity of Nell's banjo playing and takes her to live in a bamboo hut, "which he, voluptuously ascetic, had chosen as the proper abode of a propagator of Christian ideals." After several months, Nell dies "of loneliness, of severity, starved of [banjo] tinklings and sounds of mirth, of sheer desolation." The missionary, in a state of anguish, wanders along the beach clinging to Nell's banjo, haunted by the memory of her asking for the banjo on her deathbed and his refusal, even unto the end.

Once again the banjo player is a young, attractive, fashionable woman. Although she is musically within the tradition of the elevated banjo, the music is not perceived as serious, difficult, or disciplined, rather it is "puerile." The character and her music appear as an embodiment of childlike innocence. The banjo serves as a rather too-obvious symbol of rejection of the more austere aspects of Victorian culture.

Even though bourgeois Americans now played the banjo, the new meanings generated were still largely simple, informal, emotional, pastoral, and/or antimodernist. The following passage is from the 5 September 1891 issue of the *Philadelphia Music and Drama*:

> Everybody knows that the bagpipes heard anywhere but on a Scottish heath are a real tragedy. Now the banjo, while an instrument of a very different kind, is subject to certain undeniable limitations. It has been the fashion in the city. Nobody can deny that it has contributed a good deal to social gayety. But it is well understood that it only has tolerance as a musical medium when it comes forward in the drawing room or on the concert platform. On the other hand, the banjo has a positive musical charm in the country. Here we can see that it fits the surroundings. Its half barbaric twang is in harmony with the unmechanical melodies of the birds. It belongs to the same orchestra as the romantic cowbell, and considering all the poetry that has been written about the cowbell, this is no slight compliment. On the veranda, on the lake of a moonlight night, at the barn concert or on the straw ride, it is a companion full of delightful possibilities. Here, where the piano sounds conventional and the violin thin and tame, the banjo sends out its lusty note in a charmingly stimulating way. And so the young women who took up the banjo because it was the fashion without knowing altogether what they were to do with it and took it with them to the country, have doubtless found the summer merrier because the discovery has been made.[55]

This article places the banjo within a white upper-class context while granting it musical validity for its strong statement of pastoral and antimodernist sentiments. Once within this aesthetic realm, the piano sounds conventional and the violin thin, but the banjo emerges "lusty."

Rudyard Kipling wrote the poem "The Song of the Banjo" in 1894 while living in Brattleboro, Vermont. The poem was popular in the United States and for that reason I include it here; the banjo in Britain has a long and varied story not included in the present study. Kipling does not use the traditional black or blackface idea of the banjo, nor does he give his readers the feminine image of the banjo. Rather, it is a white man's banjo now, and an intensification of the above lusty and half-barbaric banjo of the 1891 *Philadelphia Music and Drama* article. Kipling's banjo is played by a soldier of imperialist Britain who battles natives, tramps through deserts and swamps, and lives a primitivist existence, which is a fitting context for the banjo. The banjo speaks:

> You couldn't pack a Broadwood [piano] half a mile—
>   You mustn't leave a fiddle in the damp—
> You couldn't raft an organ up the Nile,
>   And play it in an Equatorial swamp.
> I travel with the cooking-pots and pails—
>   I'm sandwiched 'tween the coffee and the pork—
> And when the dusty column checks and tails,
>   You should hear me spur the rearguard to a walk!

The instruments of European fine-art music just won't do for the martial ethos; an instrument that can travel with the cooking pots and speak with a lusty voice is needed. "I—the war-drum of the White Man round the world!" This is a long way from the image of the happy and gentle plantation black playing the "ol' banjo" and a long way from a Farland recital. Kipling's martial banjo is filled with a barbaric passion that sets it apart from civilized society. Though the "White Man" uses it, he uses the banjo here to express some of the darkest sentiments of the white man's culture. This, of course, is Kipling's personal vision, and one that is an exaggeration of public meanings, but not unrelated.[56]

The upper classes had accepted the banjo into their parlors and parties, but many banjoists had mistaken this move for a shift in assigned values for their instrument. People like Stewart, Baur, and Farland had hoped that by incorporating signs of respectability the banjo would be accepted into the realm of official values as it had been accepted into the presence of a "better class of people," but society had merely found a new way to use the banjo in the expression of sentimental values. In the popular culture, rather than masculine, the banjo was presented as feminine, rather than rational, it hinted of emotional or even sexual meanings, and rather than modern it was seen as half barbaric (usually only half).

Americans no longer viewed the banjo as only the object of plantation blacks and blackface minstrels; it was also an appropriate instrument for young women. Although banjo playing could help redefine feminine behavior, it also coincided with old ideas of the feminine nature. In the eyes of the dominant culture, blacks were not the only emotional, not very rational, and instinctively artistic souls (in a simple way); women were as well. And as such, the banjo seemed appropriate for them. And college men? Well, they were college boys, a privileged group allowed the luxury of extending their adolescence. And when they graduated, they would put their instruments away. Although most of the professional players and teachers were white men, the banjo is never presented (except in the banjo journals) as truly appropriate for them. It is better stationed in the hands of those who are not allowed the weighty business of running society: blacks, theater people, young women, and college boys.

Most Americans thought of the banjo, before the post–Civil War effort to elevate it, as an instrument for Southern blacks, blackface minstrels, and barrooms. By 1900, the "Negro instrument" had been accepted in more polite surroundings: recital halls, music parlors, universities, and even in the home of Mrs. Dundas Lippincott. Although many professional banjo players and manufacturers saw this as a sign of their eventual acceptance into the elite music tradition, and therefore as members of "official" American culture, bourgeois Americans had merely found new ways of expressing sentimental and antimodernist thought. Some of the young society women who took up the banjo in the 1880s were attracted to the instrument because of its exotic connotations, its half-barbaric twang. The banjo fad was an early flirtation with African-American, and therefore "un-official," artistic expression, a fascination that continued into the twentieth century.

Eventually most amateur players left their banjos for bicycles or mandolins or phonographs, and college graduates put their instruments in their attics along with other memorabilia. Twentieth-century professional players worked in vaudeville or with dance ensembles of mixed instruments playing popular music, but always remembering to include something "characteristic." Although performers no longer had to blacken their faces to play the banjo, the overwhelming idea was still that the banjo was the instrument of the Southern black man, and as such it had a role to play in the expression of American sentimental values. No amount of missionary work could change that.

Notes

1. *Stewart's Banjo and Guitar Journal*, v. 4, n. 8 (February–March 1888): p. 5.

2. Robert Lloyd Webb, *Ring the Banjar! The Banjo in America from Folklore to Factory* (Cambridge: MIT Museum, 1984), p. 15.

3. The two publications (outside of the newsletter of the American Banjo Fraternity, *The 5-Stringer* edited by Elias and Madeleine Kaufman) that show the most knowledge of this era and style of banjo are Webb, *Ring the Banjar!* and Wayne Shrubsall, "Banjo as Icon," *Journal of Popular Culture* v. 20, n. 6 (1987):pp. 31–54. Both of these publications stress parlor gentility and classical repertory.

4. See Lawrence Levine, "William Shakespeare and the American People: A Study in Cultural Transformation," *American Historical Review* v. 89, n. 1 (1984): pp. 34-66, and his book *Highbrow/Lowbrow: The Emergence of Cultural Hierarchy in America* (Cambridge: Harvard University Press, 1988) on the bifurcation of American culture.

5. This is a paraphrase from Ronald Pearsall, *Victorian Popular Music* (Newton Abbot, U.K.: David & Carle, 1973), p. 228. Pearsall is writing about the lack of a split between popular and elite music in Victorian England.

6. Jackson Lears, *No Place of Grace: Antimodernism and the Transformation of American Culture 1880-1920* (New York: Pantheon Books, 1981), p. 7.

7. Lears, *No Place of Grace.*

8. John Kasson, *Amusing the Million: Coney Island at the Turn of the Century* (New York: Hill and Wang, 1978).

9. W. J. Rorabaugh, *The Alcoholic Republic* (New York: Oxford University Press, 1979).

10. Rodney D. Olsen, "The Sentimental Idiom in Nineteenth-Century American Culture" (paper delivered 17 March 1987 at the American History Museum of the Smithsonian Institution).

11. Ann Douglas, *The Feminization of American Culture* (New York: Alfred A. Knopf, 1977).

12. The following chart from page 94 of *Banjos: The Tsumura Collection* by Akira Tsumura (Tokyo: Kodansha International Ltd., 1984) gives the major manufacturers of "classic" banjos and the approximate dates of activity. Dates in parentheses refer to years of birth and death.

Manufacturers	City	Approx. Dates
Bacon Manuf. Co.	Forest Dale, Vt.	1905-39
E. L. Bailey	Brooklyn, N.Y.	1915?-20s?
Charles Bobzin	Detroit, Mich.	1892-1915
J. H. Buckbee	New York, N.Y.	1860-97
W. A. Cole	Boston, Mass.	1890-1922
Charles E. Dobson	New York, N.Y.	(1839-1910)
Edw. C. Dobson	New York, N.Y.	(1858-1919)
George C. Dobson	Boston, Mass.	(1842-1930)
Henry C. Dobson	New York, N.Y.	(1831-1908)
A. C. Fairbanks	Boston, Mass.	1875-1904
A. A. Farland	New York, N.Y.	1890-1939
Rettberg & Lange	New York, N.Y.	1897-1929
L. B. Gatcomb	Boston, Mass.	1875-95
Lyon & Healy	Chicago, Ill.	1864-1939
J. C. Haynes	Boston, Mass.	1865-97
John F. Luscomb	Boston, Mass.	1897-1920
J. B. Schall	Chicago, Ill.	1870-1907
S. S. Stewart	Philadelphia, Pa.	1879-1914
Vega Banjo Co.	Boston, Mass.	1904-80
Fred F. Van Eps	Plainfield, N. J.	1903-29
Weymann & Son	Philadelphia, Pa.	1864-1935

13. S. S. Stewart, "How Can We Do It," *Stewart's Banjo and Guitar Journal* v. 3, n. 12 (October–November 1886): p. 1.

14. *Godey's Magazine* v. 131 (1895), back matter.

15. John F. Stratton, *Catalogue of Musical Merchandise,* in the Warshaw Collection of the National Museum of American History [NMAH], Archives Center, Smithsonian Institution.

16. *The Music Trades Review* v. 38, n. 2 (January 1904): p. 39.

17. Samuel S. Stewart, *The Rise of the Banjo,* Warshaw Collection, NMAH, Archives Center, Smithsonian, p. 8.

18. George C. Dobson, *World's Banjo Guide* (Boston: White-Smith Music Publishing Co., 1890), p. 3.

19. Stewart, *The Rise of the Banjo,* p. 7.

20. *J. C. Haynes and Company Illustrated Catalogue of Musical Instruments* (Boston, 1883–84).

21. Simon Jervis, *High Victorian Design* (Ottowa: National Gallery of Canada, 1974), p. 18; John A. Kouwenhoven, *Made in America: The Arts in Modern Civilization* (New York: Doubleday & Co., Inc., 1948), pp. 53–54.

22. Frank B. Converse, *New and Complete Method for the Banjo, with or without Master* (New York: St. Gordon & Son, 1865).

23. Thomas J. Armstrong, "A Forty-Year Banjo War," *Crescendo* v. 8, n. 2 (August 1915): p. 20.

24. *Stewart's Banjo and Guitar Journal* v. 8, n. 5 (December 1891–January 1892): p. 5.

25. *Stewart's Banjo and Guitar Journal* v. 8, n. 2 (June–July 1891): p. 3.

26. Frederic LaDelle, *How to Enter Vaudeville* (Jackson, Mich.: Frederick LaDelle Co., 1913), n.p.

27. *Stewart's Banjo and Guitar Journal* v. 10, n. 5 (December 1893–January 1894): pp. 14–15.

28. *Ibid.* v. 2, n. 5 (September 1883): p. 1.

29. The Prince's banjo playing was mentioned briefly at various times and current players of "classic banjo" still like to mention it. As an example see *Stewart's Banjo and Guitar Journal* v. 5, n. 4 (October–November 1888): p. 4.

30. *Ibid.* v. 3, n. 1 (December 1884–January 1885): p. 4.

31. *Ibid.* v. 8, n. 6 (February–March 1892): p. 5.

32. *Ibid.* v. 4, n. 8 (February–March 1888): p. 2.

33. *Ibid.* v. 8, n. 3 (December 1891–January 1892): pp. 5–6.

34. The discussion on alcohol use in the nineteenth century is largely based upon Rorabaugh, *The Alcoholic Republic.*

35. Stewart gave two installments of his novel *The Black Hercules, or The Adventures of a Banjo Player* in his journal in the August–September and October–November 1884 issues. After the second installment, he advertised the sale of the dime novel. On class associations of the dime novel see Michael Denning, *Mechanic Accents: Dime Novels and Working-Class Culture in America* (London: Verso, 1987).

36. The quote is from an undated (approximately 1904) Farland recital program in the Library of Congress Folklife Reading Room, verticle file labeled "banjo."

37. Information on the Georgetown Glee, Banjo, and Mandolin Club is from the University Archives of the Georgetown Library. Information on the Brown University Glee, Banjo, and Mandolin Club is from the University Archives at the John Hay Library of Brown University.

38. J. Lawrence Erb, "Music in the University," *Musical Quarterly* v. 3, n. 1 (January 1917): p. 32.

39. This photograph is in the Christine Dunlap Farnham Archives at Brown University.

40. Information from the Smith College Archives.

41. Walter Raymond Spalding, *Music at Harvard* (New York: Coward-McCann, Inc., 1935), pp. 180–81.

42. Henry Seidel Canby, *American Memoir* (Boston: Houghton Mifflin Co., 1947), part 2, chapter 2, "College Life."

43. The article was clipped from the paper and placed in the folder "GU Music to 1900" at the Georgetown University Archives.

44. *The Cadenza* v. 1, n. 1 (September–October 1894): p. 5.

45. Levine, *Highbrow/Lowbrow*.

46. J. H. Anker, *Stewart's Banjo and Guitar Journal* v. 5, n. 1 (April–May 1888): p. 5: "Things come about something like this: some one has been fortunate enough to take a trip South; . . . All at once it becomes fashionable to have colored talent at their entertainments or sociables, and that being scarce, all at once the world is startled by the fact that certain well-known society ladies have taken to playing this or that instrument, which has lately become very popular."

47. Printed in *The Union* and reprinted in *Stewart's Banjo and Guitar Journal* v. 5, n. 1 (April–May 1888): p. 12.

48. Roy L. McCardell, "Opper, Outcault and Company," *Everybody's Magazine* v. 12, n. 6 (June 1905): p. 768. I thank Rebecca Zurier for showing this to me.

49. *Harper's Magazine* v. 32, n. 1660 (4 August 1888): p. 576.

50. The review is reprinted in George C. D. Odell, *Annals of the New York Stage* (New York: Columbia University Press, 1927–49), v. 8, p. 136. Also on Lotta see Irene Forsyth Comer, "Lotta Crabtree and John Brougham: Collaborating Pioneers in the Development of American Musical Comedy," in *Musical Theatre in America*, ed. Glenn Loney (Westport, Conn.: Greenwood Press, 1984), pp. 99–110.

51. Odell, *Annals of the New York Stage*, v. 8, p. 136.

52. Ibid. v. 9, p. 24.

53. Julian Hawthorne, "Millicent and Rosalind," *Lippincott's* v. 44, n. 23 (January 1890): p. 34.

54. James Hopper, "Banjo Nell," *Collier's* v. 44, n. 23 (26 February 1910): pp. 15–17, 26–27.

55. Reprinted in *Stewart's Banjo and Guitar Journal* v. 8, n. 4 (October–November 1891): p. 1.

56. The only late nineteenth-century American military context of the banjo that I have found is in *Collier's* v. 3, n. 18 (24 August 1889): p. 4.

2

The Southern Black Banjo

IN 1883 A YOUNG woman from Brookline, Massachusetts, wrote a letter to her newspaper. She had read an article, originally from *The Atlanta Constitution* and reprinted in her local paper, that said Southern blacks "know little about the banjo and care a great deal less."[1] This bit of news apparently upset the young Northeasterner, and she wrote: "I should be shocked to learn that the negroes of the South know nothing of the banjo. Somehow it has been a great comfort to me to associate them with that instrument."

On 24 May 1896 the Philadelphia *Press* ran a story called "The Music Cure is the Latest."[2] The *Press* accompanied its story with an illustration of a woman lounging in her parlor surrounded by a variety of musical instruments, including several banjos. The title of the illustration is "A Boudoir Where Fair Patients Take the Music Cure," and the caption reads:

> A New York doctor has made a lucky hit by rediscovering the music cure as practiced by the ancients. The fashionable patient whose nerves need something can enjoy . . . [her] languor . . . while taking medicine in the pleasant form of a harp solo, a dreamy Chopin composition on the piano, the weird strains of Paganini on the violin or the . . . melodies played of old on light guitar and mandolin by joyous Spanish troubadours. For one who needs a mild degree of enlivening, a rattling darky melody briskly played on the banjo is recommended.

Even though the doctor used European instruments and music for more serious disorders, the American banjo could still be therapeutic for an upper-class white woman in New York City, and the banjo's value was explicitly based on its association with black Americans. Both the neurasthenic woman with banjos in her parlor and the shocked young woman from Brookline, who read that Southern blacks may not actually play the banjo, suggest the importance of the idea—rather than an experienced reality—of the Southern black banjo to many Americans. The association comforted them both.

The idea of the Southern black man as banjo player was firmly set by at least the 1840s; in the late nineteenth century the idea was more than just an association. It had become a symbol of a reactionary value system, and the import of this symbol hid behind a veil of humor or sentimentality. The figure of the Southern black banjo player stood amid an Old-South mythology, racial stereotypes, and ideas about an instrument that had never been quite accepted into the musical establishment.

In the previous chapter the analysis of banjo imagery (be it graphic, narrative, musical, or decorative) is fixed within a better-defined social context. The messages sent and received were by a coherent group: white-bourgeois Americans and those who identified with and accepted their values. The idea of the Southern black banjo, the subject of this chapter, ran deep and broad in American culture; it crossed racial lines and transcended social classes, and the communication of this idea was correspondingly complex.

In this chapter I briefly examine the reality of the Southern black banjo tradition, but most of the chapter deals with ideas about that musical tradition rather than the musical tradition itself—generally the ideas of the white middle-class and commercial culture. Although the public recognition of the banjo as Southern and black originally gave meaning to banjo performances, ultimately this idea of the banjo stifled its musical development.

What I call the "Southern black banjo" should not be confused with the early twentieth-century urban-popular banjo. This was a modernized banjo, and in popular culture images it is at least as often shown in the hands of a Euro-American as in those of an African American. I will discuss this in chapter 3. The "Southern black banjo" was often called the "ol' banjo," a designation that distinguishes it from the "elevated" banjos of chapter 1 as well as the modernized banjo of chapter 3. Until the emergence of the white mountaineer as banjo player (chapter 4), the "ol' banjo" belonged to the rural Southern black in popular culture imagery. This banjo had five strings (including the short thumb string) and was either old and simply constructed, or rustically homemade.

Current literature tells us that by the 1920s, most Americans presumed the five-string banjo to be a Southern white instrument, memory of its African-American heritage having dimmed through the passage of time.[3] But this is not true. The idea of the banjo as an instrument of rural Southern black folk animated its original acceptance into the national popular culture, and this framework for meaning did not suddenly die. Many of those who wanted to elevate the banjo tried to deny its African-American heritage, but they failed. Even today many older Americans still mentally place the banjo in the middle of an Old-South dream and in the hands of a genial black man. But for most Americans in the late twentieth century, the African roots of the banjo surprise them, and any notion of African Americans playing banjos comes from something like reading Edna Ferber's *Showboat* or a vague memory of singing Stephen Foster songs in primary school. Young people in the late twentieth century are unlikely to have participated in these sorts of activities, and so are unlikely to have any notion of an African-American banjo heritage.

This was not always so. Nineteenth-century Americans would not have been surprised that the banjo grew from African roots: they already knew that. A few vehement banjoists trying to elevate their favorite instrument would have argued the point, but most would only claim that their instrument differed greatly from the African gourd instrument. From the banjo's first appearance on the popular stage in the 1830s and well into the twentieth century, Americans considered the Southern black man to be the primary player of the banjo. Seeing blackface banjo players on stage continually reaffirmed their belief.

It is difficult to fish out the historical reality of the black banjo tradition from the swamp of white popular culture materials. Only in recent years have scholars examined the African-American banjo tradition. Dena Epstein has given conclusive evidence of the African origins for the American banjo. Robert Winans has done painstaking searches through eighteenth-century runaway slave advertisements, gathering references to musicians. Out of the 709 instrumental musicians he found, only seventeen were banjo players (compared to 627 fiddle/violin players). Eleven of the seventeen banjoists were from the Chesapeake Bay area, suggesting a regional tradition. William Tallmadge and Cece Conway have explored the connections between black tradition and the white tradition in the Southern mountains. Conway, Winans, and Kip Lornell have all done field work in the Virginia and North Carolina mountain and Piedmont regions interviewing elderly black banjoists.[4] The Southern black banjo tradition was real, but it has nearly disappeared, due in large part to the loss of its performance context: black country dances in the rural South (for example square dancing and buck-and-wing).

In the nineteenth and early twentieth centuries, serious consideration of black music focused on songs, especially the spirituals.[5] This is not surprising; folk music research in general during this time dwelt upon song. It certainly may be, as Lawrence Levine writes in *Black Culture and Black Consciousness*, that the spirituals represented the highest artistic level of black music in the nineteenth century, and so attention naturally went to this song literature rather than other musical expressions.[6] But it also reiterated what folklorists and ballad collectors were doing with the traditional music of Anglo-Americans.

The collection of songs from the rural "folk" had gained a respectability that would not come for many years to the study of something like banjo tunes. Folksong was considered the wildflower of the musical art—ennobled by its natural simplicity—whereas instrumental folk music had been tainted by its connection to social dancing. Thomas Wentworth Higginson, as expressed in his early and influential article "Negro Spirituals" (1867), sensed a similarity between collecting European ballads and African-American spirituals. In the article he assumes a familiarity on the part of his audience (a nonspecialist reader of *The Atlantic*) with the work of Sir Walter Scott and the Border Minstrelsy.

> The war brought to some of us, besides its direct experiences, many a strange fulfillment of dreams of other days. For instance, the present writer had been a faithful student of the Scottish ballads, and had always envied Sir Walter the delight of tracing them out amid their own heather, and of writing them down piecemeal from the lips of aged crones. It was a strange enjoyment, therefore, to be suddenly brought into the midst of a kindred world of unwritten songs, as simple and indigenous as the Border Minstrelsy, more uniformly plaintive, almost always more quaint, and often as essentially poetic.[7]

Writers and scholars who wanted seriously or sympathetically to examine African-American music turned to the songs, most often the spirituals. So the banjo was left to less careful consideration: the popular theater, fiction writers, song lyricists, and illustrators. Minstrel theater led the way and set the tone for others to follow. What these performers offered on stage went largely unquestioned by most of the audience. By the post-Civil War era, minstrel theater merely had to be true to earlier distortion in order to be true to the presumed black "tradition."

After Reconstruction, some Southern whites, notably Joel Chandler Harris and George Washington Cable, claimed the role of true interpreter of black culture in an attempt to counteract the image-making power of the Northern-based minstrel theater. In 1883, Joel Chandler Harris complained in an article written for *The Critic:* "It is not only difficult, but impossible, to displace the stage negro in literature with the real negro."[8] In the attempt to displace the "stage negro," Harris and Cable wrote of their personal observations of Southern rural black music. For the article in *The Critic,* Harris disagreed with the popular culture's insistence that the banjo was *the* instrument of black culture. Harris admitted that his experience was limited primarily to Georgia. Even so, when the creator of *Uncle Remus* asserted that the banjo belonged not to the "real negro," but to the stage image, it touched off a small controversy. A debate on the issue continued through letters to the editor of *The Critic* starting in December of 1883 and culminating with Harris's rebuttal of his many critics in July of 1884. Many of the letters had personal testimony about

Southern blacks playing banjos, including one from a black woman of Wayne County, Georgia.[9]

George Washington Cable, who disagreed with Harris, eventually joined the controversy, as did his brother James B. Cable, who sided with Harris. *The Critic* and the New York *Tribune* reported George W. Cable's remembrances of black banjo playing in Louisiana as a rebuttal of Harris.[10] Finally, in 1886 Cable wrote "The Dance in Place Congo,"[11] an essay full of exoticism describing the African-French traditions of old New Orleans. In it, Cable describes the use of the banjo with drums for accompanying the more African-influenced dances. Cable attempted to dignify both the banjo and Americans of African descent; Harris denied the centrality of the banjo and etched into the white mind the image of the kindly old plantation darkey. American popular culture eventually took what it wanted from both—Uncle Remus and the banjo.

Less prestigious writers also reported personal experiences with Southern black banjo players. Even the followers of the elevated banjo had some fascination for the "authentic," although they deemed it less artistic. The following is an excerpt from an article that appeared in 1893 in a banjo journal:

> While in the army I was always watching for darkey banjo players on the different plantations in the vicinity of camps where we happened to be. In September, 1863 ... our division (Gen. John W. Greary's) was halted at Murfreesboro, Tennessee, where we went into camp.... One day a contraband came to me and told me that on a certain day there would be a dance at a house in the town at which the musicians would be principally banjo players.... [We] had not gone very far into the town until we heard the squeaky tones of a violin and "ker plunk" of a banjo coming from the centre of a collection of houses.... When we reached the house we found the windows all closed either with shutters or boards, but there was a "mighty thumping and a scraping and rushing of feet" inside.... I then went to the door and boldly tried it. It was not locked. I raised the latch, opened and went in, followed by my comrades. Such a sight! I never had seen and never again expect to see anything like it again. All daylight had been shut out and the room, quite a large one, had been illuminated with tallow dips.... The musicians—one violinist and two banjo players—were on a platform at one end of the room. The assemblage, which consisted as near as I can remember of about seventy to eighty people, all dressed in the most fantastic manner imaginable. The colors of the rainbow were not a circumstance. I do not think a person could expect to see such a sight but once in a life time. The most exaggerated minstrel representation of plantation life could not equal it. Everybody present seemed to be in the excitement, soul and body. The dancers, those who did not dance, the musicians, all were keeping time to the music, some shuffling their feet, some patting, and others singing and shouting, while all were sweating as if their very lives depended upon it.... Here was a scene that I had often wished to witness, a regular plantation frolic.[12]

The soldier was already a banjoist (and had performed in minstrel acts) when this event happened, but he was astonished by the actual tradition, and he realized that the minstrel theater offered only a parody. Thirty years probably affected his memory of the occasion, but this Northerner's perception at the time had already been affected by the images and ideas about black culture he had gathered from the theater and other sources of popular culture. It is also important to note the boarded-up windows. Whether accepted factually or understood metaphorically, the image evokes the reality of separate social and artistic space. The covered windows may have created darkness, but more important, they kept out uninvited eyes. The intruding soldier and his comrades finally left after repeated requests and suggestions and finally near threats. Like these soldiers, the white creators of popular culture materials rarely got a glimpse behind the shuttered windows, and, when they did, deeply engrained biases and ideas guided their perceptions.

Nor were nineteenth-century African-American banjoists confined only to Southern rural folk culture; some worked in the professional theater. These banjoists were not necessarily Southern or rural. The most famous of black banjoists in the 1870s and 1880s was Horace Weston (1825–90),[13] a highly respected musician, and a favorite of both the public and other banjoists. In the 1880s (before the appearance of Farland) Samuel S. Stewart continually trumpeted his talent to the banjo world. His career hints at how some African-American musicians navigated the difficult course between professional skill and socially constricting racial stereotypes.

Horace Weston was the son of a free-black Connecticut dancing teacher and musician. Apparently blessed with a remarkable aptitude for music, he became skilled on the accordion, violin, cello, double bass, trombone, and guitar, and he also learned dancing—all before taking up the banjo. He became famous, however, for his banjo playing. There is no reason to suppose that the banjo was foisted upon him because he was black. While in the Navy during the Civil War, it was the banjo that he carried with him. Weston toured widely in the United States, England, France, and Germany with minstrel troupes, *Uncle Tom's Cabin* shows, and with Barnum and Bailey's Show. In the 1878 production of *Uncle Tom's Cabin* at the well-known Booth's Theater in New York, Weston was a major attraction, some thirty minutes of show time allocated for his banjo playing.[14] He had many long-term engagements in New York City at saloons and at various theaters (the Old Bowery Theater and the Old Palace Garden). Weston's wife also played banjo and sometimes performed with him.[15] The career of Horace Weston provides good evidence of the types of professional performance opportunities available to African-American musicians in the 1870s and 1880s; obviously, minstrelsy was not the only avenue open to blacks at this time. Weston played in both guitar and a sophisticated stroke style, and, though he could read music, he played the banjo by ear. Weston won many banjo contests in the United States and Europe (racially integrated contests). The following is from the obituary notice of the New York *Morning Journal* of 26 May 1890:

> Weston was, perhaps, the greatest banjoist the world has ever heard. He did not learn on Southern plantations the magic touch that drew the witchery from the strings. He was born of free parents in the Nutmeg State of Connecticut in 1825. . . . He traveled all over the world, and his cleverness on the banjo delighted and astonished people in all parts of the globe.
>
> Sixteen years ago, while traveling in England with Jarrett & Palmer's old "Uncle Tom's Cabin" Company, Weston appeared before Queen Victoria, and so entertained her with the music of his banjo that she presented him with a gold medal, which he highly prized.[16]

Even though Weston fulfilled the idea of the black man as banjo player, he contradicted the image. Here was a black man who the public viewed as one of the best professional banjo players around, regardless of color. The black banjo player in popular (white) myth was a Southern plantation worker who played simple, perhaps slightly barbaric, melodies in front of his little cabin. Weston played complicated music with a sophisticated technique in front of Queen Victoria. Weston was also a Northerner, but white banjoists used this to excuse him from the other contradictions—perhaps, they thought, his playing was sophisticated because he was a "Connecticut Yankee," and not a plantation Negro. Though the propagators of the elevated banjo wanted to distance themselves from the black associations of the instrument, they gave Weston, probably by sheer force of talent, all due respect. Being a Connecticut freeborn black helped, but most white players saw him as singularly talented and an exception to the race. Maybe his playing was "witchery" rather than skill and intelligence. The professional nickname sometimes given him, "the Black Hercules," placed him outside of the normal realm of humanity, and excused the "precocious" abilities of a black man by making him metaphorically transcendent of human characteristics such as skin color.

Although the banjoists who worked to elevate their instrument into a higher class of music and better class of people, as described in chapter 1, wanted to distance their musical practice and instrument construction from the African-American heritage, they did not avoid using this association in the generation of musical meaning. Many compositions used black themes (*Dreams of Darkey Land, Plantation Dance, Sporty Coon Dance*, etc.), some even included programmatic notes such as the 1891 piece *Cotton Blossom*: "Descriptive Medley—A dark gathering at an old:time corn:shucking (sic). . . . " The first page of the first issue of *The Cadenza*, a journal for elevated banjoists, had the poem "The Darkies' Dream" containing doggerel like:

You kin talk about yo' possum, an taters in de pan,
An de honey drippin' down—dat's good for sho'
But I'd leab 'em in er minut if de fines' in de lan'
Fer de ole banjo a hangin' on de do.[17]

Even if compositions attempted to be evocative of Southern black culture, the "blackness" of the banjo was only a meaning to be exploited and never a style to be imitated. It was assumed that although blacks played the banjo, truly artistic playing of the instrument was left to "nimbler fingers." The exception was Horace Weston, but they treated him as the exception that proved the rule. They believed that without white intervention, the banjo never could have risen from its half-barbaric state. Still it seems that middle- and upper-class white banjoists could not avoid expressing a certain attraction to black American culture. They pieced together their ideas about that culture from bits of reality, popular culture interpretations of that reality, and an escape into sentimental fantasies. The foundation of much popular thinking about black culture in the late nineteenth century came from the minstrel stage.

In the late nineteenth century, the banjos used by most professional minstrel theater banjoists were highly ornamented and expensive. Many of the fanciest banjos made by manufacturers like Stewart and Fairbanks were used by professional minstrels on the stage. However, in an apparent contradiction to the stage banjo, the banjo as spoken about in song lyrics (the popularly accepted idea of the Southern black banjo) was always the "ol' banjo." Whether old and battered or homemade (in a rough-hewn manner), the black banjoist supposedly played an instrument that reflected his estrangement from civilization. Both the "ol' banjo" and the African-American were products of nature, neither art nor artifice. Stories of the origin of the banjo often explained it as an accidental combination of natural objects: a tree limb stuck in a gourd or a tortoiseshell thoughtlessly covered with an old snake skin.[18] The banjo, like Topsy, was never born, it just grew.

The late nineteenth-century minstrel banjoist turned more and more away from the old stroke technique—the most common technique of Southern black traditional players—and adopted guitar style.[19] With the new technique, the repertory began to change as well; guitar style encouraged the more harmonically based repertory of contemporary popular and parlor song. Pieces such as Home Sweet Home and The Mocking-Bird (both done with variations) became popular show pieces. The previously popular folk-based monophonic renderings of jigs and reels became old-fashioned.

Minstrel banjoists of the late nineteenth century still had to be comedian-entertainers as well as musicians. Crowd-pleasing stunts, like banjo juggling, eventually found their way into Vaudeville. The following is an account of an 1866 performance by Frank Converse (who was an innovative step ahead of his time) in London, England: "There he played 'Yankee Doodle' with variations; imitated a church organ (with a small violin bow secreted in the palm of his hand) — played 'Trinity Bell Chimes' on two swinging banjos at the same time; finally concluding his performance with selections from 'Il Trovatore' and 'Home Sweet Home,' both played in the 'tremolo style,' which was considered sensational."[20]

The actual banjo, the repertory, and the playing style offered by the white minstrel banjoists of the late nineteenth century increasingly had little foundation in black tradition. Early minstrel banjoists of the 1840s, though problematic to assert to what extent, were more grounded in black tradition than their latter-day counterparts. But that did not really matter: what generated meaning for the audience was not the particularities of musical style nor the decoration and construction of the instrument, but rather the suggestive quality of a banjo in the hands of a make-believe black man.

Joel Chandler Harris, in the article that started the banjo controversy, included a lengthy description of an 1880s minstrel banjo player, and his perception of how minstrelsy had affected the thinking of Americans:

> The people of the whole country, including a large majority of the people of the South, . . . [have] been accustomed to associate the negro with the banjo, the bones, and the tamborine. Especially with the banjo. . . . Romance may become a little frayed around the edges, but sentiment is a very stubborn thing. It is sometimes stronger than facts; and the ideal and impossible negro will continue to exist in the public mind as a banjoist. . . .
>
> What more natural? In the negro minstrel show, which is supposed to present to us the negro as he was and is and hopes to be, an entire scene is devoted to the happy-go-lucky darkey with his banjo. The stage is cleared away; the pleasant and persuasive bass voice of Mr. Hawkins, the "interlocutor," is hushed; there is silence in the pit and gallery until a gurgling ripple of laughter, running merrily through the audience, announces the appearance of Mr. Edward McClurg, in his justly celebrated banjo act. Mr. McClurg, disguised by burnt cork, is black, and sleek, and saucy. He wears a plug hat, enormous shoes, and carries his banjo on his shoulder. He seats himself, crosses his legs, waves an enormous shoe, and looks at the audience as much as to say, "Here is where the laugh comes in." Mr. McClurg is garrulous. As he tunes his banjo (inlaid with silver and costing seventy-five dollars) he tells several stories that were in last year's newspapers, and makes various allusions that savor strongly of the plantations through which the back streets of New York City run. Passing his nimble fingers lightly over the strings, he gives "Home Sweet Home" and "The Mocking-Bird" with variations, just as they were played on the plantations that exist on the stage. To audiences in nearly every part of the country this scene is real and representative, because it falls in with their ideas of the plantation negro. . . .
>
> What the negro did not care to do, the sentiment which has grown up around the stage negro has done for him, and he will go down to history accompanied by

his banjo. A representation of negro life and character has never been put upon the stage, nor anything remotely resembling it; but, to all who have any knowledge of the negro, the plantation darkey, as he was, is a very attractive figure. . . . [It] is a silly trick of the clowns to give him over to burlesque; for his life, though abounding in humor, was concerned with all that the imagination of man has made pathetic.[21]

Through the patronage of the minstrel show the banjo moved into the commercial popular culture. The banjo and the corked-faced clown intertwined in the minds of most Americans. Recent evidence does support Harris's assertion that other musical instruments, such as the fiddle, were more common than the banjo in African-American traditional music.[22] But, as Harris said, "sentiment is a very stubborn thing." The minstrel banjoist, with his oversized shoes and exaggerated clothing, was a slick entertainer and, above all else, a clown. And, as Harris describes, he dipped into both urban and plantation themes for his material. The ideas from the minstrel stage spilled out of the theater doors into the mainstream of American culture, and carried with it the idea of the banjo.

By the late nineteenth century, the minstrel theater had lost its original, and highly standardized, format and had even moved away from the original plantation ethos. Robert C. Toll in his book *Blacking Up: The Minstrel Show in Nineteenth-Century America* provides a thorough history and analysis of the theatrical form, including its post–Civil War transformation. Early minstrelsy had made frequent use of the trickster character, but by the 1870s blacks were all contented subordinates, presenting a picture of stability and stasis to a post–Civil War America troubled by social disruption and an unknown future.[23] Although minstrels emphasized nonthreatening characterizations of blacks (creating a sense of social stability), the format and size of the late nineteenth-century minstrel show revealed a destabilization. Huge companies of "40 Count Them 40" minstrels, tiers of banjo, bones, and tamborine players, Irish and other ethnic character skits, brass bands, and even a movement away from blackface all indicated a dissolution of minstrelsy and its movement toward variety theater. Minstrelsy lost its dominance of the entertainment business in the 1890s, and by about 1920, professional minstrelsy was gone. Toll ends his book with: "The minstrel show, long after it had disappeared, left its central image – the grinning black mask – lingering on, deeply embedded in American consciousness."[24]

In the early twentieth century, as professional minstrelsy was dying, a number of writers offered the public highly nostalgic eulogies for "the one single purely native form of entertainment" – the all-American minstrel show.[25] The full-length minstrel show did not lose its dominance in American theater because of its embarrassing racism. The show just became old-fashioned and vaudeville and the moving picture shows pushed it aside. Still, the minstrel show had not really died; it lingered on until the mid-twentieth century in bits and pieces in professional theater, country music, and in amateur productions (a perennial favorite of lodges and clubs, especially for charity fund-raising).[26] Radio station WGBS in New York City ran a weekly minstrel show in the 1920s.[27] When the New Deal's Federal Theater Project started in 1935, a few minstrel troupes were supported until the NAACP complained enough to have minstrelsy excluded from federal subsidy.[28] The hundreth anniversary of the minstrel show was in 1943, and despite the country being in the middle of a fight against a racist regime abroad, a celebration of minstrelsy seemed appropriate. In New York, Radio City Music Hall staged an elaborate minstrel show in honor of the occasion, and Paramount Pictures celebrated with the 1943 film *Dixie* starring Bing Crosby as Dan Emmett (the composer of "Dixie" and member of the first minstrel troop).[29] Figure 16, a sheet music cover from the movie, serves as an example of mid-twentieth-century professional use of minstrelsy. The illustration shows the type of outlandish costume that was traditional, the huge cast and elaborate production that minstrelsy had become in its final years, and the instrument that was so strongly associated with the theatrical form.

Clearly, the minstrel show was not really dead, but after it disappeared from the professional stage it became an amateur affair, something to revive for an old-time effect, or it was a "rube" show; the last professional minstrel troupes were low-budget organizations that played to rural audiences. The banjo, by association, suffered with an amateurish, old-fashioned, or even "rube" image by mid-century.

During much of the nineteenth and twentieth centuries, professional banjo players who could not find work with a minstrel or variety troupe often found their way into medicine shows. Figure 17, a 1929 advertisement from the *Saturday Evening Post,* indicates the low level of respectability suffered by both traveling medicine salesmen and blackface banjo players in a culture increasingly devoted to the benefits of modern science. The advertisement copy tells us: "The itinerant charlatan who dispensed minstrelsy and 'painless' malpractice has fled before law and public opinion." On stage are both pseudodoctor and blackface banjo player, both charlatans, one dispensing malpractice, the other, minstrelsy. And both are shown as undesirable vestiges of a premodern America.

The imagery of the "coon songs" of the 1890s is essentially an extension of the minstrel image. Song lyricists and cover illustrators presented African Americans as outlandishly dressed clowns and they used not only old plantation cliches but also urban themes. The 1890s was a period of extreme racism in the United States and the "coon songs" of the era reflected this problem.[30] The "coon songs" of the 1890s stand apart in the history of American popular song; at no other time did racial stereotyping go to such vituperative extremes.

Fig. 16: Archives Center, NMAH, Smithsonian Institution.

The level of insult in these songs cannot be equated with the injustice of Jim Crow laws (which Southern state legislatures created and codified at this time) or the horror of lynchings, but the "coon songs" are best understood when viewed as part of a large pattern of tragically bad race relations around the turn of the century.[31]

Don't Expect Your Dentist
to Perform Miracles

The itinerant charlatan who dispensed minstrelsy and "painless" malpractice has fled before law and public opinion. Yet there remains the Quack—the dentist who claims to be able to do what the reputable, ethical dentist will not... *"All Work Guaranteed for Life"* . . . *"Free Examination and Treatment"* . . . *"Cut Rate Prices."* • • Ask, or expect, no such inducements from the man to whom you entrust your teeth, your mouth. Protect others, your acquaintances or employees, from the menace of quackery. • • The honest, ethical dentist can do a great deal for you. Give him opportunity to render you and your family the valuable service for which he is fitted. Visit him regularly —as frequently as he suggests. Accept his advice, follow his instructions. Your dentist is able to contribute to your health and comfort only if you co-operate with him. Oral and general health require that you place yourself in the care of an ethical dentist and, always, "Do As Your Dentist Tells You."

LAVORIS CHEMICAL COMPANY
Minneapolis, Minn.   Toronto, Ont.

This is Advertisement No. 2 of the Lavoris Reciprocation Program tendered the American Dentist in appreciation of more than 25 years' acceptance and good will

Fig. 17: *Saturday Evening Post*, 20 April 1929, p. 136.

In "coon songs," activities such as gambling, eating watermelon, fighting with razor blades, and stealing chickens usually overshadow banjo playing. Many "coon songs" have an urban context, but "the ol' banjo" rarely leaves the rural South. "Coon songs" with a Southern locale are generally humorous, and make an occasional reference to a banjo. The banjo acted as one sign among many that could help in the wholesale denigration of African Americans; this is exemplified by figure 18, a lithographed advertisement of 1899 for a minstrel group and the popular "coon song" *Hello! My Baby.* Maybe little white girls are made of sugar and spice and everything nice and little white boys of frogs and snails and puppy dogs' tails but little black children are made of banjos, chickens, watermelon, charcoal, minstrel clothes, dice, and tamborines. Rake it in, and turn the crank.

The dying minstrel show, the charlatan medicine show, the crude "coon song"—none of these could lead to a noble vision of the African-American banjo. Before dismissing these forms as simply evidence of white racism, however, we need to ask why white culture continued to use blackface (Al Jolson, from 1906 to 1931, never performed without blackface), and why white Americans sang "coon songs," played banjos, and later danced to ragtime.

W. E. B. DuBois wisely wrote in 1903 that the problem of the twentieth century is the problem of the color line.[32] But in the realm of popular artistic expression it seems that the crossing of that line intrigued many Americans; they were fascinated by tales of people of mixed blood "passing" for white, captivated by Sophie Tucker in blackface shouting her "coon songs" and perhaps a bit titillated at the end of the performance when she pulled off her wig to reveal her Caucasian head, thereby crossing back to where she began.[33] At the turn of the century, as Victorian middle-class values began to slip from their stronghold, white Americans continually dipped into the well of African-American culture to help in the creation of a new cultural style. White America expressed its ambivalence about its attraction to African-American expressive forms with extreme insult and ridiculous parody.

The idea of the Southern black banjo also appeared in Old-South imagery, an American culture myth nicely captured in the following 1929 passage by Thomas Wolfe:

His [the young Eugene's] feeling for the South was not so much historic as it was of the core and desire of dark romanticism. . . . And this desire of his was unquestionably enhanced by all he had read and visioned, by the romantic halo that his school history cast over the section, by the whole fantastic distortion of that period where people were said to live in "mansions," and slavery was a benevolent institution, conducted to a constant banjo-strumming, the strewn largesses of the colonel and the shuffle-dance of his happy dependents, where all women

Fig. 18: Strobridge Lithograph Company, 1899: Library of Congress, Prints and Photographs.

were pure, gentle, and all men chivalrous and brave, and the Rebel horde a
company of swagger, death-mocking cavaliers.[34]

The young Eugene Gant was hardly alone in his almost instinctual romanti-
cizing of the Old South; the mythology surrounding old Dixie has had a
peculiarly strong impact on American culture, both in the South and in the
North; Wolfe places Eugene in his thinly disguised hometown of Asheville,
North Carolina. Other ideas and images of the South existed, but the black
banjo was embedded in this idea — the Old-South myth — caught between the
broad stereotypes of white aristocracy and black happiness in servitude
("conducted to a constant banjo-strumming"). Old-South mythology had a
strong hold on the American imagination; from minstrel show plantation
scenes to *Gone with the Wind*, Americans marveled at the sight of riverboats
(always side-wheelers), plantations (always large and wealthy), fields of cotton
(always white with harvest season), and magnolias (always in bloom).

Sentimental Old-South imagery has had a long history; it appeared in
antebellum popular songs, the most enduring and influential of which are the
songs of Stephen Foster. We sometimes learn, however, from failures. For
example, the following lyric from 1852 is from a song that was meant to follow
a generalized Foster model. The lyricist, Fanny Crosby, wrote it based upon the
suggestion of the composer, George Root (under the pseudonym of Wurzel):

> Fare thee well, Kitty dear,
>> Thou art sleeping in thy grave so low,
> Nevermore, Kitty dear,
>> Wilt thou listen to my old banjo.[35]

This song was not a hit, and had no lasting influence. It does contain the
pathos of many of Foster's songs along with a picturesque reference to a banjo,
but the style is far too literary, the words not in dialect, the cause of sorrow
seems to be a lover (rather than "massa," or Little Eva, or homesickness: all
more appropriate causes for slave sorrow according to the popular culture),
and the song does not create a plantation setting other than a vague reference
to the Southern sky (later in the lyric). The next passage is from a Stephen
Foster song also dealing with a banjo player's grief over a death:

> I cannot work before tomorrow,
>> Cayse de tear drops flow.
> I try to drive away my sorrow
>> Pickin on de old banjo.
> Down in de cornfield
> Hear dat mournful sound:
> All de darkeys am a weeping,
> Massa's in de cold cold ground.

Within Old-South mythology, the black banjo player is a maudlin character, devoted to "ol' massa." It is hard to say how much Foster reflected and how much he created this sentimental idea of the Southern black banjo player. His work represented a shift toward a more sentimental idiom in the antebellum minstrel theater, a shift that was in keeping with changes in popular literature portrayals of plantation society,[36] and a shift that anticipated post–Civil War development of a highly romantic view of the Old South. Postwar portrayals of the Old South came to a nostalgic climax during the period between the two World Wars.[37] The increasing temporal distance from the Old South allowed a greater romanticization.

Although Foster died in 1864, his fame as a composer of sentimental Southern songs (Foster was a native of Pittsburgh) reached a peak at the end of the nineteenth century and during the first half of the twentieth century. In his book on Stephen Foster, William Austin[38] points out that the "pathetic plantation songs" (sentimental songs), such as *Massa's in the Cold Ground, Old Kentucky Home,* and *Old Black Joe,* owed much of their popularity to the *Uncle Tom's Cabin* shows, a classic of romantic racial stereotypes. Austin discusses how Stephen Foster was transformed into a composer of American "folk songs," the confusion of his songs with African-American spirituals, and the respectability these songs achieved in the twentieth century. It is a powerful thing to be accepted as "folk"; within a tradition of democratic rhetoric, it is difficult to argue with the message of the "folk." Generations of American school children sang, in their classrooms, lines like the following from Foster's *Old Folks at Home:* "When will I hear de banjo tumming / Down in my good old home?"

Even though professional minstrelsy of the late nineteenth century drifted away from Southern plantation themes, other theatrical forms existed for the exploitation of Old-South mythology. Sentimental depictions and fantasies about the plantation South continued well into the twentieth century. Could there ever have been a Civil War story that takes place in the North that might have rivaled the popularity of *Gone with the Wind? Uncle Tom's Cabin* shows used Old-South plantation scenes, and eventually motion pictures were able to capture those Dixie panoramas better than the confines of the stage. In 1895, a "Negro Village" was constructed in Brooklyn, New York, complete with log cabins, farm animals, and five hundred "genuinely southern negroes."[39] Patrons strolled about the plantation before the stage show.

For many Americans, attending the theater remained an immoral activity, often for good reasons.[40] They would not patronize minstrel theater or vaudeville theater, or even "Romeo and Juliet," but one show they considered socially and morally uplifting. J. Frank Davis explains in a 1925 article in *Scribner's Magazine:* "In America to-day are vast numbers of middle-aged men and women who remember that 'Uncle Tom' was the first theatrical performance they ever saw. Also the second, third, and fourth, very likely, unless 'Ten

Nights in a Barroom' [a temperance play] also happened to come to that town. I was one of those. Until I was thirteen years old I never saw a professional company of actors in anything but 'Tom' – but I had seen that sterling production five or six times."[41] *Uncle Tom's Cabin* was first dramatized in 1852 – the same year that Harriet Beecher Stowe published the novel in book form – and it remained popular until the time of the Civil War. In the 1870s the show regained and surpassed its previous popularity and hundreds of "Tommer" companies crisscrossed the country, bringing to cities and towns of all sizes "the great instructive and moral drama." Thomas Gossett estimates that at least five hundred "Tommer" companies toured the country during the 1890s alone. *Uncle Tom's Cabin*, and its various dramatic interpretations, created basic ideas about the South for many non-Southerners. The shows frequently employed banjo players, connecting once again the idea of the banjo to Southern black plantation workers, but here in a generally more sentimental and nostalgic idiom than that of the minstrel theater. In 1931 *Outlook* magazine announced: "*Uncle Tom's Cabin*, after seventy-seven years of continuous performance here, there and everywhere, has closed at last. It is hard to believe that there are no Elizas leaping from canvas ice-block to canvas ice-block, no creaking pulleys bearing Little Eva to Heaven, no snarling Simon Legrees in the world . . . for the first time since the premiere in 1853 there is now not a single company anywhere playing *Uncle Tom's Cabin*."[42]

Uncle Tom's Cabin proved popular at movie houses as well as on the stage; it was made for the cinema at least seventeen times between the years 1903 and 1929 (some versions dramatic and some satirical).[43] Universal studios created the most lavish production in 1927. It had a budget rumored between one and two million dollars, a huge sum by contemporary standards. The film has an added orchestral sound track, but not the synchronized sound of a "talkie." The score is nearly a constant medley of Stephen Foster tunes or motives from the songs, particularly *Old Kentucky Home, Old Folks at Home,* and *Old Black Joe* – all songs with a long association to the play.

Why did the public want an incessant repetition of this single story? *Uncle Tom's Cabin* was an American morality play, with some of the most unforgettable characters in American literature, characters that have since served as cultural archetypes, characters placed in a theatrical melodrama that inevitably worked its way to the moral message. Yet in post–Civil War times, it no longer delivered a message that threatened the status quo.

Uncle Tom's Cabin, as recreated on stage and screen, no longer called for social reform, and so freely lingered on in romantic portrayals of the glory of the Old South. Filmmakers often exploited the idyllic life on the Shelbys' Kentucky plantation for scenes of white gentility and black happiness in servitude. Film reviewers frequently gave special attention to spectacle scenes in the cotton fields and on the riverboats.[44]

In the novel, Harriet Beecher Stowe does not once mention banjos, but because the instrument was considered *the* instrument of plantation blacks, it appeared frequently in *Uncle Tom's Cabin* shows and films. Horace Weston, the well-known black banjoist, often worked with *Uncle Tom's Cabin* shows, and toured in Europe in 1878 with one "Tom Show." Figure 19 is an 1899 lithograph. The stage Topsy, as this illustration shows, was usually played by a grown woman (white, in blackface), though the character is supposed to be a child. Topsy was a particular favorite with audiences; the character was a vehicle for low comedy antics. To accompany her (perhaps she is singing her famous song *I'se so Wicked*) she has sidemen on guitar and banjo, and all of them are placed in a plantation setting.

In the 1927 Universal film, the banjo appears in predictable situations; it is always played by black males in plantation scenes. During a party at the Shelbys' Kentucky plantation, the white guests in the ballroom have a slave dance orchestra that looks curiously like a first-part minstrel semicircle. The dance orchestra includes a banjo. Outside the mansion, the black folk have their own dance, but their orchestra has only the bare essential—a banjo player: an elderly man in a tattered top hat strumming wildly and comedically shaking his face every now and then.

The representation of banjo playing on the benevolent Shelby plantation in the 1927 film demonstrates that many Americans happily accepted an "ideal" society based upon strict class divisions, but not just any kind of class division. It is easy to understand why many white Americans approved of a social ordering where all white people played aristocrats; poor whites and yeomen farmers were excluded from the mythology. Figure 20 is of two 1924 advertisements for sausages. Both illustrations are meant to be pleasing to the reader, and they show the two social components of the Old-South myth. All is right with the social world; the black man—barefoot and in ragged clothes—is content playing the banjo while the white woman sits upon her pony. "From a famous old plantation"—images that reassured many Americans in 1924. Every person is in his or her place, and the banjo and the riding crop are unmistakable signs of social caste.

But there was also a note of self-chastisement in the Old-South fantasy. Eugene Genovese notes that Southern planter society has offered the only developed ideology in opposition to capitalist-bourgeois culture in the United States. A reactionary ideology, but still an ideology that deserves serious historical consideration.[45] I would argue that Southern planter culture also offered Americans something less distinct than an ideology; it offered an imaginative alternative to the social values and strictures of capitalist-bourgeois society—an escape from "official culture." The ruggedness and lawlessness of the Old West did much the same, but whereas the Old West was wild, the Old South exuded security and the cultivated manners of an aristocratic (although

Fig. 19: Courier Lithograph Company, 1899: Library of Congress, Prints and Photographs.

anachronistic) social order. The Old West was a world in the making, the Old South the vestige of a lost time.

The view of Southern planter society standing in opposition to Northern industrial capitalism is not merely the observation of a Marxian historian, it

From a famous old plantation

FROM the Mickelberry plantation comes the secret of the delicious flavor of Mickelberry's Sausage. It is the secret of old-time southern seasoning. The secret of blending lean and fat young pork and delicately spicing it. Better than you ever ate—Mickelberry's Sausages, browned to a turn. Try them.

Fresh at your store daily—links or sausage meat—in the green and yellow one-pound cartons only. Eat it often!

MICKELBERRY'S FOOD PRODUCTS CO.
801-811 W. 49th Place
Telephone: BOUlevard 0430

A Southern family's secret for 75 years

SEVENTY-FIVE years ago, the Mickelberry plantation had a reputation for making wonderful sausage. The recipe has remained in the family. It is that old-time southern seasoning that makes Mickelberry's Sausage so wonderfully good to-day—so wonderfully different. Lean and fat young pork, delicately spiced. Delicious, savory sausages. What flavor!

Fresh at your store daily—links or sausage meat—in the green and yellow one-pound cartons only. Eat it often!

MICKELBERRY'S FOOD PRODUCTS CO.
801-811 W. 49th Place
Telephone: BOUlevard 0430

Fig. 20: Ayer Collection, Archives Center, NMAH, Smithsonian Institution.

was a widely accepted idea in American popular culture.[46] The idea has antebellum roots in the pro-South and proslavery arguments, as epitomized in figure 21, a lithograph of 1850 from Boston.[47] Rather than Northern industrial society, the artist contrasts the slave South with the English factory system, the most advanced industrial society of the time and presumably the model for future Northern development. The slaves are stereotypically shown, not at work, but at play—dancing to the banjo and the bones (the banjo player is much more prominent than the bones player, who melds into the dancing throng). Apparently the American slaves have no need to complain like the British factory workers; the artist here symbolizes a carefree life with the nonverbal signs of dancing bodies and banjo strumming.

The national ambivalence about differing social values as represented by contrasting images of the North and South continued long after the Civil War's destruction of the Southern social structure. There was an undeniable attraction to the supposed stability of an aristocratic social order during the rapid change of the late nineteenth and early twentieth centuries. The paternalistic view of slavery presented in figure 21 was not repudiated in the popular culture after the war. Even so, the acceptance of sentimental Old-South mythology and paternalistic interpretations of slavery were not an explicit challenge to the rational, progressive, and modernist values of official culture. Unconsciously, probably, a set of oppositions were linked together. Seemingly unrelated concepts lay on the same side of an unnamed dichotomy:

(sentimental)	(official)
nature	civilization
leisure	work
sensual	controlled
primitive	modern
emotional	rational
black	white
South	North
feminine	masculine

In this way, the labor of black workers in a cotton field appeared in popular culture imagery as essentially leisurely (all qualities from the same side of the dichotomy). When middle-class whites wanted to create more sensual leisure activities, they harvested from that same side of the dichotomy, most notably from the black expressive arts. And because it was a dichotomy, the values from one side need not threaten the dominance of the other. Both Old-South mythology and the Southern black banjo fell squarely on the side of the sentimental.

Therefore, well into the twentieth century, an Old-South fantasy had positive value even for those immersed in the ideology of "official culture." The idea of a rushed, money-obsessed, competitive Northern culture contrasted

Fig. 21: 1850 lithograph from Boston, Massachusetts. Peters Collection, NMAH, Smithsonian Institution.

sharply with Old-South mythology, and somewhere in the interaction Americans tried to find a sense of self. The following is from a 1928 Victor Records advertisement (figure 22): "Let us pause a moment, Gentlemen [sic], and welcome the past. Let us lay aside our invoices and debentures, our politics and our coal bills. . . . For tonight an old, familiar company is with us. . . . Nelly Bly is here, and Old Black Joe . . . Uncle Ned . . . the Old Folks at Home. . . . And with them their banjos and cotton bales, their slow brown rivers and their cabin doors. . . ."

Accompanying this advertisement is an intricate, yet primitivist, drawing filled with Southern scenery. The romantic white couple in the center is surrounded by mostly black figures, including a banjo player, and the requisite western-style sidewheeler steamboat. "The Old Songs Are the Best Songs," and apparently the old songs are Southern (even if the composer is Northern). Put aside modern concern with money matters, and let us welcome the sentimental past, our shared mythical Southern past.

It is not a mistake that most of the "Carry Me Back" and various geographically placed homesick songs are about the South. The Old-South stereotype of stability, being cared for by others (for example, a Mammy), and placement outside of the realm of capitalist-economic competition are also the qualities of an ideal childhood home. Old-South mythology eventually gave way to the agrarian-white mountain South of country music homesick songs; many of the qualities of the former carried over, with some transformation, to the latter. The banjo is transferred, but this story belongs to another chapter.

Romantic racialism molded the image of the Southern black banjo player, as indeed it molded the image of all blacks in the sentimental Old-South idiom. "Romantic racialism" is a term used by George M. Fredrickson in *The Black Image in the White Mind* to describe one of the major currents of white American racial thinking. The romantic racialist believed that blacks had a greater capacity for joyous expression at both work and play, a simple but sincere spirituality, an innate musicality, and overall a closeness to natural instincts and "nature" (rather than "civilization"). These ideas had roots in antebellum paternalism and in Enlightenment notions of the noble savage.

The following is from an 1856 article in a popular music journal. Although from before the time period under consideration, the passage hints at the roots of a long-standing romantic stereotype. Who could provide more of a contrast to the American white bourgeoisie than the antebellum Southern black? In this article, the reason for looking at black music was not to understand black culture, but to understand and criticize the society that white Americans were building, to criticize the official culture for its lack of sentiment. The author clearly sees black culture and character as an antithesis to middle-class white America. And the comparison does not always compliment the dominant group:

LET us pause a moment, Gentlemen, and welcome the past. Let us lay aside our invoices and debentures, our politics and our coal bills. . . . For tonight an old, familiar company is with us. . . . Nelly Bly is here, and Old Black Joe . . . Uncle Ned, Susanna, Lou'siana Belle . . . the Old Folks at Home . . . Jeanie with the light brown hair. . . . And with them their banjos and cotton bales, their slow brown rivers and their cabin doors. . . .

These old songs, written by Stephen Foster more than 75 years ago, are known all over the world. Our grandmothers sang them, and our fathers. We ourselves still love them. . . . And now here they are in their entirety, arranged by Nat Shilkret, beautifully played and sung, and collected in a convenient album for your enjoyment.

This is the latest of a long series of Victor Red Seal recordings which are bringing to the musical public the world's most beautiful and important music. Interpreted by the foremost artists and orchestras, recorded with incredible realism by the famous Orthophonic process, they bring within your home the whole horizon of the concert stage. . . . The nearest Victor dealer will gladly play you the Stephen Foster album (four double-faced records, list price $6.00). Hear it at your first opportunity! . . . Victor Talking Machine Co., Camden, New Jersey, U. S. A.

VICTOR *Red Seal* RECORDS

Fig. 22: "The Old Songs are the Best Songs." Ayer Collection, Archives Center, NMAH, Smithsonian Institution.

The only musical population of this country are [sic] the negroes of the South. Here at the North we have teachers in great numbers, who try to graft the love of music upon the tastes of our colder race.... The Negro is a natural musician. ... The African nature is full of poetry. Inferior to the white race in reason and intellect, they have more imagination, more lively feelings and a more expressive manner. In this they resemble the southern nations of Europe.... Might not our countrymen all learn a lesson from these simple children of Africa? We are a silent and reserved people.... Songless and joyless, the [white] laborer goes to his task.[48]

The romantic racialist idea of African Americans was not really taken as a model for emulation; perhaps we should learn from the "children of Africa," but we need not be like them. Even so, the persistence of the characterization on stage and in literature reveals at least a level of fascination. As social conditions changed, exponents of romantic racialism (often well-intentioned liberals) responded with appropriate transformations of the idea. The stereotypes of romantic racialism were thought complimentary in the 1920s as they appeared in such works as DuBose Heyward's *Porgy*, which was later set to music by George Gershwin as *Porgy and Bess*. In the opera, Porgy expresses his philosophy of life in what is labeled in the score as a "banjo song"—*I Got Plenty of Nothin'*—a song lyric based on romantic racialist thinking. Writers in the 1920s presented the African-Americans' supposed emotionalism and freer sexuality as an alternative to the puritanical philosophy then under attack.[49]

The creators of popular culture normally presented the black banjo player within a romantic racialist framework in an Old-South setting: his musical instrument was a product of nature rather than civilization, and he played the role of the loyal slave, happy with life's limited pleasures. The banjo player was always male. In the nineteenth century, he was often young, even a child, but by the 1920s the image of the Southern black banjoist was usually that of an elderly man. Age placed the character historically in the slave era, and made him the product of a paternalistic upbringing. The character was uneducated and untainted by the ways of the city. He lived close to nature both as a worker in the fields (though seldom shown working) and in his little cabin, usually portrayed as nothing more than a door with magnolias blooming around it.

Below is an excerpt from an 1887 Variety theater skit. In it we meet Pete, a typical example of the sentimental Old-South banjo player.

[Pete,] an old, rheumatic darky, limps on:
[Pete]: There's the ol'mansion, jest the same as wen I lef' it twenty-two years ago. Didn't think Ah'd evah live to see mah ol' home agin. 'Spose all the chillen is married an' grown up—some gone to see their Maker where Ah's goin' mahself befoh long.... (His foot touches something and he looks down to see what it is)

Goodness me! There's a banjo a layin' on the grass. Looks lak one I used to own long befoh Ah lef the old plantation. (Picks up a banjo and examines it) Why, it's mah ol' banjo been lyin' there evah since Ah lef.... [50]

At this point, Pete plays his banjo and sings of those good old days of slavery. The banjo, though it had been lying in the grass for twenty-two years, is in perfect playing condition. Pete, being ill, has come home to see "ol' massa" and to die. Both goals are eventually realized, an offstage chorus sings *Sweet By and By*, while on stage the master grieves for the passing of his loyal old slave. We are never told why Pete had not taken the banjo with him when he left the plantation. Perhaps he realized that the power of the instrument as social symbol depended upon its Old-South plantation context; it could not move easily into a new society. The "ol' banjo" belongs on the plantation and there it did not suffer the ravages of time that poor Pete suffered after emancipation. The banjo was never emancipated.

The 1927 cartoon "Felix the Cat in Uncle Tom's Crabbin'"[51] distills the sentimental black banjo to a symbolic level and completely remakes the story of *Uncle Tom's Cabin*. Felix the Cat, out for a walk, hears the sound of a banjo. Following the sound, he finds Uncle Tom sitting in front of his little cabin playing the banjo and Topsy dancing joyously in front. Felix joins the dance. Felix and Topsy are drawn very similarly; Felix is another Topsy, full of innocent joy, but he has the cunning of a cat (the Topsy character is more simpleminded in her innocence). Meanwhile, Legree, who has no interest in dancing in the sunshine, is disturbed by the banjo music while trying to sleep in his gloomy house. When Legree arrives at the cabin, he lassos the banjo with his whip and pulls it and Uncle Tom, who does not let go of his banjo, off the screen. Felix and Topsy's faces wince with each blow of the whip, which the audience surely thinks are falling upon Uncle Tom (they know how the real story goes). But as the scene shifts, we see Legree whipping the banjo and watch as the banjo splits into pieces. Just as Felix is another form of Topsy, the "ol' banjo" is a form of Uncle Tom. It can even replace Uncle Tom in his punishment and death. Neither can escape to the North, both are simple folk with a loyalty to the Old South, and both are old, passive, and subject to the white man's aggression.

The black character "Jo" in Edna Ferber's tremendously popular novel *Showboat* (1926) (who in the musical version by Oscar Hammerstein and Jerome Kern sings the song *Old Man River*) plays the banjo to accompany the singing of spirituals.

Jo's legs were crossed, one foot in its great low shapeless shoe hooked in the chair rung, his banjo cradled in his lap. The once white parchment face of the instrument was now almost as black as Jo's, what with much strumming by work-stained fingers.

"Which one, Miss Magnolia?"

"I Got Shoes," Magnolia would answer, promptly.

Jo would throw back his head, his sombre eyes half shut: . . .

The longing of a footsore, ragged, driven race expressed in the tragically childlike terms of shoes, white robes, wings, and the wise and simple insight into hypocrisy: "Ev'rybody talkin 'bout Heav'n ain't goin' there. . . ."[52]

Jo is undoubtedly a noble character, but along very predictable lines: he has a sincere though "tragically childlike" spirituality, and a naive musicality. He sings simple, earthy folksongs, and plays a naive musical instrument, one that has become an extension of Jo, its face a matching black from the constant touch of Jo's work-stained hands.

For Europeans and peoples of European extraction, there has usually been something essentially "other" about the banjo. Lute-type instruments with a vellumlike vibrating head are found in parts of Africa (e.g. the *kora* of the griot), the Middle East (e.g. the Persian *tar*), India (e.g. the Hindustani *sarod*), and East Asia (e.g. the Japanese *shamisen*), but this type of instrument was not found in western European societies—until the banjo. Its unusual—for Euro-Americans—form of construction tacitly refers to an exoticism, a half-barbaric quality, a wildness within, or perhaps even a freakishness. The Steinways, of Steinway pianos, in an 1893 interview declared the banjo "half guitar, half drum, [which] like the mule [also a mongrel] . . . has not pride of ancestry nor hope of posterity"[53]—strange fruit indeed.

The Columbia advertisement below dates from 1920. Whoever wrote the advertisement surely exaggerated the banjo's power of suggestion, but it defines the areas of exotic associations that were available to the instrument.

The music of the banjo has a fascination peculiarly its own. There is a barbaric vigor to its ringing tone and drumlike rhythm which carries us away from the staid music room of our home out under the stars over Southern levees where groups of dark-faced negroes, with shining teeth and eyes, sing plantation melodies to the strumming strings; back to the Senegambian savages with their bania, the parent of our American banjo; still further back to ancient nomadic Arabs who brought their stringed instruments to the negroes of Western Africa centuries ago.

In all the developments of the banjo, since the negro first brought it to this country, it has never lost its spell. . . . [54]

This passage shares a bucolic and uncivilized view of the banjo with the 1891 *Philadelphia Music and Drama* article quoted in chapter 1: "On the other hand, the banjo has a positive musical charm in the country. Here we can see that it fits the surroundings. Its half barbaric twang is in harmony with the unmechanical melodies of the birds. . . . " This article addressed the banjo playing of white upper-class young women, not Southern blacks. The barbaric vigor of the black banjo becomes only half barbaric in this context, but it is clear that the idea of the black banjo was used to help create meaning for the banjo-playing fad of fashionable circles in the late nineteenth century, and in ways more subtle than programatic compositions.

Rich rhythms of an old race

PLEADING and strange... restless and beautiful . . . such are the rhythms that make up the irresistible charm of negro songs and spirituals. Nobody knows how old they are, or from what distant source they sprang —nobody cares—their deep, brooding melody—the weird cadences... these are enough.

It is the amazing ability of the Orthophonic Victrola to hold the minute and fragmentary tone shadings

of the pleading, restless spirit of negro music. You will hear lower notes and higher notes than ever. You will find a new beauty and power, a new depth and sonority, to all music played on the Orthophonic Victrola. Whether the deep, rich basses of a negro song, or the strange, brooding melody of a negro spiritual —this marvelous instrument brings them all to your home, there to be played whenever you want them, again and again. , , ,

Send for Free Pamphlet, describing the miracle of

the New Orthophonic Victrola. Just send your name and address to the Victor Talking Machine Company, Camden, New Jersey, and a pamphlet describing the interesting development of the Orthophonic Victrola will be sent to you free of charge

See and hear the Orthophonic Victrola today. Your dealer will gladly demonstrate this musical miracle— any time. There are four beautiful models—the Credenza at $300—the Granada (illustrated above) at $135—the Colony at $150 and the Consolette at $85.

The New Orthophonic Victrola

VICTOR TALKING MACHINE COMPANY   CAMDEN, NEW JERSEY, U. S. A.

Fig. 23: "Rich rhythms of an old race." Ayer Collection, Archives Center, NMAH, Smithsonian Institution.

A 1927 Victrola advertisement (figure 23) includes an illustration of a group of older black men gathered around the cabin door singing; two members of the group are playing the banjo. Romanticism and exoticism form the foundation of this description of black music and banjo playing. "Rich Rhythms of an old race. . . . negro songs and spirituals. Nobody knows how old they are, or from what distant source they sprang—nobody cares—their deep, brooding melody—the weird cadences . . . these are enough."

"Weird" is a word often encountered in nineteenth- and early twentieth-century descriptions of African-American music, and writers of the period often used the same word to describe white Appalachian traditional ballads and dulcimer music. "Weird" means mysterious, exotic, and unknown, and betrays the outsider status of the writer. The "weird" or "exotic" form an opposition to the "familiar." Not only was the banjo exotic, the South was portrayed as exotic, and African Americans had a touch of the exotic as well. But Africa, the "Dark Continent," seemed yet more exotic.

A 1920 short story by Arthur Stringer from *Hearst's Magazine* entitled "The Drums of Dusk"[55] probably makes the banjo as exotic as was possible. Stringer avoids the word "banjo," as if it would pin the meaning down to something too trivial, but the illustration (though shadowy) and the written description are both clearly of a banjo. The banjo is handmade from the natural substances fitting for a home in "darkest Africa," and so returned to a state of nature. The story, a spicy form of popular literature, abounds with the characteristic 1920s questioning of civilized sexuality and the supposed freedom from social constraints that Western imperialists and intellectuals both projected onto the non-European peoples of the world. A wealthy white American woman, on a private cruise down the Nile, is bored with life, and bored with her rather effete millionaire husband, Montie. Along the Nile, she spies with her binoculars an attractive African man on a small rickety boat and "the glimmer of light on the swarthy sinewed shoulders where the ragged shirt fell almost obscenely away from the sooty smooth body that spelled strength." She spends her days watching the man from her large ship, and her evenings listening

> to that elemental drone and throb of sound made by a bull-necked negro chanting in front of his whitewashed marsh-shanty and drumming on a crudely fashioned instrument made of oiled goat-skin stretched over a grotesquely carved drum frame to which had been attached a walnut stem strung with dried gut. Yet as it pulsed and throbbed through the deepening night it both intrigued and troubled the wide-eyed listener. It awoke the war-drums in the Kraal of her own body. It disturbed something ancestral and dormant, something which seemed to leave all the rest of her life thin and shadowy.

The author could have used a different sort of experience to awaken the heroine's "war-drums," but Stringer has curiously turned to the old American image of the white folks listening from the porch of the big house (here become the deck of the cruise ship) to the evening banjo strummings of an African-American male and transforms it with exoticism into eroticism.

Although evening banjo strummings along the Nile are unquestionably more exotic than the same activity in the United States (for Americans), still, Stringer's choice of imagery indicates an intrinsic exoticism in the original Dixie image (but never an eroticism). Early twentieth-century illustrators tended to place the black banjo in one of two places: on a river shore or levee, usually with a side-wheeler riverboat in view, or in front of a little cabin on a plantation. Both locations appealed to the sense of spectacle and the exotic. Often the two locations were combined.

Figure 24, a sheet music cover from 1876, gives a closeup view of the pictorial convention of plantation blacks playing the banjo and dancing in front of a lowly cabin. The year 1876 is well before the 1890s era of "coon songs," so the art work is free of the grotesque caricatures of African Americans that appear at the end of the nineteenth century, as in figure 18 (caricatures that don't fully disappear in the United States until after the mid-twentieth century). Popular illustrations of African-American banjo players and dancers in front of a cabin tended, over time, to distance the viewer from the scene. By the 1920s pictures of this sort became shadowy silhouettes surrounded by Old-South panoramas. Details faded with distance and the twilight hour, and the imagery was awash with a generalized romanticism.[56]

The 1930 song, *When It's Sleepy Time Down South,* [57] paints with words this twentieth-century brand of Old-South imagery. It is twilight, the visual imagery is long-distance ("Pale moon shining on the fields below," etc.), people exist as a collective, generalized "folks" in contrast to ragtime and "coon songs'" tendency to focus on individuals. The lyrics have steamboats and banjos and a strong dreamlike quality:

> Steamboats on the river, a-coming, a-going,
> Splashing the night away,
> Hear those banjos ringing, the folks all a-singing,
> They dance till break of day.

It is in lyrics like the above that we find the idea of the Southern black banjo presented in its most exotic and sentimental idiom. But this path to meaning inspired more lyricists and graphic artists than performing musicians. It became a dead end for actual banjo performance because it demanded no more than a nostalgia for a mythical past. You can only play *Old Black Joe* on the banjo for so long.

The Old-South myth began to break down in the mid-twentieth century, and as this happened, the sentimental idea of the Southern black banjo lost its home. By the late twentieth century, most Americans, especially younger Americans, no longer thought of the instrument as black at all. The abandon-

Fig. 24: Detail from cover of "Down Among De Sugar Cane," 1876. Harris Collection, Brown University Library.

ment of this formerly strong image was the result of changing stereotypes of African Americans and changing public attitudes toward racism and the South.

With African-American migration to Northern urban areas and the mass appeal of black urban-based music such as jazz, white Americans' ideas about blacks changed. The old stereotypes no longer fit. A comparison of the 1927 cartoon *Uncle Tom's Crabbin'*, discussed earlier, with the 1947 cartoon *Uncle Tom's Cabana* (Loew's Inc.) gives an indication of the shift in thinking that took place in those twenty years. The 1927 cartoon had Uncle Tom playing the banjo in front of his cabin with Topsy dancing wildly. Legree whips his banjo into pieces instead of whipping Uncle Tom. The 1947 cartoon starts with a plantation scene and a music track of sweetly played orchestral versions of Foster's *Old Kentucky Home* and *Old Black Joe*. Uncle Tom sits in front of his cabin (so far the old ideas continue unchallenged), but this Uncle Tom smokes a big cigar and talks in New York City cadences. He tells us that we are about to learn the *real* story of Uncle Tom. The scene suddenly shifts to a modern city, and we learn that to keep Legree from foreclosing on his downtown cabin, Uncle Tom, with the help of a very grown-up Eva, has opened up a night club called "Uncle Tom's Cabana." This Uncle Tom does not play the banjo; he is a boogie-woogie piano player, a "Fats" Waller character. Black Americans had become part of the urban scene.

The well-entrenched notion of genetic racial differences in intelligence and temperament was not seriously challenged until the 1920s and 1930s. A small group of scholars, including Franz Boas, led the fight to establish liberal environmentalism as the working ideology in American race thinking. By the 1930s, their ideas had penetrated academic circles, but real triumph did not come until World War II. The irony of fighting Nazi racism while maintaining institutionalized segregation and racism at home was hard to ignore. Also, race relations in the nation had a detrimental effect on post–World War II efforts to charm third world countries into American spheres of influence. And the growing power of the NAACP and the Urban League began to have an effect. Official doctrine on the federal level was due for a change.

Public ideas of race slowly began to change, but the change proved less than graceful and it resulted in a general avoidance of African-American images in the popular culture, including images of black banjo players. Hollywood movies after World War II depicted a different kind of South than the sentimental Old South of the 1920s and 1930s: the Hollywood new South was largely white, and given to Gothic extremes.[58] Advertisers and popular song lyricists had commonly used black characters in their work (generally in denigrating ways) before the war, but by the mid-1950s, blacks had all but disappeared from both media.[59] It was easier to delete the image of African

Americans than to reform it. In the midst of the tensions of social change, the idea of the Southern black banjo player no longer provided a comfortable escape from the "official culture" for the mostly white audiences and consumers of American popular culture.[60]

Because of the racist imagery connected to the instrument in the national popular culture, the banjo is a problematic cultural symbol for most African Americans. Consequently, few African Americans have communicated about it to the general public. One outstanding exception to black silence on the topic of the black banjo is the 1893 painting "The Banjo Lesson" (figure 25) by Henry Ossawa Tanner (1859-1937). Tanner was the leading African-American painter of his time, known primarily for his biblical painting. He spent most of his professional life in France, as he was unable to make a living in the United States. Tanner painted "The Banjo Lesson" from a sketch he made in 1889 while visiting in Highlands, North Carolina, a small Blue Ridge mountain community. The Hampton Institute, a school founded in 1868 for the education of newly freed black Americans, acquired the painting in 1894. The Hampton University Museum still owns "The Banjo Lesson." The two figures in the painting, older man and young boy, form a warm and nurturing image in the rustic home. An unseen fireplace fills the room with a soft glow. The two are huddled together with gazes intent upon the learning of right-hand technique. Interestingly, Mary Cassatt finished her first "Banjo Lesson" in 1893 also (figure 3 is the 1894 reworking of the 1893 piece), but her teacher and student are white bourgeois women.

In 1893 Tanner's sensitive painting was at odds with the popular culture treatment of the Southern black banjo player. There is nothing derogatory here, nor any hint of Old-South mythology. These are real people in the heart of rural African-American culture. This painting, according to the impressive bibliographic research of Lynn Moody Igoe in her *250 Years of Afro-American Art: An Annotated Bibliography,* is by far Tanner's most reproduced painting (in magazines, books, etc.). The popularity and importance of "The Banjo Lesson" grew as a result of a post-Civil Rights search for symbols of the African-American heritage. "The Banjo Lesson" has been made into a popular poster, UNICEF used it for a Christmas card design, and it appears in many school textbooks.[61] Even though most images of the black banjo were demeaning or racist, particularly in the 1890s, positive images were possible—and Tanner created one, one that is still being put to work.[62]

The Jamaican-born black writer Claude McKay (1890-1948) wrote the novel *Banjo* in 1929. McKay spent many years in the United States and France, and involved himself in leftist politics until his conversion to Roman Catholicism in 1944. He was one of the leading figures in the "Negro literary renaissance" of the 1920s. McKay sets *Banjo* along the beaches of Marseilles and most of the characters are of African descent from various corners of the

Fig. 25: "The Banjo Lesson" by Henry O. Tanner, 1893. Hampton University Museum.

world. The characters "Banjo" and "Goosey" both hail from the American South. Through their dialogue, McKay expresses some of the ambivalence that many black Americans felt about the banjo:

> "Banjo! That's what you play?" exclaimed Goosey.
>
> "Sure that's what I play," replied Banjo. "Don't you like it?"
>
> "No. Banjo is bondage. It's the instrument of slavery. Banjo is Dixie. The Dixie of the land of cotton and massa and missus and black mammy. We colored folks have got to get away from all that in these enlightened progressive days. Let us play piano and violin, harp and flute. Let the white folks play the banjo if they want to keep on remembering all the Black Joes singing and the hell they made them live in."
>
> "That ain't got nothing to do with me, nigger," replied Banjo. "I play that theah instrument becaz I likes it. I don't play no Black Joe hymns. I play lively tunes. . . . "[63]

The generally racist ideas that clung to the image of the black banjo player not only encouraged the abandonment of the instrument by blacks, in the end it discouraged the survival of the instrument as a viable vehicle for music making in American culture. The continued association of the banjo with the minstrel show and the medicine show in the twentieth century gave the banjo a lowbrow and old-fashioned image. These theatrical forms had become vestiges of another day and were slowly disappearing, and they had the potential of taking the old five-string banjo with it. The black banjo was depicted in theatrical and musical performances, in illustrations, literature, and song lyrics as the instrument of a simple and childlike race, and the banjo could only be simple and childlike in return. Outside of the actual performance context, the banjo had a certain positive meaning when encased in Old-South nostalgia. But Old-South myths and medicine and minstrel shows were not contexts of meaning that would fully survive the social changes of the twentieth century, and they proved sterile grounds for the development of new meaning for a new time (at least a meaning that would lead to actual musical performance). Though the "ol' banjo" of the Old South had found strength by staking out ground that was outside of the "official culture" and part of American sentimental ethos, the specific ground staked out by the sentimental Southern black banjo was doomed to be swallowed up in the overdue social changes of the twentieth century.

By the post–World War II era, Americans had become accustomed to the image of the Southern black man playing the "ol' banjo"; this idea had been presented to the public for more than a century in the theater they attended, in the magazines that came to their homes, on the postcards they received,[64] in the books they read, the movies they saw, and on the sheet music that sat on their pianos. Some Americans even had little black Sambos on their walls with a clock set in the middle of Sambo's banjo.[65] But these images did not survive the twentieth century with its righteous challenge to racial exploitation. Henry Tanner's "The Banjo Lesson," a strong and almost singular statement of the value of this African-American rural tradition, stands alone — an isolated message without support. In the second half of the twentieth century, as revisionist history finally affected popular culture, and black migration and civil rights agitation caused a reworking of Southern realities and Southern stereotypes, the black five-string banjo player, both the real and the mythical, faded from view.

Notes

1. The letter is quoted in Joel Chandler Harris, "Plantation Music," *The Critic* v. 3, n. 95 (15 December 1883): pp. 505–6.

2. I thank Rebecca Zurier for showing this article to me.

3. For example, see Bill Malone, *Southern Music, American Music* (Lexington: University of Kentucky Press, 1979), p. 8.

4. Cecelia Conway's 1980 dissertation is entitled "The Afro-American Traditions of the Folk Banjo" (University of North Carolina); largely based upon interviews, it does explore historical questions as well. With Tommy Thompson, she wrote the article "Talking Banjo," *Southern Exposure* v. 2, n. 1 (1974): pp. 63–66. Dena Epstein includes much of her banjo research in her 1977 book *Sinful Tunes and Spirituals*, but her findings on colonial era banjos in North America and the Caribbean are clearly given in "The Folk Banjo: A Documentary History." Kip Lornell, "Pre-Blues Banjo and Fiddle," *Living Blues* v. 18 (1974): pp. 25–27. Kip Lornell and J. Roderick Moore, "On Tour with a Black String Band in the 1930s," *Goldenseal* v. 2, n. 4 (1976): pp. 9–12, 46–52; "Clarence Tross: Hardy County Banjoist," *Goldenseal* v. 3, n. 3 (1976): pp. 7–13. See Daniel W. Patterson, ed., *Arts in Earnest: North Carolina Folklife* (Durham, N.C.: Duke University Press, 1990) for "Banjos and Blues" by Kip Lornell (pp. 216–31) and "The Banjo-Song Genre" by Cecelia Conway (pp. 135–46). William Tallmadge makes a strong case for pre–Civil War introduction of the banjo in the Southern mountains by African-Americans in "The Folk Banjo and Clawhammer Performance Practice in the Upper South: A Study of Origins," *The Appalachian Experience*, ed. Barry M. Buxton (Boone, N. C.: Appalachian Consortium Press, 1983), pp. 169–79. Robert B. Winans, "The Black Banjo-Playing Tradition in Virginia and West Virginia," *Journal of the Virginia Folklore Society* v. 1 (1979): pp. 7–30; Winans, "Black Musicians in 18th-Century America."

5. The early important works on African-American music include William Francis Allen, Charles Pickard Ware, and Lucy McKim Garrison, *Slave Songs of the United States* (1867, reprinted New York: Oak Publications, 1965); *Jubilee Songs as Sung by the Fisk Jubilee Singers* (New York: Biglow & Main, 1872); *Fifty Cabin and Plantation Songs* (Hampton Singers, 1874); William Barton, *Old Plantation Hymns* (1899, reprinted New York: AMS Press, 1972); Frederick J. Work, *Folk Songs of the American Negro* (Nashville, Tenn.: Work Bros. and Hart Co., 1907); Henry Edward Krehbiel, *Afro-American Folk Songs: A Study in Racial and National Music* (New York: G. Schirmer, 1914). All are concerned with song.

6. Lawrence W. Levine, *Black Culture and Black Consciousness* (Oxford: Oxford University Press, 1977), p. 18.

7. "Negro Spirituals" by Thomas Wentworth Higginson originally appeared in the *Atlantic Monthly,* June 1867, and is reprinted in Bruce Jackson, *The Negro and His Folklore in Nineteenth-Century Periodicals* (Austin: University of Texas Press, 1967), pp. 82–102.

8. Harris, "Plantation Music," p. 505.

9. Hannah Street, letter to the editor, *The Critic* v. 3, n. 96 (22 December 1883): p. 523.

10. Lucy L. C. Bikle, *George W. Cable: His Life and Letters* (New York: Scribner's, 1928, reprinted 1967), pp. 126–28. My gratitude to Nina Silber for showing this to me.

11. George Washington Cable, "The Dance in Place Congo," originally appeared in the February 1886 issue of *Century Magazine.* It is reprinted in Jackson, *The Negro and his Folklore in Nineteenth-Century Periodicals,* pp. 189–210.

12. Albert Bauer, "Reminiscenses of a Banjo Player," *Stewart's Banjo and Guitar Journal* v. 9, n. 6 (February–March 1893): pp. 7–8.

13. The Bohee brothers were also well-known black banjo players. They spent much of their professional careers in England giving lessons to British upper-class patrons. See "The Banjo in England," *Stewart's Banjo and Guitar Journal* v. 5, n. 1 (April–May 1888): p. 3.

14. The review is an untitled clipping of 23 February 1878 in the Harvard Theater Collection, File 1.

15. *Stewart's Banjo and Guitar Journal* v. 3, n. 12 (October–November 1886): p. 15.

16. "Banjoist Weston Gone," *Morning Journal* (New York City), 26 May 1890. Other sources on Horace Weston include Thomas L. Riis, "The Music and Musicians in Nineteenth-Century Productions of *Uncle Tom's Cabin,*" *American Music* v. 4, n. 3 (1986): pp. 268–86; Eileen Southern, *Biographical Dictionary of Afro-American and African Musicians* (Westport, Conn.: Greenwood Press, 1982), as well as frequent references to him throughout the 1880s issues of *Stewart's Banjo and Guitar Journal.*

17. *The Cadenza,* v. 1, n. 1 (1894): p. 1.

18. The tortoiseshell story of banjo origins was written in "How to Build a Banjo," *The Boy's Own Paper* of 15 December 1888 and reprinted in *Mugwumps* v. 3, n. 2 (March 1974): pp. 23–25. In 1976 Elizabeth Baroody gave the readers of *Early American Life* v. 7, n. 2 (April): p. 57 an incredible description of the slave banjo as a combination of nearly unaltered natural objects: "[the] instrument was simply a straight limb from a tree, with four strings fastened to it." The only stories in which cleverness or skill is used in the creation of the first banjo are ones that credit the creation to a white person. As an apt comparison, note how the blues were created, according to the lyrics of *Birth of the Blues,* one of the biggest hit songs of the twentieth century. The blues, rather like the banjo, were created by the combination of natural sounds, not through creativity or intelligence.

19. Robert B. Winans, "The Black Banjo-Playing Tradition in Virginia and West Virginia," *Journal of the Virginia Folklore Society* v. 1 (1979): pp. 7–30.

20. Norman Howard, "A History of the Banjo" (1957), p. 7 (unpublished manuscript in the New York Public Library Special Collections at Lincoln Center).

21. Harris, "Plantation Music," pp. 505–6.

22. Winans, "Black Musicians in 18th-Century America." See also Sterling Stuckey, *Slave Culture: Nationalist Theory and the Foundations of Black America* (New York: Oxford University Press, 1987): p. 21.

23. Toll, *Blacking Up,* p. 168.

24. Ibid., p. 274.

25. These nostalgic eulogies include: Matthews Brander, "The Rise and Fall of Negro-Minstrelsy," *Scribner's Magazine* v. 57 (1915): pp. 754–59; an unsigned article, "Passing of the Minstrels," *Literary Digest* v. 62 (16 August 1919): pp. 28–29; Marian Spitzer, "The Lay of the Last Minstrels," [the title is taken from a popular Sir Walter Scott poem about a medieval minstrel] *The Saturday Evening Post* v. 197, n. 36 (7 March 1925): pp. 12–13, 117; and Daily Paskman, *"Gentlemen, Be Seated!" A Parade of the American Minstrels* (New York: Clarkson N. Potter, Inc., 1928).

26. Many amateur guides were published; as an example see Kent Walker, *Staging the Amateur Minstrel Show* (Walter H. Baker Co., 1931). As late as 1950, the Urban League of Portland, Oregon, wrote a letter to the editor of the journal of the National Educators' Association asking that public schools not allow community groups to use their facilities for staging minstrel shows. "Is It Fair?" *NEA Journal* v. 39, n. 7 (October 1950): p. 485.

27. Daily Paskman, *"Gentlemen, Be Seated!"* Paskman directed the radio minstrels.

28. Information from a conversation with Lorraine Brown, administrator of the Institute on the Federal Theatre Project at George Mason University, September 1986.

29. Unsigned, "Minstrel Shows," *Life* v. 15, no. 1 (5 July 1943): pp. 80–84; unsigned, *Time* v. 42, n. 13 (27 September 1943): pp. 48, 50.

30. Sam Dennison, *Scandalize My Name: Black Imagery in American Popular Music* (New York: Garland Publishing, Inc., 1982): especially chapter 8, "From the Gay Nineties through the First World War."

31. On race relations in the United States during the 1890s, especially on the codification of Jim Crow laws, see C. Vann Woodward, *The Strange Career of Jim Crow* (New York: Oxford University Press, 1974).

32. W. E. Burghardt Du Bois, *The Souls of Black Folk* (Greenwich, Conn.: Fawcett Publications, Inc., 1961, originally published 1903): essay 2, "The Dawn of Freedom."

33. Janet Brown, "The 'Coon-Singer' and the 'Coon Song': A Case Study of the Performer-Character Relationship," *Journal of American Culture* v. 7, n. 1–2 (spring–summer 1984): pp. 1–8.

34. Thomas Wolfe, *Look Homeward, Angel* (New York: Charles Scribner's Sons, 1957), p. 141.

35. *Fare Thee Well Kitty Dear* song and chorus by G. Friedrich Wurzel (psd.) (New York: William Hall and Son, 1852). In the collection of the Music Division of the Library of Congress.

36. The shift toward a more sentimental and paternalistic idiom in popular literature portrayals of the South is discussed in William R. Taylor, *Cavalier & Yankee: The Old South and American National Character* (Cambridge: Harvard University Press, 1979).

37. Sam Dennison in *Scandalize My Name* comes to a similar conclusion (p. 437).

38. William W. Austin, *"Susanna," "Jeanie," and "The Old Folks at Home": The Songs of Stephen C. Foster from His Time to Ours* (New York: MacMillan Publishing Company, 1975): especially chapter 12, "Jubilee singers and friends of the 'folk'."

39. Toll, *Blacking Up*, p. 262.

40. For example, see Claudia D. Johnson, "That Guilty Third Tier: Prostitution in Nineteenth-Century American Theaters," in *Victorian America*, ed. Daniel Walker Howe (Philadelphia: University of Pennsylvania Press, 1976), pp. 111-20.

41. The sources used and quoted here on the theatrical versions of *Uncle Tom's Cabin* are: J. Frank Davis, "Tom Shows," *Scribner's* v. 77, n. 4 (April 1925): pp. 350-60 (this quote from p. 350); Thomas Gossett, *Uncle Tom's Cabin and American Culture* (Dallas: Southern Methodist University Press, 1985), p. 371; Ralph Eugene Lund, "Trouping with Uncle Tom," *Century Magazine* v. 115, n. 3 (January 1928): pp. 329-37 (quote from p. 329); Riis, "The Music and Musicians in Nineteenth-Century Productions of *Uncle Tom's Cabin*."

42. Unsigned, "Death of 'Uncle Tom'," *Outlook* v. 157, n. 3 (21 January 1931): pp. 89-90.

43. Several of the early *Uncle Tom's Cabin* films are in the collections of the Library of Congress, including the Universal film discussed here.

44. For example see the review of the 1913 Universal production in *Variety* 5 September 1913.

45. Eugene D. Genovese, *In Red and Black* (Knoxville: University of Tennessee Press, 1968), pp. 315-53.

46. For the antebellum roots of popularly held notions of contrasting Northern and Southern cultures, see Taylor, *Cavalier and Yankee*.

47. Photograph from the National Museum of American History, Smithsonian Institution, iconography file of the Division of Musical History.

48. Unsigned, "Songs of the Blacks," *Dwight's Journal of Music* v. 9, n. 7 (15 November 1856): pp. 51-52, reprinted Jackson, *The Negro and his Folklore in Nineteenth-Century Periodicals*, pp. 51-54.

49. George M. Fredrickson, *The Black Image in the White Mind* (New York: Harper and Row, 1971), p. 328.

50. Douglas Gilbert, *American Vaudeville* (New York: Whittlesey House, 1940), pp. 43-44. Gilbert actually gives the date as 1878, but the text of the skit states that twenty-two years have passed since emancipation, so I suspect that he inverted the numbers and the year of this performance was actually 1887.

51. "Felix the Cat in Uncle Tom's Crabbin'," a Pat Sullivan Cartoon, 1927 Bijou Films, Inc. (E. W. Hammons presents) B/W. It is a silent film, so the sound of the banjo is represented by traveling bits of musical notation. It is in the collection of the Library of Congress.

52. Quoted from pages 120-21 of the 1935 First Modern Library Edition. The book became a musical in 1927, and is still a perennial favorite of community theaters and high schools across the country. The show was made into a film three times: 1929 (Universal), 1936 (Universal), and 1951 (MGM). *Show Boat* was the basis of the popular 1930s radio show, "The Maxwell House Show Boat Hour."

53. *Stewart's Banjo and Guitar Journal* v. 10, n. 4 (October–November 1893): p. 3.

54. This advertisement, originally from September 1920, is reprinted in Jeff Todd Titon, *Early Downhome Blues* (Urbana: University of Illinois Press, 1977), p. 230.

55. Arthur Stringer, "The Drums of Dusk," *Hearst's Magazine* v. 38, n. 1 (July 1920): pp. 11–13, 72.

56. Three examples of the "Southern-exotica" illustration style from sheet music covers: *I Love the Land of Old Black Joe* (m. Walter Donaldson l. Grant Clarke) 1920 (a moonlit, riverside cabin in the distance with a shadowy figure of a banjo player on the porch); *Heaven Is Like Dixie After All* (Jack Stern and Clarence J. Marks) 1921 (about the same as the first); the cover to the 1908 edition of James Bland's 1880 song *In the Evening By the Moonlight* (an elderly white couple sits on the porch of the main house watching the banjo playing of a distant, shadowy person in front of a little cabin, with a large moon overhead).

57. *When It's Sleepy Time Down South* (words and music by Leon Rene, Otis Rene, and Clarence Muse), Mills Music Inc., 1931. It was introduced by Clarence Muse, but is best known as Louis Armstrong's theme song.

58. See Jack Temple Kirby, *Media-Made Dixie* (Baton Rouge: Louisiana State University Press, 1978) and Edward D. C. Campbell, *The Celluloid South* (Knoxville: University of Tennessee Press, 1981): pp. 192–93.

59. John Denis Mercier, "The Evolution of the Black Image in White Consciousness, 1876–1954" (PhD dissertation, University of Pennsylvania, 1984); Earl F. Bargainnier, "Tin Pan Alley and Dixie: The South in Popular Song," *Mississippi Quarterly* v. 30, n. 4 (1977): p. 542.

60. Although the black banjo player, and the Old-South mythology that he represented, was no longer a comfortable escapist fantasy for white Americans in the 1950s, it should be remembered that white Americans were still using aspects of black culture for an escape from official culture, for example Rock and Roll.

61. Information from a conversation with Hampton University Museum curators, September 1987.

62. Other artists have sympathetically depicted the African-American banjo tradition. The best known of these works are: Thomas Eakins, "Negro Boy Dancing" (a work often compared to Tanner's—Tanner was a student of Eakins); Eastman Johnson, "The Banjo Player" and "Old Kentucky Home"; Richard N. Brooke, "A Pastoral Visit"; and William Sidney Mount, "The Banjo Player" (a portrait with an ambiguous context).

63. Claude McKay, *Banjo* (New York: Harper and Brothers, 1929; reprinted 1957, New York: Harcourt Brace Jovanovich, Inc.), p. 90.

64. A large collection of banjo postcards is reproduced in Tsumura, *Banjos: The Tsumura Collection* p. 124–28. Many of the cards are British.

65. Mercier, *The Evolution of the Black Image in White Consciousness, 1876–1954*, pp. 450–51.

3

The Modernization of the Banjo in the Early Twentieth Century

Rag time is regarded as musical slang by the highbrows, but their attitude towards it would be different if they didn't have to give the banjo credit for securing a monopoly of praise in that field. When you want real syncopated rag, well done with plenty of gravy, have it served hot on a banjo.[1]

WHEN THOMAS J. ARMSTRONG wrote this passage in 1916 for the Boston-based music magazine *The Crescendo,* it had been twenty-eight years since his "lady pupils" had performed banjo solos for the benefit concert in the Philadelphia home of Mrs. Dundas Lippincott. Gone is the aura of gentility that he and his friend S. S. Stewart[2] had tried to bestow on the banjo in the old days (Stewart died in 1898). Theirs had been a modernizing agenda, but based on nineteenth-century ideas, and predicated upon their desire for social elevation. The modernization of the banjo in the twentieth century entailed a continuation of technological innovation in instrument design and a rejection of sentimental Southern black imagery of the instrument, but by 1916, Armstrong saw that modernizing the banjo in the new century depended on its inclusion in the nascent mass culture of the twentieth century, a nonelitist cultural style that drew from African-American and working-class expressive forms.

The five-string banjo ragtime of the 1890s and the four-string banjo in jazz of the 1920s challenged the old sentimental ideas of the banjo as rural and antimodernist. The reorientation of Anglo-American culture in the early twentieth century involved a rejection of certain Victorian values and expressive arts and, through the aegis of the infant culture industry, a mediated utilization of African-American urban music and dance. It is commonplace to say that black entertainment has served white needs, and that white culture has repeatedly taken from black music to enrich its own experience. But models of appropriation and one-directional musical influence impoverish understanding and cannot satisfactorily account for the twentieth-century change in American music and musical events. This change must be viewed as an exchange process within a framework of social class and American racial ideology. Clearly, not all members of this musical dialogue came to the exchange with equal power, but, somehow, they did communicate. The banjo, unlike any other musical instrument, iconographically bridged the African- and Euro-American experience and so had a particular role to play in the expression of American fears, ambivalence, and excitement about the new music and culture of the twentieth century. Within this context, the "ol' banjo" was modernized—a kind of modernization at odds with nineteenth-century official culture, but not really a part of the sentimental ethos.

Playing techniques, advertising styles, and ideas linking class, gender, and banjo players all changed with the modernization program. The banjo's brush with modernity, however, did not last very long. In the end, the banjo's modernity depended upon its association with the jazz band; it rode piggyback into twentieth-century mass culture. As jazz evolved, the banjo, unable to adapt to new styles and new technologies, lost its place to the guitar. Once displaced, the four-string banjo slipped into the familiar world of American sentimental culture.

Manufacturers made tremendous changes in the physical form of the banjo during this period. By the 1920s the four-string banjo (lacking the short fifth string) had become the dominant form of the instrument, the five-string banjo now relegated to a grandfatherly status. Patents for the banjo peaked in the 1920s, but, by the 1930s, manufacturers had lost interest in developing new banjo designs.[3] Few new instruments were sold during the depression, and the metal rationing of World War II nearly stopped the manufacture of banjos altogether. But the predepression years of the twentieth century produced a plethora of banjo designs and banjo-like instruments.

Late nineteenth-century manufacturers, in their desire to bring the banjo into the realm of official culture, had increased the mechanical qualities of the banjo. Early twentieth-century manufacturers (often the same people), building upon earlier design innovations, worked to increase the power of the machine. Basically, the five-string banjo underwent two major changes in the early twentieth century: the addition of a resonator and the subtraction of a string (however, five-string banjos, with and without resonators, continued to be made and played). A resonator is a sort of dish that attaches to the back of the banjo, covering the back for the purpose of projecting the sound forward and away from the body of the player, creating a more powerful sound. Even though George Teed in the 1860s and Henry Dobson in the 1870s made banjos with resonators, resonators did not become popularly accepted until the flange designs of the 1920s, created by the William L. Lange Company (Paramount) and the Bacon & Day Company (followed by many others).[4] Additionally, both the flanges and the resonator gave the banjo new space for adding ornamentation. Banjos without a resonator could not compete with the flashy decoration of many of the fancy resonated banjos of the 1920s.

Professionals working in large theaters wanted more volume from their banjos. They switched to metal strings, which are louder when played with a pick than the gut or silk strings that were used before, around the turn of the century. A number of other changes in instrument design followed in order to accomodate the increased tension caused by metal strings. The popularity of the mandolin introduced the technique of using a plectrum (pick) on metal strings. Many banjoists seeking more volume, particularly those working in vaudeville, began to use plectral technique in the early years of the twentieth century. There is some evidence of theater performers playing banjo with a plectrum as early as the late 1880s and 1890s.[5] Plectrum playing made the short thumb string nonfunctional, and when strumming away on full chords (a favorite technique for vaudeville players because it was loud—the pit orchestra took care of melodic details), the thumb string, a drone, became dysfunctional. Many banjoists removed the short thumb string, and eventually manufacturers made "plectrum" banjos, the same size and tuned the same as the standard banjo, but lacking the thumb string.

Other developments of the banjo essentially grew out of the national interest in the mandolin. "The Spanish Students," a group from Madrid playing *bandurrías,* toured with great success in the United States in 1880. Shortly afterward, a number of imitative American so-called Spanish Students groups began concertizing using mandolins; thus began the mandolin fad that hit its stride during the late 1890s to early 1910s.[6] When the banjo fad waned, the mandolin fad waxed. As early as 1894, a newspaper in Omaha, Nebraska, quoted a young mandolin-playing actress as saying: "I think that the banjo is a back number among social fads."[7] Of course, the banjo and mandolin by the late 1890s traveled in the same circles. In Northern bourgeois culture, especially among college students, they were often played in the same clubs along with guitars (or in similarly organized clubs), and one teacher very often taught all three of the "light string instruments."

In an era that seemingly delighted in musical instrument inventiveness, it is not surprising that manufacturers hybridized the banjo and mandolin.[8] The first mandolin-banjo was patented in 1885, but it was not until the end of the 1890s that it gained popular acceptance.[9] The mandolin-banjo is mandolin sized, and is strung, tuned, and played with a plectrum like a mandolin, but the body is that of a banjo. The banjo body gives the mandolin a banjo-like sound. During the 1910s, the loud and percussive strumming of the mandolin-banjo, essentially a rhythm instrument in this context, became popular with dance band musicians. Manufacturers also hybridized the banjo with the guitar and the ukulele, but neither proved quite as popular for dance band work as the mandolin-banjo. The banjo-uke, like the ukulele, was popular as an amateur instrument for strumming song accompaniments. It was a private, rather than public, kind of musical instrument.

Many mandolin-banjo players objected to the sustained tone created by the mandolin-style doubled strings. Serving as the time keeper in a dance band playing syncopated music, they wanted a more staccato, percussive quality, therefore some players removed four strings of the mandolin-banjo and played just four single (rather than doubled) strings.[10] Some companies made the "banjolin," a four-string version of the mandolin-banjo. Mandolinists and violinists (the violin, mandolin, banjolin, and mandolin-banjo share the same tuning and so the same fingering) seeking employment during the dance craze of the 1910s could easily turn to the then more popular (for professional dance work) mandolin-banjo or banjolin with little difficulty.

New styles of social dancing, using the rhythms of ragtime, hit a peak of popularity around 1913–15; the tango emerged as the most popular dance of 1914. At this same time, banjo companies began to offer another four-string banjo tuned in open fifths like the banjolin, but pitched a fifth lower. Usually called the "tango banjo" when first introduced, it eventually became known as the "tenor banjo."[11] The tenor banjo quickly gained popularity for dance band playing and became the premier banjo of the 1920s. Like the plectrum banjo, manufacturers added a resonator to the tenor banjo of the 1920s and often adorned it with rich ornamentation.

Elaborate decoration hit a frenzy in the 1920s, especially on instruments for flashy vaudeville soloists. "Perloid" fingerboards, gold-plated flanges, multicolored rhinestones, and resonators decorated with scenes from faraway lands create an excessive visual gesture for most viewers today. By comparison, banjo decoration in the late nineteenth century was elaborate, but private. Fancy carving on the dark wood neck or intricate etching on the metal rim could only be seen up close. Elaborate decoration of the 1920s, public rather than private in nature, radiated out to a distant audience, giving the professional theater player a visual, as well as aural, means of communication.[12]

The terminology for the various banjo-like instruments of this period was not consistent. The mandolin-banjo was often called the banjo-mandolin, and there was also an instrument called the mandolin-banjo that had the body of a mandolin and the neck of a banjo. This instrument was a rarity, and any mention of mandolin-banjos or banjo-mandolins generally refers to the more popular mandolin-necked banjo-bodied instrument. Banjo-ukes could be referred to as "banjukes," "banjuleles," or "ukulele-banjos." Other complicated terminologies arose. The first instrument sold as a "tenor banjo" that I have found was a nine-inch rimmed banjeaurine (tuned a fourth higher than the standard five-string banjo) sold by Stewart in 1888. Also, when Stewart first introduced his piccolo banjo in 1884, he called it the "Little Wonder Mandolin Banjo," even though it had the standard five-string setup.[13] The profusion of shapes, sizes, and names reveals that banjoists and banjo-makers of the time thought of their instrument as thoroughly malleable and not bound by tradition. There is a playful aspect to their application of American technology and innovation to these unpretentious "democratic" instruments. The banjo, as a musical "machine," invited constant tinkering.

Nonbanjoists may confuse the twentieth century plectrum and the tenor banjos; both have four strings and are about the same size, but the tenor banjo has a shorter neck (nineteen rather than twenty-two frets). Jazz bands of the 1920s used either form. The plectrum banjo developed directly from the five-string banjo (the tuning is the same and so the left hand fingering is the same), and five-string players adjusting to the new music naturally tended to turn to the plectrum banjo rather than the tenor. Mandolinists had few problems adjusting to the tenor banjo, which they tuned in open fifths like the mandolin and the violin. By the 1920s the tenor banjo's popularity outdistanced that of the plectrum. For example, the Gibson banjo catalogue of 1927 devotes eight pages to tenor banjos and places toward the back of the catalogue only one page of plectrum banjos. The five-string banjo also appears in the back of the catalogue and is allowed only one page: "the original *founder* of the modern banjo family." By 1927, Gibson, and others, saw the five-string banjo as an aging grandfather deserving of respect, but rather behind the times.

Not only did makers and players view the physical form of the banjo as malleable during the period of ragtime to early jazz (1890s–1920s), likewise performance technique changed to fit with new music, new performance contexts, and new forms of the instrument. Ensemble playing, especially for dance bands, offered performance opportunities for most banjoists and required a technique completely different from that of the 1890s banjo club. Solo technique also changed during this era. A number of soloists enjoyed popularity on stage and as recording artists;[14] record companies produced a large number of recordings featuring the banjo starting in the 1890s.[15]

Before the development of electrical recording technology in the mid-1920s, musicians gathered around large collecting horns, and played as loudly as possible. Record makers had to be content with a narrow frequency range; bass frequencies were especially difficult to capture. Acoustic recording technology directly turned the musician's airwaves into soft wax etchings. Although it did not produce quality sound, it was actually a boon for the banjo. Acoustic recording equipment responded well to the banjo's frequency range, and the percussive sound of the instrument recorded very well. Although banjoists played and recorded a various repertory, many of the 1890s and early twentieth-century solo banjo recordings are of ragtime or protoragtime forms such as cakewalks, coon songs, and syncopated marches (they also recorded many standard marches). As we have seen in the previous chapters, Americans already associated the banjo with popular "characteristic" music.

Commercial recording created "stars" of the talking machine, a very new form of American success. Popular recording banjoists, such as Vess Ossman (1868–1923), shared in this modern image. Recording technology not only helped reshape public ideas of the banjo, it molded performance practice and musical learning of many subsequent banjoists. The effect of recording technology on musical learning appeared early in the life of Fred Van Eps (1878–1960), who, along with Ossman, was the most popular of commercially recorded finger-style five-string banjo players. In an interview of 1956, Van Eps described how he learned to play the banjo, and the central role the new technology of the 1890s had in his musical life:

> George W. Jenkins [a railroad conductor] . . . taught [me] parrot fashion — played it over and over and showed me where to put my fingers. It didn't take long to learn all his numbers, and I was at a dead end until I heard a record by Vess L. Ossman. . . . The first Ossman record I ever heard was "The White Star Line March." . . . I heard it in 1893 before Edison began to make cylinders. . . . So I bought a Type M Edison two-minute cylinder phonograph. It cost me $100 — a lot of money then — but I paid for it the next week by attaching 14 ear tubes, taking it to the Firemen's Fair and letting people listen at five cents a play. . . . Well, anyway, I bought all the Ossman records, and soon I was able to play them and write out the copies. My chief purpose in getting the machine was to practice making my own records, and I began to do home recordings almost as soon as I obtained it. . . . After a great deal of experimenting and home recording, I decided the time had come to try my luck as a professional recording artist. I made two cylinders at home that sounded fairly decent, so I put them under my arm and went to the Edison plant at West Orange. This was in 1897, and Edison had begun to issue brown, wax cylinders regularly the year before.[16]

And so began the recording career of Van Eps. His story illustrates how recorded sound technology engendered a remarkable change in ideas about music learning and performing. The technology becomes the performance product; it is the filter for listening, as well as a method for learning. Van Eps did not go to the Edison plant with his banjo to audition, but instead brought his recorded cylinders. Rather than live performance, it was the wax recording, as commodity and as the product of modern technology, that became the goal and that somehow seemed more real than live performance—abstract sound become object.

The earliest banjo performers on cylinder and disc (Berliner introduced flat discs in 1896, and discs and cylinders competed for about twenty-five years) played five-string banjo basically with the guitar-style technique that had developed in the later part of the nineteenth century. Other five-string banjoists, besides Ossman and Van Eps, recorded in these early years of acoustic recording, for example: Steve Clements, Parke Hunter, Ruby Brooks, as well as a number of British banjoists.

Even though the players of the most elevated classical banjo and the popular ragtime banjoists shared the same basic technique, there were differences—differences that grew out of differing ideas of the banjo. In the 1956 interview, Van Eps told of the lessons he took from Alfred Farland (the "Scientific Banjoist of Pittsburgh, Pa.").[17] When Farland asked him to play Hauser's *Cradle Song* with tremolo, he walked out in disgust. Although they shared the same basic way of playing, certain techniques, such as tremolo, he rejected as affectations. Van Eps (as well as Ossman) also objected to much of Farland's "classical" repertory (specifically music lacking the proper banjo-like rhythm) as contrary to the musical nature of the banjo; he took a stand against the elitist posturings of the most "elevated" banjoists. The playing of the popular "ragtime" banjoists was a virtuosic three-finger picking style emphasizing speed and the snappy rhythm of "characteristic" music, and they rejected the mannerisms and repertory that, for "elevated" banjoists, had conferred status upon their art.[18]

Vaudeville banjoists during the first few decades of the twentieth century moved away from the five-string banjo and the finger-style playing of musicians such as Van Eps. In the theater, unlike the recording studio, finger-style banjo was simply not loud enough. Loud four-string banjo strummings using a pick on metal strings and with orchestral accompaniment proved more impressive in the theater. Performers such as "Black Face" Eddie Ross (who recorded in 1921) strummed the chords loudly but included few melodic references—the orchestra provided musical details. Eddie Ross's role was to play loudly, to strum in rhythmically interesting patterns, and, when performing in vaudeville (rather than for a recording), to entertain in a visually interesting manner as well. Some vaudevillian performers, such as Eddie Peabody, played with a more intricate technique.

Although these vaudeville performers strummed in a manner grossly similar to typical jazz band banjoists (plectrum playing on a four-string banjo emphasizing chordal work), the performance styles differed. Jazz band banjoists were part of the rhythm section, blending into the whole, providing the foundational rhythmic pulse and chord changes, and generally only calling attention to themselves during short two-measure breaks. Unlike the varied rhythms of the vaudeville star banjoist, the jazz band banjoist tended to play in a seldom-changing straight rhythm, allowing the soloists and the drummer the freedom of rhythmic expression. Also, the stage name of Eddie Ross—"Blackface" —tells us that this performer in 1921 continued to communicate old minstrel ideas about the banjo. As professional minstrelsy died in the early twentieth century, many short minstrel acts, with banjos and blackface comedy, appeared in the variety format of vaudeville.

By the 1920s, some four-string banjoists were exploring ways to move beyond strumming or simple single-string techniques, and developing the four-string banjo as a solo instrument. The master of the tenor banjo in the 1920s, and still considered the master by many today, was Harry Reser (1896–1965). Reser and his "Cliquot Club Eskimos"—a banjo band named for their sponsor, Cliquot Club Ginger Ale—proved to be very popular radio entertainers (see figure 26).[19] Their show ran from 1925 to 1933. They made recordings and toured (always clad in their Eskimo costumes, even in the radio studio), and performed popular novelty numbers such as *Barney Google* and *Yes We Have No Bananas*. Reser also made solo recordings of popular music and "novelty rags." His superb technique and ability to bring melodic and harmonic complexity to the tenor banjo was impressive; Reser's flashy playing created the banjo counterpart of the novelty piano fad of the 1920s, Zez Confry being the leader of that movement.[20] Novelty music sold well in the 1920s, and at the time it was thought of as a jazz idiom that explored new ideas in rhythm and idiomatic special effects. The jazz influence on George Gershwin owes more to novelty music than to classic jazz. Reser, and other well-known solo banjoists of the 1920s, such as Roy Smeck, were essentially novelty banjoists. They were creative arrangers and fine technicians. But what is novel for one decade often seems kitsch in the next.

The fretted instrument clubs (performance ensembles) that had started in the 1880s continued, in a variety of altered forms, into the twentieth century. During the early years of this period, collegiate five-string banjo clubs lost popularity, but mandolin clubs did very well until the mid-1910s. The Brown University clubs exemplified the kinds of transformations that took place in fretted instrument orchestras as they moved closer to the "jazz era." At Brown University,[21] the banjo club disappeared around 1906, but the mandolin club continued into the 1920s. By 1916, the mandolin club used mandolin-banjos for ragtime numbers; the banjo tone gave that "peculiar snap" needed for "characteristic" music. A newspaper clipping from the early 1920s gives the instrumentation of the mandolin club as: eight mandolins, two banjos [probably tenor], one mando cello [a large, low-pitched version of the mandolin], three saxophones, and one drum set. This instrumentation indicates a movement towards the dance orchestra and a breakup of the fretted instrument orchestra.

The four-string banjo and other fretted instruments continued to be associated

Fig. 26: Harry Reser and his Cliquot Club Eskimos. DeVincent Collection, Archives Center, NMAH, Smithsonian Institution.

with college life even after the banjo and mandolin clubs had disbanded. This was not only because of the popularity of jazz and dance bands in universities (which generally included at least one banjo); four-string banjos and the ukulele grew popular as informal social instruments used for strumming popular song accompaniments. The ukulele was perhaps more suited in this role, being smaller, lighter, and having a gentler sound than the banjo. The ukulele first became popular around 1916 as part of the Hawaiian fad that fed popular culture hunger for new exoticisms and new kinds of "characteristic" music. Brown University had a ukulele quintet in 1916.

By the 1920s, the strictly fretted instrument orchestra, either banjo or mandolin, was no longer a part of the college scene nor was it an upper-class trend. Amateur fretted instrument clubs, however, still operated in many communities among middle- and working-class people. Many clubs featured only fretted instruments, but some included instruments such as saxophones or drums. The clubs of the 1920s (and later) rarely used the five-string banjo; when they used banjos they used tenor banjos, plectrum banjos, mandolin-banjos, or banjo-ukes. Local teachers of fretted instruments organized and directed most of the clubs. The "orchestras" (as they were usually called now, rather than "clubs") provided a performance outlet for their students and, if the group did well, advertised the services of the teacher. These groups performed light, popular music for occasions such as club meetings, church socials, and local radio broadcasts. Mandolins predominated, but the orchestras included the many forms of banjos, guitars, ukuleles, Hawaiian guitars, and perhaps drums or even a marimba for special effects. A 1929 guide for fretted instrument orchestras[22] lists 138 organizations in the United States that included banjos. Groups listed ranged in size from duos and trios, to orchestras of over one hundred players (such as the "Santos Banjo Band" of Rochester, New York). This mass approach to banjo playing had more appeal in certain parts of the country. With groups reported for twenty-six states, over 54 percent of the groups listed came from the four contiguous states of Connecticut, New York, New Jersey, and Pennsylvania—the same region that had been the center for 1890s banjo club activity.

Russell Baker, in his autobiography *Growing Up,* describes his mid-1930s childhood in a working-class family in New Jersey. His experience with formal banjo lessons suggests the change in the idea of the banjo that had occurred since the 1890s. This was no longer a fun fad for the leisure-seeking class, but musical learning—a form of work—for a working-class child whose mother hoped to culturally equip him for the climb up the social ladder:

> A door-to-door salesman had come to the house one day selling banjo lessons at bargain prices. For a trivial sum, he told my mother, he would rent me a banjo and enroll me in a new academy of musical instruction being formed in the neighboring town of Nutley [New Jersey]. . . . The salesman wanted a down payment of one dollar on the banjo rental. Lessons would be fifty cents each. Well, every civilized man ought to know a little something about music, she [his mother] reasoned.
>
> I took my rented banjo to the Nutley musical academy. It was a small single-family house. Eight or nine other students turned up, we took our seats, and a

burly red-headed man sat on the parlor windowsill and illustrated the use of the banjo pick. It was a humbling experience.[23]

Russell's lessons did not go well; if he had continued he probably would have become a member of his teacher's fretted instrument orchestra. Baker, in his autobiography, not only tells of the student experience, but he gives us a picture of the profession and business of banjo teacher—door-to-door salesmen using credit plans to coax precious dollars and cents from depression mothers, and teachers, trying to be respected "musical maestros," squeezing nine students into their living rooms for music lessons.

Even though the mandolin dominated the amateur fretted instrument orchestras of the early twentieth century, the banjo and banjo-like instruments, starting in the 1910s, became the dominant fretted string instrument of the professional dance orchestra. By the time of early jazz recordings (1917–20s), the banjo was well established as a member of the rhythm section. The period before World War I is an especially interesting one for this study, a time when the dance craze created a market for dance music ensembles that played "raggy" tunes (often called "pre-jazz" by later historians). The 1910s was a transformational time period for the banjo as well, both in its physical form— the move from mandolin through mandolin-banjo to tenor banjo—and its musical role within the ensemble.

Banjos played an important role in both the dance bands and the "Negro Symphony Orchestra" of James Reese Europe. Europe was a well-known black musician in New York City before World War I: orchestra leader, composer, organizer of the Clef Club and Tempo Club (black musicians' unions), and a commercial recording celebrity (see figure 27). During the war he directed the 369th Infantry "Hell Fighters" Jazz Band. His life was cut tragically short when he was murdered in 1919. Before the war, the strumming of both mandolins and banjos (primarily mandolin-banjos and banjolins) formed a vital component of Europe's distinctive sound. With the "Negro Symphony Orchestra," Europe worked to encourage the development of an African-American orchestral style that would not imitate white orchestral traditions. In his words: "You see, we colored people have our own music that is part of us. . . . It's us; it's the product of our souls; it's been created by the sufferings and miseries of our race. . . . Whatever success I have had has come from a realization of the advantages of sticking to the music of my own people."[24] One of the distinguishing sounds of the orchestra, according to Europe, was the strong rhythmic quality created by the strumming of the mandolins and banjos. But it was not the African-American connotations of the banjo that mattered to Europe, it was the rhythmic force that the banjo created. For him, the essence of African-American music was rhythm, and banjo-like instruments merely helped in the creation of that rhythmic sensibility.

Fig. 27: James Reese Europe with Clef Club members, 1914. Schomburg Center for Research in Black Culture. The New York Public Library. Astor, Lenox and Tilden Foundations.

James Reese Europe's groups are today the best known of the northern prejazz ensembles; trying to uncover what other musicians created is difficult. It is problematic to use commercially available orchestrations to reconstruct "typical" playing styles of the less-renowned syncopated music ensembles.[25] Although it seems that most, but certainly not all, prejazz bands played by note (including James Reese Europe's groups), this should not be mistaken for playing the score as written. Photographs of dance bands from the first three decades of the twentieth century show so many groups of idiosyncratic instrumentation that it is clear that a good deal of arranging and orchestration, or rearranging previous arrangements, took place within each group. Playing from notation did not prevent players from embellishing (for example "ragging") their part, and one instrument often played parts originally written for another instrument (for example a euphonium could play from a written cello part). George L. Lansing, a long-time professional (white) banjoist in Boston, wrote an article for banjoists about his own approach to dance band orchestration during the prewar dance craze. In it, "banjo" refers to the standard five-string banjo, which for dance work he advocated playing with a plectrum, rather than in the traditional finger style.[26]

> For two years I have been furnishing banjo orchestras for dancing, often having three teams out on the same evening. It seems to me that with such an experience I may be permitted to make a few suggestions regarding [the] most effective form of banjo instrumentation. For a small orchestra of three pieces, a mandolin-banjo, banjo and piano. If no piano is used, the guitar-banjo is the best substitute. I always use piano if possible. As the orchestra is enlarged, the following instruments are added respectively, drums, mandolin-banjo, trombone, banjo, saxaphone [*sic*] or cornet, mandolin-banjo, banjo, double bass.
>
> I do not advocate the banjo for lead although it is effective on melody at times like the cornet or 'cello and in view of this fact, I would say the possibilities of the banjo are almost unlimited. For instance when the drummer is playing bells, the banjoist can play the accompaniment with the piano. If the performer is clever, he can rag the part as the drummer does. The banjo can also take the cello part or the trombone or bass.
>
> As a rule I prefer to read from the piano score as it usually has the melody cued in. This gives one considerable latitude to choose from as it contains besides the melody, the bass and accompaniment.[27]

The realities for professional dance band musicians made the written score, and commercially available orchestrations guidelines for performance rather than a prescription. For the players of the late nineteenth century who had hoped to elevate their instrument, strict adherence to a written score gave proof of their legitimacy in the musical world. But throughout the 1910s to 1920s, most professional banjoists moved consistently away from the authority of notation. From ragging the rhythms to improvising the breaks, musical legitimacy no longer depended on the idea of the artistic primacy of the permanent text.

Not only published orchestrations, but commercial recordings are also a problematic source of information on dance band orchestration in the early twentieth century. Early acoustic recording technology could not properly capture the sound of many instruments, including drums (except for those ever-present woodblocks) and so one wonders if the banjo, a member of the rhythm section that happened to record very well—neither guitar nor mandolin recorded well—might have been used in the recording studio to take up the slack. This, of course, would lead to recorded performances that were rather different from live performances. Even so, whether in a recording studio or in a dance hall, by the 1920s big-voiced banjos strumming in a straight rhythm provided the essential pulse for a music that many thought of as wildly syncopated.

This leads to the question of why jazz bands discarded the four-string banjo in favor of the guitar in the 1930s. This should be thought of not as a failure for the banjo, but as a success for the guitar. And one may ask why they used the banjo in the first place. The banjo became the dominant (though never obligatory) fretted instrument in dance orchestras because of its percussive punch and great volume—especially after the addition of resonators—qualities highly valued in both the recording studio and in noisy dance halls. Before the banjo established itself in this position, other instruments vied for its place. James Reese Europe frequently used multiple mandolins in his Clef Club Orchestras and his own Society Orchestra. Early New Orleans musicians seem to have had a preference for the guitar. The only known photograph of Buddy Bolden and his band (taken about 1895) shows two cornet players, a trombonist, clarinetist, string bass player, and a guitarist.[28] Early New Orleans jazz banjoists Johnny St. Cyr, Bill Johnson (also a bass player), and Bud Scott all started on guitar.[29] "Jelly Roll" Morton's first popular music ensemble included bass, mandolin, and Morton on the Spanish guitar.[30] But the guitar of that time, usually referred to as the "Spanish guitar," was a quiet-sounding, low-tension gut-strung instrument. Musical instrument designers of the 1920s, primarily at the Martin and Gibson companies, developed steel-strung guitars and finally Gibson and Epiphone began making the arch-top steel-strung guitar in 1934. With the arch-top design, the guitar was now loud enough to be able to hold its own in the jazz ensemble. Jazz in the 1930s did mellow from the rough and tumble sounds of the 1920s. It was a musical compromise between the 1920s jazz band and the society orchestra that produced the highly popular and profitable big band jazz sound of the 1930s and 1940s.[31] And the less percussive, though now audible, sound of the guitar blended nicely into the whole.

In general, players of fretted string instruments are able to switch to other fretted string instruments without too much trouble. This is not true for the five-string banjo, which, because of the short thumb string, has an idiosyncratic technique. But by the 1910s and 1920s, the banjo in the dance orchestra or jazz band was almost always a steel-strung plectrum-played version of the banjo, one lacking the problems implicit in the short drone string. It is not surprising to find that fretted string instrument players switched instruments, and that many jazz banjoists became guitarists in the 1930s. Even so, when jazz bands switched to the guitar sound in the 1930s, many banjoists preferred to play the four-string arch-top guitar (tenor guitar), which they tuned like their four-string banjo.

The five-string ragtime banjo playing of musicians such as Vess Ossman and Fred Van Eps provided a transition from nineteenth-century guitar-style banjo, and the ideas associated with it, to the twentieth century use of the banjo in prejazz and jazz. Although Ossman and Van Eps recorded ragtime — the modern music of the turn-of-the-century popular music industry — the banjo imagery employed still drew upon a sense of otherness from the presumed white middle-class customers that the record companies were seeking to attract. Much of the syncopated music called ragtime from the 1890s to 1910s still had strong connections to minstrelsy and "coon songs," genres that made the music more other by dealing in Southern black stereotypes and minstrel imagery. For example, even though Ossman did not perform in minstrel shows and did not "black up" to play the banjo, advertisements for his recordings often used references to Southern black stereotypes or minstrelsy.[32] The turn-of-the-century idea of the modern banjo in popular music still drew from the idea of the Southern black banjo.

By the 1920s, neither the minstrel nor the Southern black imagery of the banjo could sell many instruments; maybe it could sell sausages (as in figure 20 of chapter 2), but not new banjos. It was the five-string banjo, not the modernized four-string version, that had these old associations. The 1927 Sears and Roebuck Catalogue makes the distinction clear.[33] On the top of page 673, the mail order firm offers six models of tenor banjos and includes an illustration of a modern, tuxedoed, white dance band with a conductor, two trumpeters, a pianist, and a banjo player front and center. On the bottom of the page, they offer four models of five-string banjos accompanied with an illustration of two black-face minstrels. The five-string banjo referred to a popular culture past, and salesmen realized that the best way to sell the old five-string banjo was through an appeal to a sense of tradition and nostalgia. The catalogue for Carl Fischer, Inc. of 1925–26 explained the value of the "regular banjo" (the five-string banjo) to its customers in this way: "The traditions of the Plantation, Minstrel, College Banjo and Glee Clubs are too strongly entrenched in the heart of America to permit the old five-string banjo to become obsolete. Regardless of the popularity of the Tenor Banjo, the five-string instrument still has quite a following. For certain kinds of music nothing can take its place."[34]

And those certain kinds of music are decidedly old-fashioned. In the popular mind, the modern dance band banjo, steel-strung and plectrum played, rejected the old ideas of the banjo, and the five-string banjo remained behind to bear the tradition, safely rooted in the old sentimental imagery.

During both the "elevation" and the "modernization" of the banjo, players and manufacturers of the instrument denied the idea of the "ol' banjo" as applicable to their style of playing and making the banjo. The two eras shared much, even many of the same people (such as Thomas J. Armstrong who appears in the opening quotes of both this chapter and chapter 1). Yet, advertisements reveal an essential change in the presentation of the idea of the banjo from the late nineteenth-century era of "elevation" to the early twentieth-century "modernization" of the banjo. Whereas late nineteenth-century advertisers tried to sell the banjo by convincing potential customers of its social prestige, early twentieth-century advertisers presented the banjo as a ticket to a money-making career. During the 1910s and 1920s, both writers and advertisers in *The Crescendo* (a magazine for banjo, guitar, and mandolin players) continued to depict the mandolin as an amateur instrument for club playing and middle-class socializing, but they increasingly portrayed the banjo as a working instrument for professional dance orchestras and, to a lesser extent, as a vaudevillian instrument.

Figure 28 is a 1914 advertisement from *The Crescendo*. Most of the Vega advertisements of this time in *The Crescendo*, a musically conservative publication, are still for five-string banjos with celebrity endorsements testifying to the high quality of the instrument. But here, for the mandolin-banjo that had become an important part of the "tango" orchestra around 1914, the appeal is clearly profitability. The headline screams "DOUBLE PAY" to the working musician, and for the working music teacher the copy informs them that "For the teacher this Tango craze should prove a Bonanza when properly handled." By 1919 the tenor banjo had usurped the position of the mandolin-banjo, and so the Wm. C. Stahl company of Milwaukee, Wisconsin, informed readers that "Piano, Drums and Tenor Banjo! That's the dance combination in small places everywhere; that's the cabaret combination, the jazz combination, too. No matter how small the orchestra, the tenor banjo comes first."[35] The subtext: if you play the tenor banjo, you should have no problem finding work with a popular music group.

With the change in advertising style from a pitch for social elitism to professional profitability, there was a change in the presumed audience from leisure-seeking upper- and middle-class people to wage-earning middle- and working-class young men. As such, advertisers by the 1920s often presented the banjo as an easy way to make big dollars in fashionable settings. During the 1920s, the magazine *Smart Set*, which catered to a youth- and fashion-conscious clientele, ran many advertisements for mail order music lessons and instruments, especially for the banjo and the saxophone. One Wurlitzer advertisement of 1925 includes a photograph of a tuxedoed young man with the headline "Couldn't Play a Note—Now Makes $100.00 a week. . . . Read Bill Carola's story in his own words—" "When I sent for your catalog, I wanted a Tenor Banjo, but I hesitated a long time as I didn't know a note of music. I finally decided to try it a week, as you offered, and at the end of that time I found I could pick a few notes. Then I started the correspondence course you furnished, and in seven months, even before the final payments on the Banjo were due, I had taken my place in a professional orchestra. Now I am making $100 a week, three times what I made as a clerk."[36]

Fig. 28: 1914 Advertisement from *The Crescendo*.

This was not just any way to make money, it was a way that included elegant clothing, smart restaurants, and participation in the social occasions of the "fast set." Unlike the social appeal for the leisure-seeking banjoist of the 1890s who might join his peers in forming a club, the social appeal for the 1920s four-string banjoist often reads more as using your new (or future) musical skill to open social doors that would normally be closed. And the appeal was both monetary and social, as this 1927 Gibson catalogue blurb makes clear:

Social Popularity Assured the Banjoist

The Gibson Banjo is the modern "Open Sesame" to a world of good times, fun and happiness. . . .
Ability to play the banjo soon places one in position to pick and choose from scores of social invitations. Everywhere, the banjoist is assured of a hearty welcome. . . .
It is comparatively easy for the ambitious banjoist to interest his "pal" or an acquaintance in working up a banjo "team", or perhaps organize several players into a quartette or a small "Banjo Band."
Such combinations have wonderful possibilities . . . not only from a social angle . . . but also for financial profit. The Gibson Company will gladly furnish helpful suggestions.[37]

The emphasis on the professional possibilities of the banjo not only changed the earlier focus on a leisure-seeking class to an appeal to the nonelitist masses, it also established the modern banjo within the male domain. The earlier movement to elevate the banjo was strongly feminine in character. But in the 1910s and 1920s, with the emphasis upon professional playing, the image, and the reality, was strongly male. Young women appear in popular magazine photographs and illustrations playing the banjo-uke, but rarely the four-string banjo.[38] Professional groups did not use the quiet-sounding banjo-uke; it remained an amateur instrument.

The popular image of the four-string banjo player by the 1920s was not just male, but *young* male. Popular dance music of the 1920s (then almost always considered "jazz," although scholarly usage of the term since has restricted the meaning of the word) was a new music geared toward the new youth culture of the 1920s.[39] The jazz life and art of 1920s youth culture challenged Victorian ideas of respectable expressive behavior.

Many historians in recent years have written of the years 1880–1920 as a time of transformation in American culture.[40] The 1920s is viewed as a time of arrival of new cultural forms for white middle- and upper-class Americans, forms most fully expressed in the youth culture of the decade. Americans caught up in the modern life style of the 1920s led a social life of less formality and increased heterosocial activity than had their parents, with a greater acceptance of consumer and leisure values. The 1880s–90s banjo fad among young bourgeois women had been one expression of their desire for an increased informality and acceptance of new social roles and leisure values. By the 1920s that freedom of expression had expanded. Young women were no longer depicted as merely playing half-barbaric banjos, but rather dancing, drinking, petting, spending too much money and time on nonedifying leisure pursuits, and running with "that jazz-mad crowd." This image rejected many of the official values of Victorian culture, without an indulgence in sentimental values. The quest for the "up-to-date" (modernism rather than antimodernism), the focus on public life (rather than a longing for home), and a preference for urban expressions (rather than pastoral imagery) all contradict the ideal of "sentimental culture." Still, primitivism, exoticism, and African-American music and dance – all traditionally connected to sentimental ideas – played an important role in the new expressive forms of the 1910s and 1920s, but they were used in the attempt to create something vitally new and forward looking rather than sentimental and backward looking.

Within this framework of new expressive behaviors in American culture, a further reading of the ostentatious decoration of some banjos from the 1920s is possible. For comparison, Larry May,[41] in an analysis of changing architectural and decorative styles of movie theaters, views the appearance of lavish theaters in the late 1910s and 1920s as a sort of democratic display of consumer values. Movie theaters became rich palaces open to all classes (no separate seating for different social classes) for the reasonable price of a movie ticket. Many of the movie palaces used exoticism to create the atmosphere of the Near East, or the "nights in the gardens of Spain." The use of exotic and primitive motifs "signaled a release from everyday inhibitions, tapping the quest for post-Victorian freedom."[42]

The most elaborate of the 1920s banjos used similar modes of decoration – lavish display of unashamed opulence: gold-plating, embedded rhinestones, and intricate Indian Chief pegheads. The Gibson Florentine banjo ("The World's Finest, Most Luxurious Banjo . . . " featuring "Florentine designs of the Renaissance period") and the Bella Voce model (with a "strikingly beautiful Spanish Floral design displaying the graceful lyre, lute and other symbols alluding to the Goddess of the Muse") both use exoticism as an important part of their consumer appeal.[43] Some banjo manufacturers simply gave their high quality banjo models names like "De Luxe," but many incorporated exoticism (although never an African exoticism) into their allusions to luxury: the Bacon "Sultana," Epiphone "Alhambra," Ludwig "Toreador," and the Leedy "Hollander" are all examples. These banjos snubbed refinement and classical restraint while embracing the most audacious aesthetics and avarice of the new consumer ethos.

On a deeper level, the structure of jazz music and the social forms of dancing in the cabaret created more open-ended and interactive expressive forms. Traditional Western aesthetics privileges artistic forms set apart (on a stage, in a set literary genre, placed in a frame) and concretized (in a score, in a written text, made of imperishable materials) with single and distinguishable creators (composer, author, artist). Jazz, the great icon of the "jazz era," violated these standards. The performance spaces of cabarets and nightclubs moved toward an integration of performance and audience space.[44] The improvisatory nature of the music challenged ideals of the composer and the role of notation as a means of giving permanent form to the essentially ephemeral art that is music.

For many bourgeois Americans, these new forms of expression not only violated old artistic norms, they were an affront to established morality. There would not have been a problem if ragtime, jazz, and their respective dances (especially the dances) had remained in their proper places—the vice districts, the theater, or any place out of sight from genteel eyes—but during the 1910s and 1920s, with the help of the increasingly pervasive mass media, these forms invaded white culture on all social levels.

For most of the moral critics, the threat of jazz or ragtime was not the music as an abstract sound object, it was the music as event and as a symbol of a lifestyle that threatened civilized society. This was the social and performance context for the modern banjo of the 1910s and 1920s, and so it deserves some exploration. Moralistic objections flourished during the prejazz dance craze of the 1910s, and it should be noted that moral indignation against ragtime did not really gather steam until this time. Although the music had been popular since the late 1890s, it was the ragtime *dancing* of the 1910s that concerned the moral critics. Social reformers tended to focus on the dance, especially the dancing of young women, and the implied deterioration of maidenly virtue as the real threats to society.[45]

Many of the popular dances of the 1910s came from African-American culture or from famous vice districts such as the Barbary Coast of San Francisco. Dances such as the "Grizzly Bear," "Bunny Hug," and the "Shimmy" involved body movements considered lewd by bourgeois Anglo-Americans. The upholders of Victorian standards of behavior fought the battle on two sides: members of both the white working class and the white upper classes violated those standards. The "newly wealthy" often flouted Victorian restraint while many youth of the upper and middle classes rejected bourgeois decorum with an aristocratic contempt. Working-class youth, especially children of immigrants in the urban North, turned to popular culture forms with roots in African-American culture during their leisure time rather than fully accept the uplifting activities designed by middle-class reformers. One 1913 magazine article about "tough girls" and "idle boys" explained it this way: "In the last three or four years, since the arrival of the 'nigger' dances and the 'rags' and the 'turkey trots,' dancing has become a public obsession. Like the gambling game of craps,—which has supplanted or changed the habits of boyhood from the traditions of sport of northern Europe to the games of the negro,—

this new dancing is a curious recrudescence, apparently originating from the same source as the gambling game . . . in the crude and heathen sexual customs of middle Africa. . . . "[46]

Even the popular instrumental combinations—for example "Piano, Drums and Tenor Banjo!"—were unorthodox for the time with a heavy use of those half-barbaric instruments that had no place in a proper orchestra or band. Music and dance provided central symbols of a larger valual realignment, but dance was the physical enactment of the abstract suggestions of the music. So it was dance, especially during the 1910s, that aroused the most ire from the guardians of civilization.

Even so, a middle ground existed. For the socially reputable patrons of the 1910s dance fad, Vernon and Irene Castle personified the proper approach to the dangers of twentieth-century popular expressive culture. Rather than reject the new music and dance as immoral, they presented a mediated form. They and other fashionable white dance teams of the era, in attempting to reform ill-mannered dancing, wrote instruction books (at times overtly aimed at working-class youth—the worst violators).[47] Figure 29 is a list of rules by the Castles, a guide to reformation.

The list of "do nots" indicates that this was precisely what dancers were doing; they were using movements out of line with Anglo-American ideas of proper body deportment and enjoying too much body contact while dancing. The Castles also suggest dropping dances such as the "Grizzly Bear," the "Turkey Trot," and the "Bunny Hug," all dances strongly associated with African-American culture. They advocated the Latin American "Tango" and "Maxixe," as well as the "One-step" and "Hesitation Waltz"—dances not associated with African-American culture or with American vice districts. The Argentine *tango* came from the working-class neighborhoods of Buenos Aires, and long had illicit connotations, in the same manner as the African-American dances did in the United States.[48] But the American "tango" dancers always presented the dance as having gone through the civilizing effects of Parisian adaptation, and it was in Paris that they learned the dance.

Although members of the upper classes danced the dances of working-class youth and of African-Americans, they often did so in a more refined manner and chose those dances that seemed less tainted. A useful illustration of the social-class marking of dance style is the 1918 film *Amarilly of Clothes-Line Alley* starring Mary Pickford as the Irish tenement dweller, Amarilly.[49] In the film, we are taken to both an upper-class nightclub and a working-class dance hall. In the nightclub, well-dressed patrons move gracefully with a modicum of distance kept between partners; in the dancehall, the young working-class couples, in inelegant surroundings, press their bodies together while dancing on the too-crowded floor. The film also includes several shots of dance orchestras (a silent film)—the workers who create the music needed for the preferred

CASTLE HOUSE SUGGESTIONS
FOR CORRECT DANCING

Do not wriggle the shoulders.

Do not shake the hips.

Do not twist the body.

Do not flounce the elbows.

Do not pump the arms.

Do not hop--glide instead.

Avoid low, fantastic, and acrobatic dips.

Stand far enough away from each other to allow free movement of the body in order to dance gracefully and comfortably.

The gentleman should rest his hand lightly against the lady's back, touching her with the finger-tips and wrist only, or, if preferred, with the inside of the wrist and the back of the thumb.

The gentleman's left hand and forearm should be held up in the air parallel with his body, with the hand extended, holding the lady's hand lightly on his palm. The arm should never be straightened out.

Remember you are at a social gathering, and not in a gymnasium.

Drop the Turkey Trot, the Grizzly Bear, the Bunny Hug, etc. These dances are ugly, ungraceful, and out of fashion.

Fig. 29: Rules for correct dancing from the 1914 instruction book *Modern Dancing* by Mr. and Mrs. Vernon Castle.

activity of dancing. At the nightclub, the band is on a balcony, nearly out of sight, keeping working musicians neatly removed from wealthy patrons. The instruments visible are saxophone, piano, two violins, bass, and a strummed plectrum banjo. At the working-class "Cyclone Cafe," the music is provided by black musicians wearing old clothing and playing drums (trap set with bass drum), saxophone, clarinet, piano, and mandolin-banjo (they are clearly musicians actually playing, unfortunately, silently). The band plays on the dance floor, in full view, integrating performance and audience space, unlike the musicians in the nightclub. Dancers, drinkers, and musicians all share in the total occasion.

It may be that the filmmakers embellished reality by having black musicians play at the Cyclone Cafe, an Irish-American working-class bar. But since colonial times, black musicians have traditionally played dance music for upper-class white social occasions.[50] So it should not be too surprising that the music that Vernon and Irene Castle (the fashionable dancers for New York's better set) danced to was the music of black Americans, in particular the music of James Reese Europe.[51] Europe, largely through his association with the Castles, became a celebrity. "Europe's Society Orchestra" recorded with Victor in 1913 and 1914. These recordings are important examples of Northeastern prejazz music. Much of the excitement of pieces such as *Too Much Mustard* (Victor 35359) and *El Irresistible* (Victor 35360) derives from the prominent strumming rhythm of the multiple mandolin-banjos (or banjolins) and mandolins that were always a part of his many dance orchestras as well as his "Negro Symphony Orchestra." Even if the socialite dancers tried to present themselves as interpreters of Latin American-derived (via Paris) dances rather than African-American, they were still dancing to black American music, and to the strumming of banjo-like instruments.[52] And even though the Castles and other dance manual writers declared the "Grizzly Bear" and the "Bunny Hug" as out of fashion in 1914, white American youth still danced these same dances in the mid-1920s.[53]

The upholders of white genteel culture were shocked to see their own children behave in what seemed a grotesque parody of black culture. Figure 30 is a 1926 cartoon from the music establishment magazine *Musical America*. Here the cartoonist presents an elitist view of the noblity of "authentic" black music: the idealized song of the plantation South when black music was a safe and Southern-exotic folk expression rather than a commercially successful product of African-American urban culture. In contrast, the inset shows the depravity of white jazz culture, that is white indulgence in what was viewed as black urban expressive behaviors (the urban forms of black culture believed, by highbrows, to be degenerate). Dancing, alcohol (during prohibition), and jazz music (represented here by the banjo) are destroying white civilization. The woman displays too much of her body and behaves in an unseemly, even immoral, fashion; her dance literally based upon a bottle of alcohol. The men leer at her; one plays the banjo, and one plays the bottle (fingering the same chord). The symbol that unites the jazz club and the plantation is the banjo. Americans associated the banjo with both jazz and the old plantation, and the presence of the banjo was thought by some to be evidence of the black origins of jazz. But in the hands of a white man in a nightclub, it becomes a sign of societal (racial?) degeneracy.

A Contrast in Origin and Mood—The Spiritual of the Negro's Yesterday, and Today's Jazz, as Epitomized by Dick Spencer

Fig. 30: *Musical America,* 13 February 1926, p. 3.

Figure 31 is another elitist depiction of the banjo in the hands of a white man. The young man, still childlike with his round face and chubby cheeks, serenades his flapper girlfriend using a banjo. Yes, it is a lowbrow instrument, but, according to the caption, it is ideal for certain occasions, i.e., the young romance of musical illiterates. This 1923 illustration is from an article by Robert Haven Schauffler, an advocate of the music appreciation movement. The essence of his article, "Jazz May Be Lowbrow, But—," is distilled in the introduction: "From mouth-organ jazz to enjoying Kreisler is a long jump. Maybe the mission of jazz trash is to help folks leap that gap. The pep and punch of these savage instruments from Hawaii and Africa may lure our musical illiterates to learn."[54] He was trying to make peace with the music of

The banjo may be lowbrow, but it is ideal for certain occasions

Fig. 31. *Collier's*, 25 August 1923, p. 20.

the "lowbrows" that had come to such prominence by the 1920s. Perhaps playing the banjo will eventually lead this man to buy the recordings of Fritz Kreisler; he will eventually tire of the simplicity of "jazz trash" and see the banjo for what it is—a child's toy.

The proponents of high culture felt their position as the arbiters of taste eroding as profits dictated the future course of the recording industry, and in a few years, the broadcast industry as well. In the end, the late nineteenth-century development of an artistic split between highbrow and lowbrow was of limited benefit to highbrows; it separated them from the masses of Americans. Their attacks on jazz were a struggle for cultural authority. The banjo—which already had a long history as an instrument unacceptable to the official culture—was thus fitting for the highbrow as a symbol for jazz.

In contrast, manufacturers did not present banjo players in their advertisements as lowbrow or childish, nor would banjo players view themselves as such. Figure 32 is from the front of a 1930 pamphlet for Weymann banjos. In keeping with the theme of professionalization, discussed earlier, Weymann created an image of success and glamour for the attractive male banjoists shown here strategically placed in front of a microphone. Weymann gives us the modern young man of the twentieth century, a great contrast to the image of the male banjo players in figures 30 and 31.

Fig. 32: From the collection of the Archive of Folk
Culture, Library of Congress.

Whether the idea of the modern four-string banjo player was positively
or negatively portrayed, the popular culture typically depicted the banjoist
as a young white male. Although there were some professional women banjoists in vaudeville, and even an entire chorus line of nineteen young women
banjoists for awhile in the Zeigfield Follies,[55] in general, women were no
longer thought of as banjo players. Although white Americans recognized
African-American males as jazz musicians, the idea of the African American
connected specifically to the banjo still tended to resolve into Old-South
imagery rather than the idea of the modern banjo. And finally, the "jazz life"
being connected to youth culture, the modern banjo of the 1910s and especially the 1920s did not belong to the old master, but to the young, even
adolescent, musician.

But what does this say about changing ideas of manhood in the twentieth
century?[56] The ideal late nineteenth-century middle-class man was industrious,
rational, dependable, and in control of his impulses. He would not choose the
life of a jazz band banjoist. College boys could still play banjos and be excused
as adolescents, but adult working men should have better things to do.
Although Bill Carola in the 1920s found financial success (now makes $100
per week, three times what he earned as a clerk), his occupation was tied to the
questionable culture of the twentieth-century entertainment industry. The
true Victorian male tamed the frontier or sought success in the business world

through hard work and self-discipline (and good luck), not through a career that indulged in expressive behavior in environments that promoted sexual and social informality. Rather than taming, civilizing, and disciplining the self, the jazz life encouraged the loosening of social restraint. But by the 1920s, Bill Carola's story could be presented as a modern kind of success story—to a certain audience, of course.

Not that new standards of male behavior had found full acceptance; old values persisted, values that did not include banjo playing as acceptable male work. In the following passage, written in 1933, dissonance creates humor when an upper-class Englishman with generally Victorian behavior learns to play the banjo-uke, an artifact of twentieth-century American mass culture. This is not only inappropriate as male work, the banjo-uke is in questionable taste as a leisure activity due to its less than aristocratic associations. Bertram Wooster, the feckless gentleman of P. G. Wodehouse's novels, upon hearing some American vaudevillians, decides to take up the banjo-uke (here called "banjolele"). Not only does Bertie take his new hobby rather too seriously, as if it were work (something Bertie knows little about), he has even chosen the banjolele, taking on the lowbrow connotations of both banjo and ukulele:

> Those who know Bertram Wooster best are aware that he is a man of sudden strong enthusiasms and that, when in the grip of one of these, he becomes a remorseless machine—tense, absorbed, single-minded. It was so in the matter of this banjolele-playing of mine. Since the night at the Alhambra when the supreme virtuosity of Ben Bloom and his Sixteen Baltimore Buddies had fired me to take up the study of the instrument, not a day had passed without its couple of hours' assiduous practice. And I was twanging the strings like one inspired when the door opened . . . [57]

An upper-class amateur, like Bertie Wooster, who chose to play banjo with serious intent lacked not only good taste and common sense, but he perhaps appeared a bit effete or childish as well. In contrast, professional jazz band musicians, although expressive, did not appear particularly feckless, just uncivilized; they were white men who had lost all sense of propriety and were returning, behavior-wise, to the jungle from whence this music had come. Additionally, with the possible exception of the drums, the banjo, more than the other instruments of the modern dance orchestra, had that half-barbaric image.

Figure 33, a 1926 cartoon from the *Saturday Evening Post*, depicts the out-of-control jazz band, including, naturally, a banjo player. Contorted bodies and faces give evidence of the lack of self-control—unseemly male behavior—implicit in the apparently barbaric music. Of course, the early jazz tendency among many white musicians to play "nut jazz" (a form of jazz that imitated animal sounds and indulged in novel instrumental special effects) certainly helped to establish this sort of generalized jazz imagery in the minds of many,[58] but by 1926 jazz had progressed far beyond the eccentricities of "nut jazz." As one *New York Times* journalist wrote, even Tchaikovsky at his most moving did not cause listeners (and musicians) to loose decorum of bodily control, as did jazz.[59] Figure 30 also illustrates this sentiment. In the present illustration (33), it is the musicians, not the listeners, who have lost decorum of bodily control. The patrons must resort to extraordinary technological measures in order to maintain a sense of public propriety and bypass the savagery of new music.

But if the image of jazz music and musicians flew in the face of public

Device for Making Yourself Heard in a Restaurant

Fig. 33: Reprinted from *The Saturday Evening Post* (6 February 1926, p. 104), The Curtis Publishing Co.

standards of male behavior, why did it achieve such resounding popularity in the 1920s? By the 1920s many Americans wanted to challenge Victorian ("Puritanical") standards of behavior; jazz and other expressive forms of what were thought to be more primitive, hence freer, peoples provided ammunition for the attack. The passage below from banjoist Eddie Condon's autobiography illustrates this point well. He and his band had a job to play for an elegant Newport party in 1928. Knowing that this Newport gathering was expecting Viennese waltzes, the young musicians nervously set up their equipment:

> I looked around; [Gene] Krupa was adjusting a tom-tom. The artillery was ready.... Eight seconds later everyone in the room was staring at us.... The guests automatically began drinking more champagne. They couldn't talk because we were playing too loud; between sets we pushed them out of the way to get at the champagne. "Extraordinary demonstration of the freed libido," I heard one matron mutter. "Lady," I said, "will you hold this glass while I get some caviar?" "Extraordinary creature!" she said, but she took the glass and held it while I got some eggs.[60]

These young jazz musicians felt free to attack social propriety. Condon even metaphorically presents their musical instruments as weapons, weapons used to disrupt normal social interaction. Some party goers chose to interpret the loud music and rude behavior as expressions of freed behavior. By attending this performance event, reserved patrons partook of the jazz-inspired liberation from Victorian restraint.

Eddie Condon's autobiography of 1947 provides an interesting comparison to Fred Van Eps's interview of 1956—a study in contrasting ideas of male behavior. Although both men were professional white banjoists from small towns and inauspicious families, they presented themselves and their music in strikingly different ways. Van Eps, the famous five-string ragtime banjoist, though he performed a music that led to the jazz music that Condon loved, still explained himself in much the same manner as did the elevated banjoists of the late nineteenth century. In the interview, Van Eps delights in talking about technique (the rational and work-oriented part of music making) and recording technology. He always presents himself as a successful working musician and, after his performing career, as a good businessman. Eddie Condon, the jazz-age version of musicianly male behavior, writes informally about his life as a jazz player relishing stories about lacking money and respectability, chasing girls, drinking too much, and playing and listening to the music that had captured his imagination. Van Eps complimented the playing of the Van Eps Trio by simply explaining that "The Trio played with almost metronomic precision."[61] It is hard to imagine Van Eps writing about music the way that Condon describes his first hearing of King Oliver's band in Chicago. Although Condon also appreciates musical precision (planned with

a calipers), he encases this appreciation with an extremely subjective emotionalism: "It was hypnosis at first hearing. Everyone was playing what he wanted
to play and it was all mixed together as if someone had planned it with a set of
micrometer calipers; notes I had never heard were peeling off the edges and
dropping through the middle; there was a tone from the trumpets like warm
rain on a cold day. Freeman and MacPartland and I were immobilized; the
music poured into us like daylight running down a dark hole."[62] These white
adolescents from the midwest did not need to hide behind a wall of gentility or
a mask of burnt cork; they were ready to accept the music of those New
Orleans black musicians as artistically profound. Jazz shaped their artistic
sensibility and gave meaning to their lives, and they made the music their
own.

For Eddie Condon, it was not the banjo that fueled his musical drive, it was
jazz. It was not the banjoist Johnny St. Cyr that immobilized him that night,
but the front men, particularly Louis Armstrong and King Oliver, and the
polyphonic and rhythmic sweep of the totality. Van Eps quit his performing
career when the five-string banjo fell from public favor; Condon switched to
the four-string guitar (tuned like the banjo) when the banjo fell from grace in
the jazz band. Fred Van Eps continued to play the banjo in private; Eddie
Condon continued to play jazz in public.

Condon was never a flashy solo player and never had the technical skill of
Van Eps; he is remembered as more of a band leader and promoter of jazz
than as a great jazz player. Yet, in a sense, Condon is a perfect representative of
the jazz banjoist because he used the banjo for entry into the world of jazz,
never expecting to be in the spotlight. It was the music and lifestyle of jazz that
mattered to him, not the banjo. The banjo was never a central instrument to
jazz, although highbrow critics used it as a demeaning symbol for a music they
disliked. The banjo, in the end, had merely hitched a ride with the new music
of ragtime and jazz into modernization.

During the Depression of the 1930s, jazz became respectable, but not until
submitting to change. "Swing," the most popular jazz form of the 1930s,
developed a compromise style lying between collectively improvised jazz (New
Orleans style) and the society jazz/dance orchestras like Paul Whiteman's
group. Jazz became more controlled, arranged, and refined. The punchy 2/4
rhythm gave way to a smoother 4/4. At this same time, jazz bands discarded
the banjo in favor of the guitar; by the time jazz had become respectable, the
banjo was no longer a part of it.

After World War II "traditional" jazz—collectively improvised jazz associated
with "New Orleans Jazz" rather than the highly arranged "swing" or "big
band" jazz of the 1930s and 1940s—enjoyed a small revival. Eddie Condon
blazed the trail with his radio-broadcasted concerts of traditional jazz at New
York's Town Hall during the War. Condon and other jazz musicians' devotion

to the idea of a less-restrictive highly improvised music for small ensembles easily translated, for other musicians, into a devotion to a revival or recreation of old music. "Dixieland" revival jazz became a music that referred to the past, a music encased with nostalgia. And it was in this music that the four-string banjo again found a home in the jazz idiom. But the essence of this revival for the banjo was really regression. Four-string banjoists of the early twentieth century, through their association to current popular music trends, had seized a modernizing agenda. But now in the second half of the century, four-string banjoists abandoned modernity for a return to sentimentality.

Besides the Dixieland revival (an ensemble of mixed instruments with the banjo in the rhythm section), the four-string banjo itself enjoyed a revival shortly after World War II. Mike Pingatore, formerly the featured banjoist with Paul Whiteman's orchestra in the 1920s, had a hit record in 1948 with a revival of the 1924 song *I'm Looking Over a Four-Leaf Clover* showcasing the banjo, of course. During the 1950s and early 1960s, many four-string banjoists joined together to form banjo bands that strummed old songs for sing-alongs. They usually wore pseudo-1890s costuming of striped jackets, string ties, and straw hats while the audience threw peanut shells on the floor. These groups conflated Gay Nineties, Roaring Twenties, and Mississippi riverboat nostalgia — and managed to create a series of successful nightclubs out of the conflation.[63] Shakey's Pizza parlors became patrons of this kind of banjo music in the 1970s. Plectrum and tenor players dominate the Fretted Instrument Guild of America, and so this music can be heard at the annual FIGA conventions. Most fans of the four-string banjo today view banjoists Harry Reser and Eddie Peabody as the great past masters, and recreating an old Reser arrangement is the proof of a banjoist's instrumental mastery.

Banjo players and manufacturers of the 1910s and 1920s, finding their instrument particularly well adapted to the demands of dance orchestra playing, took advantage of the opportunity to modernize their image. During the late nineteenth century, the desire for modernization had taken the form of a conscious attempt at elevation and the hope for acceptance into the offical culture. It was an attempted escape from the idea of the "ol' banjo" of the stereotyped Southern black man and the low-class image of the minstrel performer. But the banjo could not fully escape this framework of meaning. By the 1910s, the popular music of the burgeoning culture industry opened an avenue to modernization that lay outside of the official values of Victorian culture, but even this escape from sentimental culture proved to be temporary. When jazz musicians exchanged their banjos for guitars, the banjo nearly disappeared from American popular culture, except in Southern white country music. The four-string banjo's post–World War II revival, limited in its popular appeal and dependent on Old-South and old-time nostalgia, drew deeply from the well of American sentimental culture.

Notes

1. Thomas J. Armstrong, "Banjoists Round Table," *The Crescendo* v. 9, n. 3 (September 1916): p. 20.

2. Armstrong had been a frequent contributor to Stewart's *Journal*, especially on the topic of banjo club orchestration. Armstrong was active in Philadelphia, where Stewart was located, and the two men seemed to have had a strong professional relationship.

3. For detailed information on banjo patents see Thomas Adler, "The Physical Development of the Banjo," *New York Folklore Quarterly* v. 28, n. 3: pp. 187–208; Tsumura, *Banjos: The Tsumura Collection*, pp. 144–66.

4. Webb, *Ring the Banjar!*, pp. 26–28.

5. Thomas J. Armstrong, "Banjoists Round Table," *The Crescendo* v. 6, n. 6 (December 1913): p. 24.

6. The best source for the "Spanish Students" and their imitators is Scott Hambly, "Mandolins in the United States since 1880: An Industrial and Sociocultural History of Form," PhD dissertation (1977), chapters 3 and 4.

7. The quote is from a newspaper clipping that was sent in by a reader to S. S. Stewart, which he reprinted in his *Stewart's Banjo and Guitar Journal* v. 10, n. 6 (February–March 1894): p. 9.

8. For technical details of various hybridizations of mandolins and banjos see Hambly, "Mandolins in the United States since 1880," chapter 7.

9. Ibid., pp. 218, 233.

10. *The Crescendo* v. 11, n. 5 (November 1918): p. 20. Also, see the photographs in Robert Kimball and William Bolcom, *Reminiscing with Sissle and Blake* (New York: Viking Press, 1973), pp. 52, 53, and 58. The photographs are from 1910–16. Almost all of the mandolin-banjos are actually banjolins—i.e., they have four strings, not eight. Even the mandolin-banjo in the photograph on page 52 appears to have only four strings (although there are eight pegs).

11. The Sears and Roebuck Catalogue introduced its tenor banjo in 1917 as the "Tango Banjo." By 1920, they sold the instrument as the "Tenor Tango Banjo," and by 1924, it was simply called the "Tenor Banjo." Another example—Lyon and Healy continued to sell the "Tango-Banjo" until at least 1919 (advertisement in *The Cadenza* v. 26, n. 1, p. 2). However, the instrument was sold by some as the "Tenor Banjo" as early as 1915 (Vega advertisement in *The Crescendo* v. 7, n. 9, p. 1).

12. For color photographs of highly decorated banjos of the 1920s and 1930s see Tsumura, *Banjos: The Tsumura Collection* and Webb, *Ring the Banjar!* (plates 35–37).

13. *Stewart's Banjo and Guitar Journal* v. 11, n. 10 (June–July 1884): p. 3.

14. For an overview of the banjo in ragtime see Lowell H. Schreyer, "The Banjo in Ragtime," *Ragtime: Its History, Composers, and Music*, ed. John Edward Hasse (New York: Schirmer Books, 1985), pp. 54–69.

15. The recordings that have been re-released by Folkways Records under the album title "Those Ragtime Banjos" are useful examples and includes recordings by Vess Ossman, Fred Van Eps, "Blackface" Eddie Ross, Harry Reser, and Roy Smeck.

16. The Van Eps's interview with Jim Walsh appeared in the January through April 1956 issues of *Hobbies* Magazine (v. 60, n. 11: 31–33; v. 60, n. 12: 32–36; v. 61, n.

1: 30–35; v. 61, n. 2: 29–35). This passage is from v. 60, n. 2 (January 1956): p. 32. Walsh also did a very good series of articles on Vess Ossman that ran from September 1948 to January 1949 in *Hobbies*.

17. Ibid. v. 61, n. 2 (April 1956): p. 31.

18. Alfred Farland recorded nineteen wax cylinders in 1900; only three of them were clearly in the popular or "characteristic" vein. These cylinders appear to have never been released or advertised by a major company, and are extremely rare. Elias and Madeleine Kaufman, "Alfred A. Farland," *5 Stringer* n. 140 (winter 1980): pp. 1, 12–20.

19. Susan Renee Smulyan, "'And Now a Word from Our Sponsors...': Commercialization of American Broadcast Radio, 1920–1934," PhD dissertation (1985): pp. 104–8.

20. Ronald Riddle, "Novelty Piano Music," in Hasse, *Ragtime: Its History, Composers, and Music*, pp. 285–93.

21. Information from the Brown University Archives.

22. National Bureau for the Advancement of Music, *Fretted Instrument Orchestras* (New York, 1929), pp. 51–98.

23. Russell Baker, *Growing Up* (New York: Congdon & Weed, Inc., 1982), p. 121.

24. This quote appeared in an interview article "Negro's Place in Music," *Evening Post* (New York) 13 March 1914. The article is reprinted in Kimball and Bolcom, *Reminiscing with Sissle and Blake*, pp. 60–61.

25. For a discussion of ragtime orchestration from the turn-of-the-century as evidenced by commercial stock arrangements see Thornton Hagert, "Band and Orchestral Ragtime," in Hasse, *Ragtime*, pp. 268–84.

26. Although Lansing, a long-time finger-style banjoist, advocated playing accompaniment parts with a pick for dance orchestra work, this technique was not yet unanimous. The (Fred) Van Eps Trio, a dance music ensemble that recorded extensively between 1912–20, is a striking exception.

27. George Lansing, "The Banjo Tangle," *The Crescendo* v. 8, n. 3 (September 1915): p. 20.

28. This photograph is reproduced in Frank Tirro, *Jazz: A History* (New York: W. W. Norton & Company, 1977), p. 71.

29. The information on Bud Scott is from Nat Shapiro and Nat Hentoff, *Hear Me Talkin' To Ya* (New York: Dover Publications, 1966), p. 33, and the information on Johnny St. Cyr and Bill Johnson is from their entries in John Chilton, *Who's Who Of Jazz*.

30. Shapiro and Hentoff, *Hear Me Talkin' To Ya*, p. 29.

31. Neil Leonard, *Jazz and the White Americans: The Acceptance of a New Art Form* (Chicago: University of Chicago Press, 1962); Gunther Schuller in *Early Jazz: Its Roots and Musical Development* (New York: Oxford University Press, 1968) discusses the technical-musical development of swing.

32. Edison advertised Vess Ossman's recordings with illustrations of blackface minstrels, for example see the *American Magazine*, April 1907, supplementary advertisement section. Also see advertisement copy from Columbia records that is reprinted in this work, chapter 2, "Music of the Banjo." This advertisement is for recordings by both Van Eps and Ossman.

33. *Sears and Roebuck Catalogue,* n. 155 (fall/winter 1927–28): p. 673.

34. Catalogue of Carl Fischer, Inc. 1925–26: p. 27. Warshaw Collection, Archives Center, NMAH, Smithsonian Institution.

35. *The Crescendo* v. 11, n. 11 (May 1919): p. 2.

36. *Smart Set* v. 76, n. 6 (August 1925): p. 87.

37. Catalogue of the Gibson Company, *The Banjo* (1927): p. 8. Reprinted 1974 by *Mugwumps.*

38. Examples of advertisement illustrations of young women playing banjo-ukuleles: *Women's Home Companion* April 1930, p. 175; *Saturday Evening Post* 31 May 1930 (p. 150), 28 February 1931 (p. 122), and 30 May 1931 (p. 41).

39. On the development of white middle-class, mostly collegiate, youth culture in the 1920s, see Paula S. Fass, *The Damned and the Beautiful: American Youth in the 1920s* (Oxford: Oxford University Press, '1977), especially pages 300–306 on jazz as a symbol of liberation.

40. Two prominent examples, and important works for this study, are Lewis A. Erenberg, *Steppin' Out: New York Nightlife and the Transformation of American Culture, 1890–1930* (Chicago: University of Chicago Press, 1981) and Lears, *No Place of Grace.*

41. Larry May, *Screening Out the Past: The Birth of Mass Culture and the Motion Picture Industry* (Chicago: University of Chicago Press, 1980), pp. 154–58.

42. Ibid., p. 156.

43. The 1927 catalogue of the Gibson Company, *The Banjo,* pp. 12–13.

44. Erenberg, *Steppin' Out,* chapter 4: "Action Environment: The Informal Structure of the Cabaret."

45. There are several recent books that discuss early twentieth century (up through the 1920s) social dancing: Erenberg, *Steppin' Out;* Kathy Peiss, *Cheap Amusements: Working Women and Leisure in Turn-of-the-Century New York* (Philadelphia: Temple University Press, 1986), especially chapter 4, "Dance Madness"; Fass, *The Damned and the Beautiful,* see especially pages 300–306.

46. George Kibbe Turner, "The Puzzle of the Underworld," *McClures* v. 41 (July 1913): pp. 99–111.

47. Examples of dance manuals from 1914 include Mr. and Mrs. Vernon Castle, *Modern Dancing;* Monsieur Maurice, *The Tango and Other Dances;* and J. S. Hopkins, *The Tango and Other Up-to-Date Dances.*

48. Julie M. Taylor, "Tango: Theme of Class and Nation," *Ethnomusicology* v. 20, n. 2 (1976): pp. 273–91.

49. *Amarilly of Clothes-Line Alley,* Famous Players-Lasky Corporation, 1918. In the collection of the Library of Congress, Division of Motion Pictures.

50. Eileen Southern, *The Music of Black Americans: A History* 2d. ed. (New York: W. W. Norton & Co.), p. 338.

51. On Europe, see R. Reid Badger, "James Reese Europe and the Prehistory of Jazz," *American Music* v. 7, n. 1 (1989): pp. 48–67; Samuel B. Charters and Leonard Kunstadt, *Jazz: A History of the New York Scene* (Garden City, N.Y.: Doubleday, 1962), chapter 2–"Castle Walk," and chapter 5–"Hellfighters"; Schuller, *Early Jazz,* pp. 247–251; Kimball and Bolcom in *Reminiscing with Sissle and Blake* include many fine photographs of Europe and his various ensembles.

52. The Castles, however, did not belittle the importance of James Reese Europe's music in their own dancing success (they gave him credit for the development of the foxtrot), and it appears that a sincere friendship existed between Europe and the Castles.

53. Ella Gardner, *Public Dance Halls* (Washington, D.C.: U.S. Department of Labor, 1929), pp. 19–20.

54. Robert Haven Schauffler, "Jazz May Be Lowbrow, But—," *Collier's* v. 72 (25 August 1923): pp. 10, 20. Schauffler clearly knows little about jazz music, and uses the term broadly.

55. A photograph of the "'Ingenues,' formerly of the Ziegfeld Follies" appears in National Bureau for the Advancement of Music, *Fretted Instrument Orchestras*, p. 13.

56. There has been little work done on concepts of male behavior. For this discussion, I rely primarily upon the 1982 Brandeis PhD dissertation by Anthony Rotundo, "Manhood in America: The Northern Middle Class, 1770–1920," and Elliott J. Gorn, *The Manly Art: Bare-Knuckle Prize Fighting in America* (Ithaca: Cornell University Press, 1986).

57. P. G. Wodehouse, *Thank You, Jeeves* (London: H. Jenkins, 1934), edition by Perennial Library, pp. 10–11. I thank Steven Reber for showing this to me.

58. Charters and Kunstadt, *Jazz: A History of the New York Scene*, pp. 77–81.

59. Leonard, *Jazz and the White Americans*, pp. 32–33.

60. Eddie Condon, *We Called It Music: A Generation of Jazz* (New York: Henry Holt and Co., 1947), p. 173.

61. Jim Walsh, "Fred Van Eps," *Hobbies* v. 60, n. 12 (February 1956): p. 35.

62. Condon, *We Called It Music*, p. 107.

63. The vertical file "Banjo" in the Folklife Reading Room at the Library of Congress has a good collection of newspaper and magazine clippings on the 1950s and 1960s four-string banjo revival. See also the *FIGA News* (Fretted Instrument Guild of America), an organization dominated by four-string banjoist, for the conflation of Old South, Gay Nineties, and Roaring Twenties imagery. On the beginnings of the postwar banjo boom, see "Dat Yam Rag," *New Yorker* v. 24, n. 31 (25 September 1948): pp. 23–24.

4

The Southern White Banjo

THE IDEA OF THE five-string banjo remained that of the "ol' banjo" for most Americans in the twentieth century, but through time, it changed from a plantation black to a mountain white. Figure 34 is a 1936 drawing by Charles Pollock, older brother of Jackson Pollock and student of Thomas Hart Benton.[1] Pollock drew it for the cover of a song sheet produced by the music section of the Resettlement Administration, the section headed by musicologist Charles Seeger, father of Pete Seeger. Pollock's mountaineer banjo player shares much with the black banjo player of figure 24 in chapter 2. Both play a solo banjo on the porch of a little Southern cabin. But the similarities of content only serve to set up the striking differences between the illustrations. The mountaineer banjo player is alone, and does not provide the music for social dancing like his African-American counterpart. The solitude of the mountaineer banjo player suggests a pensive mood, a mood that popular illustrators never allowed black banjo players. Pollock takes us onto the porch, and we look out at the world from the house rather than stare at the strangeness of the cabin scene as outsiders. He asks us to partake of the occasion, to be a part of the musical moment, to see ourselves on that mountain porch.

American culture has repeatedly used the banjo in the expression of a sentimental ethos at odds with, though not overtly antagonistic to, official values. The popular culture idea of the five-string banjo as played by the Southern white mountaineer exists within the sentimental genre: the banjo became an antimodern machine. Pollock's drawing of the mountaineer banjoist in figure 34 demonstrates how the idea of the Southern white banjo shared

DOWN *in the* VALLEY

Fig. 34: 1936 drawing by Charles Pollock. Kenneth S. Goldstein Folklore Collection, University of Mississippi.

large structures of meaning with the idea of the Southern black banjo, yet particularities of the image were remade into a new sentimental idea based upon prevailing notions about the nature of Anglo-Americans. Transformation to an Anglo-American white setting incorporated the idea of a "folk" to help explain the apparent liminality of a native-born Anglo-American subculture.

In this chapter, both local understanding and outside perceptions of the banjo are explored. In the early twentieth century, outsiders' construction of authenticity for the banjo as Appalachian folk artifact depended upon ideas about the otherness of Southern mountain life and art. The explanation of Appalachian otherness in terms of European folklore theories and historic metaphors eventually paved the way for a redefinition of the five-string banjo (not its urban cousin the four-string banjo). While this was happening, Southern musicians were reshaping local traditions into a new popular/commercial music: hillbilly—later called "country"—music. Southern music, both traditional and commercial, created different images of the banjo. After World War II, the two streams (local and outsider) of thought interacted and sometimes overlapped as bluegrass musicians and folk revivalists discovered one another.

By the late twentieth century, most Americans thought of the banjo as Southern, rural, and white, and many particularly associated it with the southern Appalachian mountains. The plantation setting for the banjo had nearly disappeared in the popular media by the 1950s, and the association of blacks with the banjo continually lessened in the minds of Americans; this was especially true for young people. Out of this fresh association of the banjo with Southern rural white culture, musicians created new meanings to revive an old instrument in the national popular culture. The new meanings did not frontally attack the old sentimental idiom, such as the movement to "elevate" the banjo had done, but made artful compromises with old ideas of the five-string banjo, creating a new sentimental idea of the banjo.

Asking exactly how and when "mountain whites" began to play the banjo presupposes a monolithic culture and an isolation that misleads the questioner. The banjo was a very popular instrument in the nineteenth century, due largely to minstrel theater, and it is hardly surprising that its popularity eventually spread to the rural-white Southerner. Debating who taught the mountaineer, the black folk banjoist or the professional minstrel,[2] avoids the likelihood of multiple causation, and perpetuates a perspective of the mountain South as homogeneously distinct from the whole of American culture. Not to belittle the strength of regionalism, it is still important to acknowledge the interconnectedness of American lives. People from the mountain South came in contact with minstrels, black Americans both traveled through and lived in the mountains bringing their musical traditions with them, white Southerners moved in and out of the mountain area, the banjo has enjoyed a strong tradition in the Piedmont region, and young men from Appalachia served in the armies of both sides during the Civil War, bringing home new ideas and new music.[3]

In the rural South, both black and white musicians have used the five-string banjo with the fiddle for the performance of dance music since, at least, the late nineteenth century. The banjo proved to be a fine complement giving a less-embellished and strongly rhythmic version of the melody that the fiddler produced. Black musicians developed a tradition of duo banjo playing and a repertory of banjo songs.[4] In the white tradition, musicians also used the banjo for song accompaniment. There are many references to the banjo being used in the performance of British and Anglo-American ballads, although the early scholars of the ballad largely ignored the instrument in their work. Both men and women played instrumental music, but playing outside of the home for community or commercial occasions was largely limited to men.

While early twentieth century folksong collectors competed to see which state could collect the most versions of Child ballads,[5] they gave native song scant attention, and nearly ignored instrumental music. In 1909 Louise Rand Bascom published in the *Journal of American Folklore* a singular, for that time, account of instrumental music in western North Carolina. Bascom was also a fiction writer, and her writing style, even in an academic journal, reflects her other vocation. And it is this fictive/descriptive style of writing that frees her from turn-of-the-century obligations to prove scholarly legitimacy through "scientific" concerns with classification systems and diffusion patterns. Freed from the constraints of contemporary ideas of scholarship, the author gives her readers descriptions, anecdotes, and opinions. Fiddlers' conventions (where both fiddlers and banjoists competed), native ballads, singing style, and the role of women are all subjects that she briefly discusses. And she writes: "The mountaineer who cannot draw music from the violin, the banjo, or the 'French harp,' is probably nonexistent, and not infrequently one may see a gaunt idler squatting by the roadside, picking the banjo, and at the same time working the 'French harp,' held in place by a wire around the player's neck. The fiddle is always a battered heirloom; the banjo is home-made, and very cleverly fashioned, too, with its drum-head of cat's hide, its wooden parts of hickory (there are no frets)."[6]

John C. Campbell wrote briefly of music in his posthumously published book *The Southern Highlander and his Homeland* (1921). Campbell spent many years working in the mountains, and traveling and researching mountain life for the Russell Sage Foundation. His writing reveals the variety of life in the mountains during the early years of the twentieth century. Although he writes very little about music, his short references are valuable commentary on instrumental music. After mentioning fiddlers as dance musicians and the rarity of dulcimers, especially outside of Kentucky, Campbell turns to the banjo: "Strangely enough, the banjo touches at times a deeper note than the violin, perhaps from association. It is more generally played throughout the Highlands, and breathes the life of many a lonely hearth far in the hills. Usually, however, it is off with all the gaiety of the Mountain frolic on 'Turkey in the Straw,' 'Possum up a Gum Stump,' 'Sugar in the Gourd,' or 'Sourwood Mountain.'"[7]

Perhaps the banjo seemed "strange" to Campbell in this context because in the larger society of the 1910s and 1920s, the banjo was still too strongly associated with plantation blacks, old upper-class fads, lowbrow theater, and the jazzed-up urban dance orchestra.

The Southern rural-white banjoists who grew up in the early twentieth century often learned on homemade instruments.[8] If they learned on a factory-made banjo, it was usually because an older relative already played and allowed the youngster to use the banjo; music making was often a family activity and most musicians came from musically inclined families. People made their homemade banjos from many materials; old pie tins or cigar boxes fitted with a neck and fishing line sufficed for the beginner.[9] Charlie Poole, a famous hillbilly musician of the 1920s and 1930s, made his first banjo from a gourd,[10] (probably unknowingly) following an old African tradition. Some musicians made well-crafted wooden banjos with an ingenious design that eliminated the need for the metal brackets and shoes. This type of banjo became popular among folk music revivalists in the 1960s. Most Southern rural musicians considered a homemade banjo to be a beginner's instrument. If the beginner persevered, he or she scraped together the money for a factory-made banjo; homemade instruments could not match the power and bright tone of banjos with metal tone-rings and brackets for tightening the head.

The most common technique among rural Southern banjoists was down-picking rather than up-picking. In chapter 1 the difference between the nineteenth-century down-picking "stroke" style was contrasted with the up-picking "guitar" style. Downpicking in the Southern tradition is usually called "clawhammer," "rapping," or "frailing" rather than "stroke"; I will use the term "clawhammer." Although the basic action for making the string sound is the same in clawhammer and in stroke, there are some fundamental musical differences between the Southern tradition and the minstrel style that appears in the published method books of the mid-nineteenth century.[11] Early minstrel banjo music, although usually monophonic, tended in its melodic structure to be more harmonically based than much of the repertory of Southern traditional music. The tuning of the minstrel instrument was rarely changed (unlike the variety of tunings used by most Southern rural banjoists), and the tuning almost always used in minstrel banjo (eAEG#B, later transposed to gCGBD) is rarely found in the Southern tradition. The minstrel banjoist, unlike the traditional Southern banjoist, frequently used 6/8 time and triplets in his playing.[12]

A look at the finer points of technique among older traditional banjo players today reveals a wide array of idiosyncratic approaches to the banjo, including two- and three-finger up-picking styles, and a mixing of up- and down-picking. Younger players today (both from the rural South and outsiders) tend to avoid idiosyncrasies and fall squarely into one of two camps: bluegrass or clawhammer. Instruction books, records, and tapes as well as contest playing have encouraged the standardization of styles with its rigid categories for marketing and competition. Currently, the most common technique is the rapid three-finger (two fingers plus thumb) up-picking bluegrass style associated with Earl Scruggs.

As was discussed in chapter 2, American culture has traditionally mythologized the South—it was the exoticism within: our national Other. The mountain region of the South shared in this characterization, and in the twentieth century it has been perhaps even more myth-ridden than the old Plantation South: until recently, little serious historical work has been done on the region. This mythical South differed from the "Old South." Rather than an aristocratic order based upon a system of racial caste, the mountain South was seen as a world of small farmers, a place untainted by a history of slavery, and a world set apart from the stresses of modernization—an imaginative realm in tune with the sentimental values of antimodernism, pastoralism, and nostalgia, and out of touch with the official values of progress, technology, and capitalist development.

Rodger Cunningham, in *Apples on the Flood: The Southern Mountain Experience,* views the otherness of Appalachia (more appropriately the Celtic people of Appalachia) as a long-standing historical reality. The Celtic people who settled in the Southern mountains continued a centuries-old tradition of peripheralization from politically dominant centers. Appalachian stereotyping is thus only the most recent response to a long-term cultural drama. David Hackett Fischer in *Albion's Seed: Four British Folkways in America* also sees the cultural difference of the Southern backcountry as a part of centuries-old traditions. Fischer's voluminous research on American and British folkways is impressive, but such bold strokes are both compelling and dangerous. For example, his tracing of Appalachian violence and feuding traditions to northern British folkways appears convincing, but carefully researched local histories often contradict such generalities. Altina Waller in *Feud: Hatfields, McCoys, and Social Change in Appalachia, 1860–1900* demonstrates that even in the Tug Valley of late nineteenth century/early twentieth century feud fame, a lawsuit and a trip to the county courthouse were much more common than violence. The violent occurrences in Tug Valley had more to do with the economic tensions of modernization than centuries old feuding traditions. Appalachian historiography needs more local histories before sweeping statements can be safely made.

Henry Shapiro, in his book *Appalachia on Our Mind,* traces the development of the idea of Appalachian otherness, of how the mountainous regions of eight Southern states came to be seen by outsiders as a distinct region with a homogeneous culture, and finally how the region came to be thought of as the repository of America's "folk" culture. Local-color fiction writers, benevolent aid societies and their associated educational institutions, arts and crafts revivalists, and folksong collectors all played a role in creating the distinctive otherness that has welded the region together in the American imagination. David Whisnant in *All That Is Native and Fine* powerfully demonstrates how interaction between a native culture and a dominant culture with artificial ideas about native authenticity can lead to cultural intervention. When outsiders claim specialized knowledge about native culture, they in essence are claiming the power to define that culture. Whisnant shows how this situation played out in several Appalachian case studies.

Rather than lament the effects of the politics of culture, we need to understand the motivations and preconceptions that guided the politics of culture. What were the dominant culture's ideas of Appalachia? What did the dominant culture want from their mythologized ideas of the region? How did Appalachian otherness fulfill certain fantasies and reflect ideologies of non-Appalachians, and how did the banjo fit into all of this?

The Southern mountain region is geologically comprised of the Cumberlands, the Alleghenies, the Blue Ridge chain, and the greater Appalachian valley, formations that run through the Southern states of Alabama, Georgia, South Carolina, North Carolina, Virginia, West Virginia, Kentucky, and Tennessee (the mountains also extend north into Maryland, Pennsylvania, and New York). In the late eighteenth century the mountains were the frontier and a barrier to westward expansion and those who lived in the mountains lived, by necessity, in frontier conditions. But by the late nineteenth century, with national expansion into the West and with the rapid growth of industrial capitalism, the existence of an area so close to the Eastern seaboard, yet still so rural and economically "undeveloped," proved to be an enigma to many Americans who lived outside of the region. Life in Appalachia was different from other American lives (though never homogeneous), and it was especially different from contemporary urban life. What concerns us here is how those from outside of the region interpreted and defined that difference. Over time, writers and missionaries cultivated the idea of a homogeneous, mountain culture: an almost completely isolated people of pure Anglo-Saxon blood who still lived in frontier conditions, sang the ancient ballads that Sir Walter Scott had made so popular, spoke an older form of English, and continued Celtic feuding traditions.

For those who approved of the direction that American society was taking around the turn of the century, Appalachia seemed to be a problem that needed solving and the mountaineers a people in need of uplift. The "mountain whites" appeared to be a native-born labor force waiting to be industrialized and loyal 100 percent Americans ready to defend the country; but they needed to be brought into mainstream American culture. The largesses of benevolent aid after the Civil War primarily went to the newly freed blacks of the South, but as frustration set in and problems appeared insurmountable, the "discovery" of mountain whites as a group in need of benevolent aid was a relief.[13] Here was a group—because native-born and white—that showed some promise for full economic and social integration into modern society. Many also saw them as a leaven to the hordes of immigrants, then forming most of the working class, who brought with them strange customs and dangerous political ideas.

Along with positive conceptions of Appalachian potential, there developed strong negative stereotypes of mountain people. Many depictions of Southern mountain life used themes of poverty, ignorance, illicit moonshining, and especially feuding. Feuds became a favorite topic during and after the flaring of actual feuds, especially in Kentucky, during the early years of the twentieth century.[14] Extended family feuds even affected state politics, and the press, specifically the *New York Times*, eagerly covered these stories. Some of D. W. Griffith's films, for example "The Feud and the Turkey" (1908), "The Mountaineer's Honor" (1909), and "A Feud in the Kentucky Hills" (1912) further popularized the idea that violence was a pervasive aspect of mountain life.[15] Even in these films, however, mountain culture is presented ambivalently. Although their world is violent, it is also inextricably bound to nature. Mountaineers, as children of nature, can either degenerate into savagery or freely develop in noble simplicity (for example the beautiful and innocent mountain girl played by Mary Pickford in "A Feud in the Kentucky Hills" and "The Mountaineer's Honor").

Those Americans who either disapproved of or had reservations about the direction of turn-of-the-century society were a minority, but they could draw from both old and new ideologies that criticized the emerging corporate capitalist order. Many began to doubt the claims of the moral and social beneficence of unending and unfettered material progress. The British antimodernist critique of the quality of labor in the industrial society, begun by Ruskin in the mid-1850s and followed by Morris in the later half of the century, lamented the effects of modern machine labor and praised the creative work of the medieval craftsman. Thus began the arts and crafts movement that sought to end the alienation of factory work and promote the revitalization of the craft tradition. The philosophy crossed the Atlantic to the United States, losing its socialist bite, and finding a home with prominant Bostonians seeking aesthetic reform, bored white-collar workers seeking therapeutic activity, and social reformers trying to educate working-class youth in useful activities.[16] Nevertheless, American antimodernist or "sentimental" critiques of "official" Victorian values should be viewed as arising from the material and social conditions of the United States in the late nineteenth century, and not as mere reflections of European movements.

Many of the admirers of Appalachian otherness, in addition to antimodernist sentiments, re-expressed older American ideals of republican simplicity. Hastily stated and simplified, republican virtue—an ideological product of the revolutionary era—consisted of those morals deemed necessary for the proper working of a republic that eschewed European systems of monarchy and aristocracy. It has been a recurring (though changing) theme in American intellectual history.[17] Writers, especially popular writers, when describing Appalachian life often employed ideas inherited from this traditional value system:

the distrust of luxury and consumer desires and the moral degeneracy these may engender, the evils of the industrial society, the virtue of a spartan simple life, the desire for an egalitarian social structure, and a vision of the true American type as the self-sufficient small farmer. These values should be recognized as truly conservative, sharing little with progressive socialist thought of the time.

Although Appalachia was often presented as backward and degenerate, many people who accepted newer antimodernist values and kept alive older republican ideals were attracted to the otherness of Appalachia. Like those who had used descriptions of Southern black culture as a means of criticizing Anglo-American culture, praising the native simplicity of the mountaineers implicitly criticized "official" bourgeois values. The following excerpt from *Lippincott's Magazine* of 1875 compares the perceived virtuous simplicity of Appalachian life to the crass materialism of urban life using old republican ideas and a late nineteenth century fear of over-civilization:

> In these villages we found thoroughbred men and women, clothed in homespun of their own making, reading their old shelves of standard books: they were cheerful and gay, full of shrewd common sense and feeling, but utterly ignorant of all the comforts which have grown into necessities to people in cities. . . . Palpable facts like these were calculated to shake the old notions of busy, money making Philadelphians. After all, were Chestnut street and Broadway all wrong in their ideas of the essentials of life? . . . certainly there was utterly dropped out of that life all the hurry and anxious gnawing care which have made the men of the Northern States lean of body and morbid of mind, and the women neuralgic and ill-tempered.[18]

From the waning years of the nineteenth century and into the first half of the twentieth century, many professional folklorists and Appalachian popularizers shared something of the spirit of antimodernism and a turn-of-the-century version of republicanism. The early generation of professionals in the late nineteenth century were primarily philologists with a profound attraction to old English and Teutonic culture. The tracking of old ballad texts satisfied the desire for preindustrial expressive culture, art forms that were touched with the romantic wildness somehow implicit in anonymity. The next generation, partaking of the ethos of the strenuous life, donned their tramping boots and headed for the field to track down, in the wild, the last fading flowers of folk song. Whether they explored for themselves or sent their college students scurrying for songs, they remembered to maintain their mantle of science by holding fast to contemporary scholarly concerns with classification, diffusion, and evolution. Although professionals worked with Appalachian materials, they worked in other areas of the country as well. But the popular mind tended to direct folkloristic concerns towards Appalachia (also popular were the cowboy folk song collections of John Lomax). Popularizers – song collectors, local-color fiction writers, and festival promoters – were free from contemporary "scientific" concerns, and so were more likely to write descriptions or create events that involved the banjo. Their "sentimental" Appalachia reached a large audience, and often their work dissolved into popular myth making, creating an Appalachia truly "other" from the rest of America.

Part of the perceived otherness of Appalachia resulted from the racial and ethnic composition of the mountain South. Conventional portrayals of Appalachia usually describe an all-white native-born population. But the two earliest depictions of Appalachian banjo players that I have found are both of black banjo players. One depiction is an image that was discussed in chapter 2 (figure 25), Henry Tanner's "The Banjo Lesson." Tanner made the sketch in 1889 in Highlands, North Carolina, a small mountain community in the Blue Ridge near the borders of South Carolina and Georgia.

The earliest image of an Appalachian banjo player that I have found is an illustration of an elderly black banjoist in the 1885 *Century Magazine* short story "Hodson's Hide-Out" by Maurice Thompson.[19] The story is a strange one – an inverse of the standard "Carry me back to Dear Old Dixie" type stories or songs. A young ornithologist, working for the Smithsonian Institution, is in the Appalachian mountains of Alabama doing research. He encounters a strange mountaineer who insists that the scientist is his son who was lost in the war, and the mountaineer forces the scientist to return "home." Back at the mountaineer's cabin, we meet Jord, an old black man who plays the banjo and is still being kept in slavery; the mountaineer refused emancipation and their mountain isolation has allowed this legal infraction to continue unnoticed by the outside world. The story ends with the scientist aiding Jord's escape to freedom. This story is unlike other Appalachian tales that were appearing in the popular magazines in the late nineteenth century. It is a nightmarish parody of the "going home to the South" motif. The mountaineer is degraded and a slaveholder – most local-color writers regularly told their readers that the mountaineers hated slavery and had sided with the Union during the war. Even the nature idyll, a convention of Appalachian local-color writing, is here inversed; the beauty of nature is more the possession of the government ornithologist than the mountain dweller. The story avoids Southern and mountaineer sentimentalism, and sides with the official culture of government and science. Above all else, what makes this Appalachian tale unlike others is the inclusion of a black character.

The black population of the mountainous areas of the South was much smaller than that of the rest of the South; African Americans, although not evenly distributed in the region, made up 16.2 percent of the population of the Southern Appalachian region in 1860, 14 percent in 1900.[20] These figures, however, are much higher than the literature, both popular and scholarly, would lead a reader to expect. Scholars and popular writers frequently presented Appalachia as the last bastion of Anglo-Saxon purity in a country awash with immigrants and race problems. And in comparison to northern urban areas, the region did not attract immigrants (except to some coal mining areas), nor did it have the race problems that began to affect the urban North during and after World War I.

Within such a context, not only were Appalachian blacks made invisible, but non-Anglo-Saxon ethnic groups seemingly disappeared.[21] For example, Josiah Combs, linguist and ballad scholar, in his book of 1925 adamantly asserts that the population of the mountains is "more truly English than England" and any notion of Celtic intrusion into the mountains is fallacious. He complains that the American government shows slight interest in Appalachians, "choosing rather to busy itself with undesirable types of foreigners in the slums of the greater American cities." So it is not surprising that Combs tucks into a footnote information on a 12 percent black population in the mountain South. He adds that this number is too small to have affected musical practice in the region,[22] which is clearly untrue. Musical change does not happen by majority rule. In the twentieth century, especially after the 1930s, African Americans migrated out of the Southern mountain area in large numbers, leaving behind a very small black population in the region.[23]

But how did the banjo, an instrument that was so strongly associated with black Americans, come to be seen as a white American instrument? What were the connecting links between the concepts of these two cultures, Southern black and mountain white, that cleared the way for Americans to reformulate their idea of the banjo? James C. Klotter, in "The Black South and White Appalachia," notes how late nineteenth-century accounts of white Appalachia resembled accounts of Southern rural blacks—both were poor, ignorant, living in shabby little cabins, retaining old superstitions, and both were suppressed by the wealthy elite of the plantation South. Klotter contends that the similarity of descriptions of these two groups "allowed some reformers to turn with clear conscience away from blacks to aid Appalachia."[24] If the similarity of outsiders' ideas about these two groups facilitated the transfer of benevolent aid, perhaps it explains the transfer of the banjo.

Stereotypes of black Southerners and white Appalachians shared more than the banjo and the role of recipient of (mostly Northern) benevolent aid. Plantation frolics became mountain frolics; cabins on the levee became cabins on the mountainside. African-American spirituals had fulfilled some Americans' felt need for a native folk music in the nineteenth century; white Appalachia played that role in the twentieth century. Turn-of-the-century and twentieth-century descriptions of mountaineers often included comparisons of native dialect to old English as found in Shakespeare and Chaucer, but prior to this, language scholars in the 1880s found remnants of Shakespeare in Southern black speech (as rendered by Joel Chandler Harris in *Uncle Remus*).[25] But even though similarities of description existed, there was a fundamental difference in popular culture images of blacks and mountaineers. Like the drawing by Charles Pollock in figure 34 and the illustration from chapter 2 (figure 24), basic elements are shared. Based on the artist's perspective, we stare as outsiders at the strangeness of the black banjo player, yet Pollock asks us to see ourselves on the porch of the white man. How could American popular culture, in the days of eugenics, assign "pure Anglo-Saxons" to a position of peasantry, poverty, and ignorance? How could Anglo-Americans be so unsuccessful, according to the official values, in contemporary America?

Historic metaphor allowed the Anglo-Americans of the Southern mountains to exist outside the official values; by placing them imaginatively in the past, poverty turned into pioneer simplicity and cultural isolation into Anglo-Saxon cultural survival. The dialect studies reveal an essential difference in black and mountaineer stereotypes. Although passages from *Uncle Remus* were compared to passages from Shakespeare, no one ever tried to turn black Americans into "Elizabethans of today." They were the wrong race, and white America perceived them as simply incapable of being fully modern people.

The popularizing writers, song collectors, settlement school teachers, and folk music festival promoters who chose to define the otherness of Appalachia were a small group before World War II, but they were powerful in laying the foundation upon which later ideas would be built. These interpreters of mountain culture explained the mountain white's lack of modernization and integration into official twentieth-century culture as the result of an extreme isolation that created a sort of time warp. Mountain culture was not degenerate, just temporally displaced. The mountain whites were transplanted "Highlanders," "Elizabethans of today," or "our contemporary ancestors;" they lived like our pioneer fathers and sang the songs and danced the dances of "merrie olde England." Travel into the mountains became travel through time. Exactly which time is never clear.

It is a longer journey from northern Ohio to eastern Kentucky than from America to Europe; for one day's ride brings us into the eighteenth century. (1899)[26]

The farther one goes from a railroad, the quainter sounds the English. Forty miles on horseback bring[s] one near to Chaucer's time. . . . (1910)[27]

But perhaps this is the very reason why each year her festival has attracted a wider audience, why so many people are planning to visit Ashland – to drive back into the seventeenth century via Kentucky roads, on this coming Sunday in June. (1934)[28]

Sitting there, I had a strange otherworldly feeling. It was as if, in crossing the mountains with Mr. Pentland, I had crossed into another time, another century, back to the days of the American frontier. (1967)[29]

Historic metaphor, especially the "Elizabethans of Today" metaphor, fit well with the late nineteenth-century cult of romantic Anglo-Saxonism, the growing interest in things medieval, and the continuing concern about the possible ill effects of immigration. These were especially the concerns and interests of the elite and intellectual classes of the northeast, the expression of a class reaction to rapid social change.[30] Old British and Scottish ballads were popular reading, the works of Sir Walter Scott were in vogue, and tales of medieval chivalry soothed Anglo-Americans' fears that modern civilization was making their ethnic group and class effete and neurasthenic.

Although professional folklorists and scholars of the ballad did not use these metaphors so blatantly as did the popularizers, early ballad research grew in this cultural garden. The first American ballad scholars, such as Child, Kittredge, and Gummere, worked primarily as philologists, pioneers in the new field of Medieval Studies, and as scholars of Chaucer and Shakespeare.

Why did participants in "high culture" value and use artistic expressions from "folk culture?" Folk culture has long held higher prestige than mass culture in the institutions of high culture. This relationship is better understood when viewed as a reaction against the growing power of mass culture. Mass culture was (and often still is) seen as the destroyer of both high and folk culture,[31] and folk culture was often presented as the foundation of "civilization" (i.e. high culture). Another reason for this relationship is that members of high culture had the power to define folk culture. By definition, members of folk culture were outside commercial or academic means of communication and so could not define themselves; those who crossed the barrier either did so in the terms of the high culture (as academics) or they "went commercial" (crossing into mass culture). In any case, the study and use of folk culture by educated outsiders should be recognized as within the interests of high culture and its battle with the forces of mass culture.

The field of folklore, up until mid-century, essentially shared in the use of historic metaphor: folk authenticity resided in the past, and "the folk" that folklorists searched for were people still expressing the culture of that nearly lost past. The term "folk" was generally used by members of the upper classes in reference to the rural working class, rather than in reference to the urban working class; agricultural life connoted a sense of past and stability. It was a way for the dominant classes to define what was most noble and most worth preserving in the lower classes. But it would be a mistake to dismiss bourgeois interest in the "folkness" of Appalachian whites as merely an expression of cultural dominance; many of these people were profoundly attracted to the otherness of the Anglo-American experience as lived in the Southern mountains. They saw a banality in the materialism of early twentieth-century America, and an alternative in the conservative preindustrial life and art of Appalachia. Uninspired by the official values of progress and change, they sought a sense of past and community.

The discovery during the first two decades of the twentieth century that so many of the old English and Scottish ballads still lived in the Southern mountains reinforced notions of Appalachia as an Elizabethan museum and repository of the dominant group's folk heritage. Years before Cecil Sharp told the world that more old British ballads were to be found in the Southern mountains of the United States than in the British Isles, middle-class Americans were told of the tradition in the popular writing of the day. Local-color fiction writers even incorporated ballads into their stories to give an added touch of antiquarian authenticity.[32] The *Literary Digest* reported in 1917, "The Kentucky Mountains are being ransacked by enthusiastic folk-song gatherers of these lyric remnants of the past."[33] Folksong collectors discovered the old ballads in other parts of the United States, but Ohio and Vermont did not kindle the popular imagination like the mythical mountains of the South.

By the 1930s an allusion to the Elizabethan quality of mountain culture had become a commonplace of popular literature.[34] The metaphor began to affect reality and actual musical events. School teachers instructed their Appalachian pupils in the art of old English sword dances and Morris dances — dances that had never existed in the mountains, and their revival by folklorists in England had been more disinternment than rejuvenation.[35] In an interview of 1934, Jean Thomas, an Appalachian "popularizer" and the creator and director of the American Folk Song Festival in Kentucky, described her opening for the festival:

> You see, I open the festival with a piper walking down the mountainside playing a silver flute and followed by little Lincolnshire dancers in authentic costumes . . . and the children dance an old Lincolnshire dance that still survives in our Kentucky hills. At the back of the main stage is a semi-circle of pretty mountain girls dressed as Elizabethan ladies-in-waiting. . . . My minstrels are seated on the backless benches in front of the stage. They have their dulcimers, guitars, banjos, harmonicas and accordians. The program shows the authentic steps of America's ballad history. We aim, through song, to build up a picture of mountain life as it has been lived in these hills since the seventeenth century.[36]

When listing the instruments that her "minstrels" played, Jean Thomas gave first mention to the dulcimer. Both scholars and Appalachian popularizers (categories not always easily distinguished) preferred the plucked dulcimer to other instruments. Not that the plucked dulcimer was English in origin (it developed from a German prototype), but its unusual shape and technique lent it an exoticism that they viewed as a surviving medievalism. Also, unlike the fiddle and the banjo, the dulcimer had no connection to social dancing, an activity viewed skeptically by many Christians of both highland and lowland. The dulcimer was an instrument more suited for home use, and genteel folksong collectors and settlement school teachers approved of the domestic setting for music making just as middle-class Americans cultivated music making in their parlors. Settlement schools encouraged dulcimer making and playing, and marketed homemade dulcimers, along with other "arts and crafts" items, to outside benefactors. Folk music collectors and festival organizers likewise advanced the cause of the plucked dulcimer as the most Appalachian of instruments.

Also, many associated the dulcimer with women, and in the middle-class thinking of the time it was the role of women to nurture culture and morality, and remain somehow changeless in the face of the social upheaval that took place outside of their realm of domestic tranquility. The popular idea of Appalachia was, in a way, a feminine one; its changeless, nature-bound self contrasting with the urban-masculine restless search for progress and power. Negative portrayals of mountain life generally resulted from an intrusion of masculine traits in the form of violent feuding and lawless moonshining. The passive female of Appalachia fell prey to environmentally misplaced masculine aggression.

The banjo was widely played in the mountainous regions of the South, but for most outsiders in the early twentieth century, the banjo had other, often more tawdry, connotations. The banjo, as an instrument used for dance music and in the theater, undoubtedly had some lowly connotations for more pious local people as well.[37] Perhaps this was why the banjo was so easily dismissed by many of the early ballad hunters.

Josiah Combs in his 1925 *Folk-Songs of the Southern United States* laments "For the damsel with the 'dulcimore' is retreating before the boy with the banjo."[38] Combs presents the two instruments with gendered identities and his use of the word "damsel" is revealingly archaic, expressing his longing for the changelessness of mountain life and the feminine nature. His "damsel with the dulcimore" is endangered by the boy with the banjo—masculine restlessness and contagion from the outside world. Howard Brockway in a 1917 article for *The Art World*, after praising the dulcimer as the truly indigenous instrument of the mountains, writes: "When we reached small towns which were in communication by stage with the nearest railroad we found banjoes and guitars. . . . The great deposit of beautiful folk-songs in the Appalachian Region is bound to suffer contamination and to be utterly obliterated".[39] Brockway incorrectly saw the guitar and the banjo as equally new arrivals; the banjo had a longer history in the Southern mountains than he realized. Brockway presents the banjo as a threat to native simplicity and the Anglo-Saxon heritage.

Below is an excerpt from the 1912 *Century Magazine* short story "Hard-

Hearted Barbary Allen" by Lucy Furman. Furman was a house mother at the Hindman settlement school in Kentucky.

> Beneath the musket, on the "fireboard," lay a spindle-shaped, wooden object, black with age. "A dulcimer," Aunt Polly Ann explained. "My man made it, too, always-ago. Dulcimers used to be all the music there was in this country, but banjos is coming in now."
>
> Miss Loring [a settlement school worker] knew that the dulcimer was an ancient musical instrument very popular in England three centuries ago. She gazed upon the interesting survival with reverence, and expressed a wish to hear it played.
>
> "Beldory she'll pick and sing for you . . . "
>
> Often had she [Miss Loring] read and heard of the old English ballad "Barbara Allen"; never had she thought to encounter it in the flesh. As she listened to the old song, long since forgotten by the rest of the world, but here a warm household possession; as she gazed at Beldora, so young, so fair against the background of ancient loom and gray log wall, she felt as one may to whom the curtain of the past is for an instant lifted, and a vision of dead-and-gone generations vouchsafed.[40]

The ballad and the dulcimer were tickets to another time, the romanticized time of the "old stock's" ancestors. The banjo threatened the sanctity of that vision. Miss Loring's reverential gaze upon the dulcimer fits with the almost mystical quality of old-English racial heritage that was ascribed to the mountaineers, an inheritance used to excuse their failure in capitalist America. "Their manners are gentle, gracious, and unembarrassed, so that in talking with them one forgets their bare feet, ragged clothes, and crass ignorance, and in his heart bows anew to the inextinguishable excellence of the Anglo-Saxon race."[41] At a time when eugenics found wide public acceptance, discussions of "racial inheritance" should not be excused as mere metaphor.

Ideas, unlike events, cannot be confined to a point in time. Although Elizabethan metaphors and the damsel with the dulcimer are literary products of the turn of the century, the expression of these ideas continued through the century. Catherine Marshall's popular novel *Christy* of 1967 is a rerun of early twentieth-century fictional treatment of mountain culture.[42] Missionary-school teachers, moonshining, feuds, dulcimers, ballads, mountain words from Shakespeare, and travel into the mountains as a way to travel into the past—if she had written the book fifty years earlier, not much would have been written differently. In the book, the banjo only appears at the dance, an occasion of questionable morality. Marshall introduces the dulcimer as evidence of the noble and ancient heritage of the mountain folk; it is shown at the center of domestic life, played by the father of the enlightened and tranquil Spencer family.

The dulcimer was domesticated and the banjo had a wildness that threatened the nobler aspects of mountain culture and the sanctity of home. The dulcimer is always shown at home, and usually played by a woman, the representative of domesticity. Figure 35 is an illustration from the previously quoted story "Hard-Hearted Barbary Allen." On the porch are gathered the women: three generations of mountain women (and a male baby), and the settlement school teacher (seated on the far right). The grandaughter—the damsel with the dulcimer—plays the old English ballads surrounded by family, spinning wheel, and loom: signs of a simple yet productive and upright domestic life.

"THE MUSIC WAS WEIRD, BUT ATTRACTIVE; THE TUNE SHE PLAYED, MINOR, LONG-DRAWN, AND HAUNTING"

Fig. 35: *The Century Magazine*, March 1912, p. 740.

But the boy with the banjo—and the banjo is almost always presented as the instrument of young men and boys in Southern mountain imagery of the early twentieth century—is at least susceptible to change if not an actual agent of change. Although writers sometimes place the banjo at an evening fireside in a cabin, the boy with the banjo is apt to wander away from home, away from the domestic context.[43] Figure 36 is a 1922 illustration from *Harper's Magazine*.[44] Here we see life "among the less orthodox." This is not a proper home, but an evil parody of a home. As the author tells us, this is a sleeping shed for lumber camp men. The one woman, wife of one of the lumber men, serves as the cook. Laundry is strung up, and the men drink and play cards. Unlike the setting for the dulcimer player in figure 35, the banjo player of figure 36 makes music by the hearth of a place lacking in domestic virtue, a place of moral decay.

Evidence suggests that young men and boys were most frequently the banjoists as the popular image indicates, but this says nothing about the authenticity of the instrument to regional culture. The banjo, for these popular literature writers, was not yet an authentic Appalachian artifact.

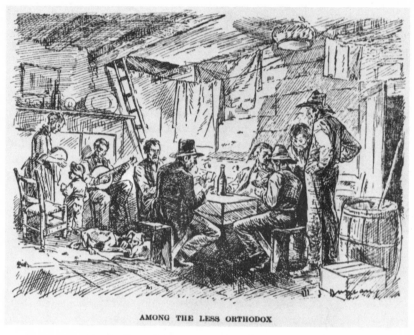

AMONG THE LESS ORTHODOX

Fig. 36: *Harper's Magazine*, September 1922, p. 459.

Authenticity is a slippery concept, an idea central to the discussion here, and a concept that lies at the heart of the history of the fields of folklore and ethnomusicology. Scholars of folk and non-Western music have traditionally preferred to study music that displayed stability (lack of historical change) and uniformity, these characteristics being accepted as signs of authenticity. An early and classic treatment of the idea of authenticity is Walter Benjamin's essay "The Work of Art in the Age of Mechanical Reproduction."[45] Benjamin is concerned with aesthetic authenticity in the face of the theoretically infinite reproducibility of the art object in twentieth-century technological culture. This is a rather different view of the question, one concerned with Western industrial culture rather than folk and traditional societies. Yet it forces us to see the Western intellectual search for authentic musics and cultures within its own cultural context. The historical concern with the authentic seems to coincide with the industrial society and the time of a growing mass culture.

Authenticity does not reside in the object, rather it is the result of a matching of characteristics of the object with an external claim or set of values. Those who set the values are asserting power over the object; they claim the power to legitimize or devalue the object. For the folksong and folklore collectors working in Appalachia in the early twentieth century, authenticity was located in the past, particularly in the Anglo-Saxon past. They valued cultural stability over the technological change of modern America, handicraft to the machine-made, and they valued purity over the dynamics of ethnic and racial pluralism.

This system of values grew from a strain of thought in Western culture that goes back to at least Rousseau:[46] society, and the inevitable artifice needed to maintain social order, made humans inauthentic beings. During the late nineteenth through early twentieth centuries, many dissatisfied Westerners tried to dive below what seemed to them the constructs of civilization to find their authentic self, and to do this they used their own conceptions of "exotic" peoples of the world (thought "uncivilized" in a positive, though condescending, sense). Whether it was Gauguin using Tahitian culture, Stravinsky creating a vision of ancient Russian rituals, or Percy MacKay (poet and dramatist) using Appalachian culture, each sought an authenticity predicated upon the comparative lack of societal artifice, as well as a distance from the acquisitive and mechanical values of contemporary Western culture. The "wild flower" of folksong (a frequently used metaphor) symbolized the lack of artifice and the organic quality ascribed to folk culture.

Even though the banjo was widely played in the mountain South, and was used in the performance of traditional music (even to accompany that most "authentic" of forms, the Child ballad), the early twentieth-century idea of the banjo did not line up with concepts of Appalachian authenticity. To be authentically Appalachian, the banjo needed to share in the otherness that defined Appalachia, and the qualities that defined the authentic self, free from the artifice of industrial culture. The banjo as factory-made musical machine, and the banjo as urban dance orchestra or popular theater instrument mitigated against the idea of the banjo as Appalachian artifact. And the banjo as African-American called into question the supposed purity of Anglo-Saxon culture as preserved in the mountains. The plucked dulcimer, of which little was known, hence much could be created, was "authentic."

Given the barriers to the authenticity of the banjo as Appalachian artifact, it is possible to project the several strategies available for the construction of authenticity. In the popular mind, the ol' five-string banjo needed to be separated from its flashier urban cousins that appeared in popular theater and dance orchestras. Stressing the rusticity of the instrument as found in the mountains and the equally rustic performance contexts did much to create a separate sphere for the southern white banjo. And the simplicity of the mountain banjo bespoke a disinterest in material acquisition indicative of personal authenticity. Both popular and scholarly literature (what little scholarly literature deigned to mention the instrument) of the time always placed the southern white banjo in the mountains, ignoring areas such as the piedmont. In doing this, the southern white banjo not only imaginatively resided in the most mythologized section of the South, but also in the most Anglo-Saxon part of the country. Placing it in a mentally segregated zone, the banjo lost some of its African-American meaning. The association of the banjo with black culture, however, would not begin to truly disappear until a mid-twentieth-century popular culture avoidance of the image of the black banjo player. An easy strategy, and a well-used one, was the rejection of the factory-made banjo for the homemade. The homemade banjo basked in the ideology of the arts and crafts revival and turned what before had appeared as an importation into an organic part of the community. Additionally, the homemade banjo lacked the machine-like quality that northern manufacturers had developed for the banjo over the years. Finally, some writers began to accept the boy with the banjo as a positive part of mountain culture, rather than as a threat to social stability. His implicit wildness need not be shown as dangerous, but rather as an unwillingness to "reform" to dominant culture values.

Both popularizing scholars and popular literature writers used these strategies on the banjo, as is shown by the following three examples. Robert Winslow Gordon was a professional folklorist and the founder of the Archive of American Folk Song at the Library of Congress. He also authored many articles and columns for popular magazines. Gordon was an innovative and dedicated field-worker who with a spirit of adventure roamed about the country searching for folksongs much like a naturalist gathering specimens. He wrote an article on banjo songs for the *New York Times Magazine* in 1928.[47] Gordon clearly sees the banjo songs as traditional, but he values them because he sees them as one step on the evolutionary ladder that leads to the ballad. The instrument used to accompany these songs, and which gives its name to the repertory, the banjo, is presented as a prop that is used while authenticity is created (while the songs are sung). Still, Gordon, in his descriptive writing, places the banjo in the heart of rustic mountain culture and creates some authenticity for banjo players by linguistically marking them as "banjer-pickers"—he makes them more other, less like himself and his readers. Gordon also describes the typical banjo player as a young man, a slightly older version of the "boy with the banjo."

John Fox, Jr. (1863–1919), an extremely popular novelist from the turn of the century, does not present the banjo as a threat to native culture, but as a natural part of it. He, too, uses the image of the boy with the banjo, but sees this boy as an untamed child of nature—a true offspring of the mountains. Fox's different view of the banjo may result from his different introduction to mountain culture. By far, most fiction writers and folksong collectors around the turn of the century spent their time in the mountains under the patronage of one or more of the missionary settlement schools, and they were guided in their research by the teachers and pupils there. These schools encouraged those aspects of local culture that coincided with their own middle-class ideas of propriety. John Fox, Jr., friend of Teddy Roosevelt and former Rough Rider, came to the mountains as a coal company executive. The somewhat untamed wildness attributed to the banjo, and to mountain life, was an attractive feature for him; it indicated an opposition to what seemed to many to be the over-civilized state of American middle-class life.

The main character of Fox's very popular novel of 1903, *The Little Shepherd of Kingdom Come,* is a boy with a banjo. This book sold over a million copies and was on the best-seller list for both 1903 and 1904.[48] The protagonist is Chad, a little boy of the mountains, an orphaned waif, and banjo player. Fox includes the names of the pieces Chad plays—"Shady Grove," "Sugar Hill," "Sourwood Mountain," etc.—giving an early, although slim, account of regional instrumental repertory. Later in the story, Chad goes to live with a wealthy relative in the Kentucky Bluegrass. Chad and his white upper-class friends spend time wandering the antebellum plantation:

> Passing old Mammy's cabin that night before supper, the three boys had stopped to listen to old Tom play [banjo], and after a few tunes, Chad could stand it no longer.
>
> "I foller pickin' the banjer a leetle," he said shyly, and thereupon he had taken the rude instrument and made the old negro's eyes stretch with amazement, while Dan rolled in the grass with delight, and every negro who heard ran toward the boy. After supper, Dan brought the banjo into the house and made Chad play on the porch, to the delight of them all. And there, too, the servants gathered, and even old Mammy was observed slyly shaking her foot—so that Margaret clapped her hands and laughed the old woman into great confusion.[49]

Chad delighted and amazed all, both black and white, by playing an instrument that lowlanders thought of as black. Fox's acknowledgment of contrasting banjo traditions is an occasion for humor (and an occasion for the banjo to be allowed in the "big house"), but he does not question the legitimacy of Chad's music.[50]

John Fox made a literary visit back to Chad's old mountain home in 1910. In the *Scribner's Magazine* story "On Horseback to Kingdom Come," Fox describes environmental deterioration and culture change in the mountains—

the result of the coal industry's lack of respect for wilderness, and the taming influence of contact with modern American society. He writes of the deforestation and heavy black smoke that comes from each passing railroad engine. With some sadness, he notes that homes look different; painted houses and latticed porches now decorate the enlarged hamlet of Kingdom Come. Even the people behave differently than during the time Chad had lived there; folks are not surprised to see a stranger, and young people have the manners of settlement school training. We meet a young boy: "He was a sturdy, good-looking lad with a nice face, and he might have posed for Chad except that there was no suggestion of the waif about him, his hair was neatly parted in the middle, and his banjo was modern and new. But the tunes were the same old tunes that Chad had thrummed—'Sourwood Mountain,' 'Turkey in the Straw,' etc.—and he surely made the instrument hum."[51] For Fox, the banjo was not a threat to native ways, as it had been for Lucy Furman and Josiah Combs; modernization and industrialization were the threats. The boy with the banjo was a positive image for Fox, but not just any boy, and not just any banjo. The unnamed boy in the 1910 story lacked the freedom and touch of wildness that had endeared Chad, a true boy of the mountains, to the narrator. His hair was neatly parted and his banjo modern and new—both he and the banjo had been tamed, just as mountain culture was being tamed by the forces of modernization.

If the banjo, generically, was not considered an authentic Appalachian artifact in the early twentieth century, still the right kind of banjo played by the right kind of person could be considered part of a legitimate mountain tradition. Fox certainly acknowledged the most powerful idea of the banjo for that time period: an instrument of black plantation workers. But this did not deny the possibility of a southern white, particularly a mountain white, idea of the banjo. The traditional sentimental ideas of the banjo as pastoral, untamed, and antimodern certainly fit with prevailing notions of Appalachian otherness. "Modern and new" banjos did not fit Appalachian otherness, but old and worn, or rough and homemade did.

Louise Rand Bascom, who wrote the 1909 article on music in western North Carolina for the *Journal of American Folklore*, turned to fiction writing in 1916. The main character in her *Harper's Magazine* story is Andy Coe, a young mountaineer who makes and plays the banjo.[52] The story is illustrated by Watson Barratt and includes five illustrations of Andy toting his homemade banjo. Andy lives with his mother and younger siblings, but as the story opens he has decided to leave his mountain home: the young man with the banjo is prone to wander away from the old ways. Andy had met Mr. Murdock, a vacationer at a nearby mountain resort, and was greatly impressed with his ability to read music. Mr. Murdock promises to teach Andy how to read music if he will join him in New York City. Andy goes to the city only to be used as a vaudeville exhibition. Murdock had no intention of teaching him to read music because it would have destroyed his "primitiveness" and thus ruined him as a theatrical commodity. Andy, filled with anger, leaves the city—a place filled with noisy trains, litter, and perfumed women—and returns home, "whar folks is folks." Although the boy with the (homemade) banjo was dangerously close to abandoning his authentic self, in the end he chooses fidelity to mountain simplicity. Louise Rand Bascom not only presents the homemade banjo as a legitimate Appalachian artifact and Andy's music as authentic, she also makes a strong complaint against the economic exploitation of native art. Still, Andy is depicted as a childlike character, not suited for higher education and unable to manage life in modern America. Bascom's story seems to deny the possibility of traditional musicians navigating the larger world with dignity; her story denies the lives of people like Buell Kazee and Bascom Lamar Lunsford.

By the mid-twentieth century, many of the challenges to the banjo's authenticity as Southern rural-white artifact had lessened. Competing ideas about the banjo weakened: professional minstrelsy was dead, amateur minstrelsy was nearly dead, the "elevation" of the five-string banjo was an almost forgotten fad, black imagery of the banjo was becoming taboo, guitars had long since replaced banjos in jazz, and bejeweled tenor banjos were not easily confused with the "ol' banjo" of the rural South anyway. At the same time, Southern white hillbilly and country musicians were creating a national market for their music and influencing popular ideas of the banjo.

Originally southeastern-based, early country music, called "hillbilly" music for many years, gained a national presence through the broadcasting of powerful radio stations and the large migration of southern rural whites—and their musical preferences—to the nation's industrial centers. Within commercial hillbilly music, regional styles mingled and local musics became nationalized. Broadcasters and record company executives discovered a market in the 1920s for white hillbilly musicians like Fiddlin' John Carson, Gid Tanner and the Skillet Lickers, and Charlie Poole and the North Carolina Ramblers. If folklorists saw traditional Southern instrumental music as an imperfect, not fully evolved, form of folk music (as compared to the unaccompanied ballads), the entrepreneurs of the recording industry apparently did not share in that value system. The early commercialization of hillbilly music was dominated by instrumentalists, and the songs they sang. An important exception is the singer Vernon Dalhart, but it was not until the arrival of Jimmie Rodgers in the late 1920s that the focus of hillbilly music turned away from string band performances to the singing star.

Although people tend to view hillbilly music as an Anglo-American musical expression, much of the repertory and style was shared with and derived from Southern African-American musicians. There are several reasons for the poor documentation of African-American hillbilly music. The recording companies wanted to keep their "race" and "hillbilly" offerings distinct for marketing purposes; they concentrated on the blues and left black string bands largely unrecorded. In the early twentieth century, segregation was the way of the South, so it can hardly be surprising that radio broadcasts of the popular barn dance shows rarely included black musicians.[53] In a deeper sense, hillbilly music would not have been if not for its African-American inheritance, the banjo being only a tangible representative of what is mostly intangible: elements of style and repertory developed in a dialogic relationship between Anglo- and African-America.

Most of the first hillbilly recordings, in the 1920s, were of small ensembles of string instruments. The most popular instruments of the hillbilly "string band" were fiddle, banjo, and guitar, with the fiddle playing lead, and often with a vocal added. Musicians used a wide variety of other instruments as well, from accordions to kazoos. Songs came from many sources: traditional ballads, nineteenth-century sentimental Tin Pan Alley creations, old Gospel songs, minstrel tunes, new songs about a recent disaster, etc. The banjo, though part of the ensemble, was rarely featured in a solo; the fiddle dominated the group. The banjo was either an ensemble instrument or singers used it to accompany songs (for example the 1920s recordings of Buell Kazee), but it was not considered as an instrument of great soloist potential. In the 1930s, as hillbilly music became less of a regional music and more of a national music, musicians used the five-string banjo less and less. The five-string banjo did not have a strong heritage to build upon outside of the southeastern mountain and piedmont regions, and so the innovative country music styles (such as Western Swing) of the 1930s and early 1940s coming out of Texas, Oklahoma, and later, California, relied on the rhythm playing of guitars or jazz-inspired four-string banjos.

Charlie Poole (1892–1931), along with Uncle Dave Macon, is the closest thing to an early hillbilly star banjoist.[54] Old-timers in southwestern Virginia still like to talk about Charlie Poole and play his tunes.[55] Although he played well, his fame is actually due more to his singing and his lifestyle than to his virtuosity on the banjo. Charlie Poole and the North Carolina Ramblers recorded from 1925 until 1930. Many of their songs, such as "Don't Let Your Deal Go Down" and "White House Blues," did well commercially and still enjoy popularity among fans of old-time music. Charlie Poole was also one of the earliest examples of a country music star who lived fast, drank hard, and died young from self-destructive behavior. This was surely part of the public's fascination with Poole. Poole was a textile mill worker from North Carolina who turned professional musician in the mid-1920s.[56] By the late 1920s, his band was turning toward a more modern, vaudevillian-influenced sound.

Later additions to the band included a tenor banjo player, and a ukelele player who could yodel. Charlie Poole's own playing on the five-string banjo was innovative for most of the traditional banjo players who listened to him. He used a three-finger up-picking style, without picks, and most often used the C tuning: all characteristics of the ragtime and classic banjo players from the North. He was a fan of Fred Van Eps. Poole heard Van Eps play in Chicago and he recorded his own versions of two 1917 Van Eps's recordings.[57] In many ways, Charlie Poole is the epitome of the "boy with the banjo:" his music came from Southern roots, but his wandering ways led to divorce, alcoholism, and a desire to push against the walls of musical tradition.

Charlie Poole was unusual for a hillbilly five-string banjo player—he was not a musical traditionalist and not a comedian. In most of the early string bands, the banjo player had the role of comic, big shoes and all. The usual role of the hillbilly five-string banjo player drew heavily upon the old minstrel and medicine show heritage. Banjo players were supposed to be funny, they often dressed in ridiculous costumes, and as the century progressed, the country music banjoist embodied old-fashioned musical values.

Uncle Dave Macon had a long career with the *Grand Ole Opry* (from 1925 until just before his death in 1952) as a keeper of the tradition, old-time banjo player, and singer of old familiar songs. Yet his popularity resulted more from his talents as an entertainer than as a musician. Even though he was a fine old-time player, the banjo really served as a prop while Uncle Dave entertained with songs and jokes and trick playing. Uncle Dave Macon preserved not only nineteenth-century Southern traditional music, he also practiced nineteenth-century theatrical entertainment. The five-string banjo was the perfect tool; long associated with minstrel theater and comedy, Uncle Dave and other banjo players (for example "Stringbean") continued this association for country music audiences well into the twentieth century.[58]

During the 1930s, professional country musicians used five-string banjos infrequently, preferring instead the gentler sounds of guitar and mandolin duets or western-influenced instrumentations. By 1938 even the Sears and Roebuck catalogue, the great supplier of musical instruments to rural America, ceased to offer five-string banjos. The few country musicians who continued to play the banjo did so as old-fashioned traditionalists and comedians. When "Grandpa" Jones turned away from modern country music in the late 1940s to become a vehement traditionalist, he turned to the five-string banjo. Before that time he had preferred to play the guitar.[59]

It is said[60] that when the young Earl Scruggs first played banjo at the *Grand Ole Opry* in 1945 with his flashy new technique, Uncle Dave Macon's only response was "He ain't one damned bit funny." The story is perhaps apocryphal, but it tells us how Earl Scruggs changed not only banjo technique, but challenged accepted ideas about the role of the banjo in country music. It was not just his technique that transformed the banjo. Earl Scruggs took professional banjo playing out of the minstrel tradition, which had still defined the performance practices of professional hillbilly and country banjoists.

Blackface minstrelsy still had a healthy existence in the South as an amateur affair during the first half of the twentieth century, and minstrel-inspired acts worked the medicine show and vaudeville circuits. Hillbilly string bands, early bluegrass bands, and the *Grand Ole Opry* all occasionally used blackface comedy acts in their performances. The jokes, techniques, and theatrical ethos of minstrelsy resonated beyond the form proper, beyond the black mask.[61] In most photographs of early 1920s hillbilly musicians, the bands appear in suits and neckties with their instruments in hand. This unmediated presentation of self did not last long; with professionalization came the adaptation of regional conventions of professional theater, conventions rooted in the minstrel theater, though not always willingly adopted. The exaggerated hayseed imagery that became such a lasting part of country music was a show business affectation, a transformation of the blackface mask into a new clown face. From the early days of the *Grand Ole Opry* to the television show *Hee Haw,* the mark of the minstrel is clear, only the color of the mask has changed.

The banjo player was especially susceptible to "whiteface" minstrelsy. Ridiculous costumes, oversized shoes, and comedy gags were part of being a banjo player. Even if "Snuffy" Jenkins played the banjo with a three-finger technique close to Scruggs style before Scruggs, Jenkins never left behind the minstrel banjo; photographs always show him in droopy overalls, a ragged little hat, and oversized shoes.[62] The dapper costuming and lively theatrics of Uncle Dave Macon owed much to his early exposure to the world of vaudeville and medicine shows. Bill Monroe had banjoist-comedian "Stringbean" as a member of the Blue Grass boys until 1945. His value to the band was not his banjo playing, but his theatrical (minstrel) skills. After Stringbean left the band, a new banjo player became a Blue Grass boy—Earl Scruggs.

Scruggs did not transform the banjo only by refusing the role of minstrel, he created new musical territory for the instrument. Scruggs used a Gibson Mastertone with metal strings, played in a three-finger (thumb plus two fingers) up-picking style with metal picks to create a loud and powerful tone. At the core of his technique were "rolls"—a variety of patterns for right hand alternations between the two fingers and the thumb, formulas that could be creatively manipulated to produce a flurry of seemingly constant fast-moving notes. Within this powerful sounding race of bright-toned notes, syncopation played an important role in driving the rhythm further. Scruggs, and the bluegrass banjoists that followed, often played in the upper positions that had been previously explored by both "classical" and vaudevillian players, but was new territory for both traditional and old-time country music banjoists. In the high-powered jazz-influenced string band style that Monroe and his band were developing, Scruggs's new technique dramatically increased the banjo's musical capabilities and allowed it soloist stature within the group. And for many (most?) subsequent bluegrass bands, the banjo player became the lead soloist of the ensemble. And Uncle Dave was right about Earl Scruggs—he wasn't funny.

Even bluegrass musicians were not completely immune to the role of minstrel comedian. Earl Scruggs and Lester Flatt played cousin Earl and cousin Lester (their parts were somewhat more dignified than the hillbilly-turned-millionaire Clampett family roles) on the television program *The Beverly Hillbillies*, a show that trafficked in the broadest of Appalachian stereotypes. The Dillards, a well-known bluegrass band, appeared frequently on *The Andy Griffith Show*[63] as a moonshine-loving, somewhat deranged mountaineer family called the Darling family. In both instances, the "whiteface" hillbilly mask dropped away when the music started: the musical occasion in bluegrass was not the time for comic self-effacement, but a time for tight ensemble playing and the display of technical prowess. These shows did, however, connect the sound of bluegrass music and bluegrass banjo to hillbilly stereotypes for millions of Americans.

Even though Earl Scruggs played the cousin of the Clampett family, the poker-faced virtuoso was not performing his music in the tradition of the minstrel-comedian. Perhaps Scruggs can be compared to Alfred Farland, the "Scientific Banjoist of Pittsburgh, Pa." Farland also took the banjo out of the minstrel tradition by refusing the role of comic, refusing the costume and makeup traditional to the professional banjoist, and by developing an outstanding technique. But Earl Scruggs's innovation has proven to be of more lasting consequence than Farland's: Scruggs's imitators are legion forty-five years after his initial appearance with the Blue Grass Boys, and other bluegrass banjoists explain their innovations by comparison to "classic" Scruggs style.

Whereas Alfred Farland et al. sought the elevation of the banjo by mounting a frontal attack on the old sentimental ideas of the instrument, Scruggs and other bluegrass banjoists elevated the banjo in country music through an artful compromise. The banjo was empowered with a new technique and legitimized as a full member of the string band with soloist capabilities, but both the ensemble it played in and the repertory it played were strongly nostalgic, antimodernist, and filled with agrarian imagery—in short, sentimental. Not only was bluegrass imagery strongly Southern, it was strongly Southeastern, refusing to give into the cowboy imagery so popular in country music in the 1940s and 1950s, or the more upscale imagery adopted by the 1970s. But it was only by musical empowerment, by putting the old music "in overdrive," that the Southeastern string band tradition could continue in the world of commercial country music. The bluegrass banjo, with its mad rush of sparkling notes, stood as the most noticeable symbol of this musical transformation, and so the banjo became even more strongly tied to ideas about white rural Southeasterners and the conservative music they made.

Country and hillbilly music was a different musical dialect from the popular music coming out of New York and Hollywood, and as such, country music was implicitly a form of cultural opposition to the dominant culture of the northeast. With time, and with the growing commercial power of country music, implicit opposition became explicit. When Ernest Tubb, heading a *Grand Ole Opry* unit, walked onto the stage at Carnegie Hall in New York in 1947, he exclaimed, "My, but this place sure could hold a lot of hay."[64] The hall was packed and the unit grossed $9,000.[65] The music and hence the culture of the poor white folks of the rural south had invaded a bastion of elite northeastern urban culture. Just the thought of loading Carnegie Hall with hay was a way of explicitly announcing cultural opposition to the class and society to which the hall referred.

Within the oppositional genre of country music, bluegrass stood as an internal opposition to trends in commercial country music. Bluegrass was obstinately conservative, refusing electrification and drum sets, and holding fast to a song repertory centered on the old themes of home and farm, mother and heaven. In the rest of country music, the five-string banjo had become a marginal instrument by the 1930s; only performers, such as "Grandpa" Jones, who were self-consciously anachronistic continued to regularly use the five-string banjo. So the banjo was relegated to the most sentimental and antimodernist subgenre in country music—bluegrass. And there it thrived.

It is problematic to speak of *the* folk music revival. When closely examined, the concept crumbles apart into pieces of ideas. R. Serge Denisoff in his book *Great Day Coming* leaves his readers with the impression that the impetus for the popularization of folk music came from the political left, especially from Stalinist circles. There is some truth to this, but Denisoff paints an overly cynical, almost conspiratorial, view of the American left and its role in the folk music revival. Robbie Lieberman, in *My Song Is My Weapon: People's Songs, American Communism, and the Politics of Culture, 1930–1950,* demonstrates that rather than Stalinist, members of the "People's Songs" organization (a group—and a magazine—that Denisoff writes extensively about) saw themselves as part of both Popular Front ideology and New Deal politics. Many of the songs and the people (for example Pete Seeger and Woody Guthrie) who came out of "People's Songs" have had a powerful presence in American culture and cannot be dismissed as marginal figures even if their personal politics lay at the fringes of American life.[66]

The real complexity arises with the acknowledgment that interest in American folk music and the desire to preserve and revitalize it are older and broader than any one particular political movement. How can we reconcile the image of Pete Seeger, always with banjo in hand, singing radical union songs, with the picture of Henry Ford, patron of old-time music, advocating an American square dance revival? Both men attacked the twentieth-century culture industry, particularly as manifested in the music of Tin Pan Alley, and encouraged their own preferred genre of people's music. But Henry Ford turned to old-time music and square dance out of a reactionary impulse: a desire to rein in what seemed to him a galloping irrationality and subversive morality allowed expression in jazz-age music and dance.

Most of the pre–World War II folk music revivalism in the United States sprang from a conservative impulse. Henry Ford tried to use old-time dance music to turn back the social clock to a time before the values of the culture industry had infiltrated middle-class society.[67] Ford did this without the intellectual framework of the German romantic idea of the "folk": he celebrated the Common Man.[68] Ford recorded many traditional instrumentalists from around the country in the 1920s with the hope that this would lead to an eventual standardization of old-time music and dance. Thus rationalized, the process of mass producing a culture industry of his own choosing would be more efficient. Henry Ford's revival was based on his industrial ideology, and was not a denial of the beneficence of the industrial society after all, but rather a fear of the growing mass culture. Dancing to jazz music seemed as irrational to him as painting cars in different colors.

Folk entrepreneurs organized the first folk festivals in the late 1920s and 1930s, and overall, they shared in a conservative impulse. The news media documented these events and presented them to the reading public.[69] Jean Thomas and her American Folk Song Festival (begun in 1930) looked to Elizabethan England as the artistic ancestor of mountain music—a truly preindustrial folk fantasy. John Powell and Annabelle Buchanan began the White Top Folk Festival in 1931 to encourage a revival of folk music among the white natives of the Southern mountains. They, too, looked for the survival of preindustrial musical expressions, and they actively asserted power over musicians' choices of repertory and style. The racial and social world view articulated in the White Top festival by its organizers was conservative to the point of being reactionary.[70] Bascom Lamar Lunsford established his folk music and dance festival to help preserve his own sense of artistic and social past in the face of rapid change in Asheville, North Carolina.[71]

In retrospect, even the leftist artistic expressions and interests of the New Deal era, including folk music, were at core conservative: the desire to restore what had been lost to a world gone sour. This has led to a sometimes confusing marriage of radical ideology with a retrograde aesthetic.[72] Warren Susman has questioned just how ideological the "Red Decade" really was,[73] and a look at much of the artistic life of the political left in the 1930s only supports Susman's suspicion of an ideological softness. The leftist origins of the American folk music revival in the late 1930s exudes more of the folksy warmth of a Thomas Hart Benton painting[74] than the ideological toughness of a Bertolt Brecht play. Although their motivations were different, in the end Pete Seeger and Henry Ford do share this much: a sentimental glorification of the American Common Man.

In 1936, a sixteen-year-old Pete Seeger traveled South with his father, musicologist Charles Seeger. During the trip the two attended the Asheville "Mountain Dance and Folk Festival," the first of the series of folk festivals that appeared in the 1930s. The festival had been started in 1928 by Bascom Lamar Lunsford, a native of the area, collector of old songs, banjoist, fiddler, dancer, former teacher, and lawyer. Lunsford was, as David Whisnant writes, "finding the way between the old and the new." Asheville was a boomtown and tourist resort in the early part of the twentieth century. The growth of the town and influx of outsiders threatened traditional local culture. Lunsford developed a festival that both catered to outsider interest and encouraged the preservation of local music and dance. He knew that he could not contain modernization, and it is doubtful that he would have wanted to do that. Lunsford's goal was the conservation of the old-time local music and dance that he loved. His goal was direct and his manner dignified but never condescending; Lunsford's festival proved popular with natives and outsiders alike. Both Seegers enjoyed the show.[75]

Years later, Pete Seeger wrote of this trip and mentioned two things: his youthful shock upon seeing terrible poverty and his delight at seeing and hearing his first five-string banjo at the Asheville festival (played by Aunt Samantha Bumgarner).[76] The young Seeger was predisposed to notice the banjo playing; he had already been strumming a four-string banjo in his school jazz band. He was struck, on a strictly musical level, by the sound and rhythm of this other form of the instrument to which he had already felt some kinship. But the social context constructed the framework of meaning for the musical moment; the two were inseparable. Traveling with his father, who was involved with leftist political groups and was an early member of the Communist Party-supported Composers' Collective,[77] the young Pete Seeger was predisposed to view Southern rural poverty within a particular ideological framework. Pete Seeger was an early "red diaper baby"; he subscribed to the Communist literary magazine *New Masses* at the tender age of thirteen.[78] But the trip South brought him in direct contact with that other America. Adolescent encounter with social injustice and an introduction to the five-string banjo came at the same time. For Pete Seeger, the five-string banjo became a metaphor for the rural working class and the nobility of folk culture. There was nothing clownish (minstrel-like) about his idea of the five-string banjo. For Seeger the four-string banjo had been ruined by the athletic exhibitions of commercial performers, but the five-string banjo exuded the honesty of working-class folk.

Although members of "People's Songs," particularly "The Almanac Singers," worked tirelessly during the 1940s, and "The Weavers" achieved some mainstream popularity in the early 1950s, it was not until the late 1950s and early 1960s that folk music revivalism gained a large, overwhelmingly youthful, audience; some date the beginning of the revival with the 1958 Kingston Trio recording of "Tom Dooley." White American youth during most of the twentieth century have repeatedly used the music of liminal social groups as a vehicle for the creation of a youth culture at odds with their parent's culture. Jazz, rhythm and blues, rock and roll, and folk music all had roots in the lower classes, especially the Southern white and black working class. Commercial folk music (often referred to as "protest song" in the 1960s) enjoyed its largest audiences and greatest economic success during a low period for rock and roll. Although the Kingston Trio probably did more to popularize the banjo at the time (they also probably did more to depoliticize folk music than anyone else), for the truly dedicated followers of the revival, Pete Seeger and his ever-present banjo, along with Woody Guthrie, emerged as a father figure for the whole movement. It was a Pete Seeger concert in 1954 that inspired Kingston Trio member Dave Guard to learn to play the banjo.

At the same time that the folk-protest song movement flourished among mostly Northern youth (the movement's center was in New York City), a related folk music revivalism developed. Deviating from the singer-songwriter model of the folk-protest song movement, others, such as the members of the New Lost City Ramblers and the Greenbriar Boys, began to re-create actual performance styles and repertory of traditional Southern musicians, especially Southeastern stringbands. The practice grew out of the folk music revival, but their musical interests naturally led these Northeastern musicians to the "discovery" of bluegrass. Bluegrass probably would not have survived as a commercial form into the 1960s without the support of the folk music revival; revivalists were even the first to define bluegrass as a distinct genre.[79] But bluegrass, and the banjo style that helped define it, grew from different roots than did the folk-protest song movement. The banjo, strongly identified with Pete Seeger and Earl Scruggs, was an important symbol in both folk-protest music and bluegrass. Even though there was musical overlap (and a shared segment of the audience), there was also a tendency for an ideological split between players of folk banjo and bluegrass banjo (see figure 37).

Although there has always been an overlap, by the late 1960s, bluegrass and folk-revival inspired "Old-Time" (capitalized here so as not to be confused with the generalized adjective) banjo players had differentiated themselves. Old-Time musicians turned to the recreation of prebluegrass string band music, which they considered to be more authentically folk than bluegrass. Bluegrass banjo players and Old-Time banjo players valued different types of

Fig. 37: *Sing Out!*, January 1962, p. 71.

instruments, had different techniques and repertories, and had different musical philosophies. Old-Time music had stronger ties to the folk music revival, and Old-Time musicians believed in the moral rightness of their preservationist and anticommercial approach to Southern music.

In the cartoon of figure 37, the counter-culture clothing, hairstyles, and the disparaging comment about Earl Scruggs's politics indicate that these are not bluegrass players, but followers of the folk music revival. Although both the Southern bluegrasser and the Northern revivalist/Old-Time musician were oppositional to dominant culture values, they stood opposed in different ways, with different political outlooks and different ideas of public dress and behavior. Bluegrass still had a large following from the rural South in addition to its large following from outside of the area, which included folk music revivalists. As a result, many bluegrass events have had a sometimes uneasy mixture of conservative working-class Southerners and youthful middle-class liberals.

There is another clue in figure 37 that these are not bluegrass musicians: the banjo player is a woman. In Southeastern tradition, women often play the banjo. Women banjo players, such as Lily May Ledford and Cousin Emmy (Cynthia May Carver), are well-known entertainers from the early years of Country music. Currently, Dolly Parton and Barbara Mandrell are examples of banjo-playing female Country music stars. In Old-Time music, there are many women banjo players. But, with the exception of family bands, very few women up through the 1970s played professional bluegrass, and very few women played bluegrass banjo. Bluegrass has been a male-dominated music, and performances, especially for informal pick-up bands, tend to have the competitive spirit of an athletic contest (another traditionally male-dominated world).[80]

The folk-music-as-protest goal of the folk music revival, by 1970, was eclipsed by the goal of authentic performance by Old-Time musicians. Pete Seeger's approach to the banjo illustrates the folk-protest music philosophy; he played in a variety of styles, some of his own making, using whatever technique best supported the message-making musical moment. In comparison, the dedicated Old-Time banjo player typically studied the techniques of elderly skilled players from the Southern mountains (especially clawhammer style), perhaps traveling South for field work or simply to pick a few tunes with the "real" tradition bearers. Some moved to the mountain South. Like the folklorists, ballad hunters, and local-color writers before him or her, the concept of authenticity directed the Old-Time banjoist's music. But unlike the prewar seekers of folk authenticity, Old-Time musicians did not merely seek the authentic; they worked to become authentic performers themselves. By the 1950s, some professional folklorists also became inclusive in their ideas of "the folk"; everyone, in some way, was a "folk," and the expanded scholarly definition of the word fit well with the ideas of the folk music revival.

Bluegrass players (both Southerners and non-Southerners) also had tradition and concepts of authenticity, but they based their tradition on individuals (for example Scruggs, Don Reno, Ralph Stanley) and a commercially recorded repertory. Old-Time banjoists, even though they mined early hillbilly recordings for repertory, based their concepts of tradition and authenticity upon ideas of "the folk" and a distinctly antimodern and anticommercial ideology. And they chose instruments, repertory, and a performance style that reflected their ideas.

Bluegrass and Old-Time banjo players share ideas about their instrument that spring from American sentimental values.[81] Even though it has been a part of the popular culture for over a hundred years, the banjo still suggests an exoticism to most Americans and has a half-barbaric quality that is appealing to many. Robert Cantwell writes in 1984: "Earl Scruggs tamed the wildness that is still in the banjo; but he did not domesticate it."[82] Americans originally saw the banjo's innate wildness as an African inheritance, but later attributed this to its Southern mountain origins. The Southern-white banjo maintains its bucolic connotations. For both Old-Time and bluegrass players, the banjo still has an old-timey folk quality, an antimodernist aesthetic that they value.

Bluegrass banjoists are especially fond of the mechanical quality of their instrument; the nuts and brackets, flanges, tailpiece, and bridge invite constant mechanical adjustment. Because of the modernizing innovations of banjo manufacturers at the end of the nineteenth century and during the 1920s, the banjo is a machine, inviting manipulation. This would seem to be a denial of the sentimental idea of the banjo, but late twentieth-century Americans are so drawn to technology that they even use it in their escape from modern society; one has only to look at the high technology of current camping equipment for evidence. Many Old-Time banjoists are drawn to the gadgetry of the banjo as well, but bluegrass banjoists tend to spend more time on the mechanical setup of their instrument—the technology is a source of joy. The setup (i.e., adjusting string and head tension, adjusting neck angle, choosing string gauge, selecting the type of bridge and tailpiece) can significantly change the sound of the banjo. Bluegrass banjos are usually designed and set up to maximize a bright and sustained tone, a quality very different from the sound of the original African gourd-resonated banjo, although there has been a recent trend toward a darker sound (for example Bela Fleck).

The most sought-after instrument for bluegrass banjoists is the prewar Gibson Mastertone, a powerful instrument with a back resonator, and the instrument played by Earl Scruggs and other bluegrass notables. Old-Time banjo players prefer open-backed banjos patterned after the "elevated" banjos from the turn of the century. Metal strings and geared pegs have replaced the original gut strings and violin-type pegs, and the usual result is a banjo too loud for Old-Time music. The banjo player in the Old-Time band generally uses clawhammer technique to back up the fiddle lead and only rarely takes a solo. Most Old-Time banjo players place either foam rubber or a sock behind the head to dampen the tone a bit so that the banjo will blend better with the other instruments. Old-time banjo players usually set up their instrument for a darker timbre than bluegrass players.

The most prized instruments for Old-Time musicians are the actual high-quality banjos from the turn of the century. On the first page of the preface of *Complete Banjo Repair*[83] is a photograph of the most coveted of Old-Time banjos: the Fairbanks "Whyte Laydie." Knowing about A. C. Fairbanks and for whom he was making his banjos (see chapter 1), the photograph is ironic. Not only is the banjo strung with metal strings, given a high-tension tailpiece, and has a head discolored from playing in clawhammer (i.e., stroke) style rather than guitar style, but the banjo is placed on a woodpile. Fairbanks would have preferred his handiwork to appear in more fashionable surroundings, but modern ideas, which are really old ideas, place the banjo in a less civilized context.

Figure 38 is from a 1963 advertising pamphlet for Ode banjos. The banjo shown is much like the turn-of-the-century instruments that were marketed as "musical mechanisms" with elitist or modernist names like "The Imperial" or "The Electric." But the Ode advertisement teaches potential customers a different lesson about the meaning of the banjo. The banjo is purposely behind the trend, it is a part of nature, and a path to preindustrial craft values. Although it no longer takes the form of the "ol' banjo" of chapter 2, the idea of the banjo, presented in this Ode advertisement, recapitulates the familiar theme of sentimental pastoralism. It is a protest against "indifferent machinery" and the technological culture born of the official values of American society. It is also a protest against the degraded and alienated state of work in corporate America; it is a conservative plea for a renewed, craft-oriented, work ethic.[84] The banjo is still used in the expression of sentimental values.

Early twentieth-century fiction and folklore writers viewed the banjo as only an accompaniment to Appalachian-folk authenticity, an authenticity that resided in the ballad or folksong, not in the banjo. Some could find authenticity in the homemade or rustic banjo, because it was the product of native craft and so considered an organic part of the "folk" community. For folk music revivalists of the 1960s, the five-string banjo, generically, was a true Appalachian-folk object, but deeper levels of banjo authenticity still rested upon the privileging of low-technology handicraft as illustrated by the popularity of Frank Proffitt's banjos (starting in the 1960s). As Frank Warner wrote in 1963, "Frank was becoming a symbol in the rising tide of interest in the authentic."[85] Proffitt played and made, for sale, wooden, fretless banjos. His mail order business did so well that he eventually got several neighbors to help make "Frank Proffitt banjos." The design, learned from his father, did not have metal

Fig. 38: Advertisement for ODE Banjos, 1963. Archive of Folk Culture, Library of Congress.

brackets or geared tuners; the eye saw only wood, strings, and a skin head. Proffitt's banjo no longer had the look of a machine. It gave visual testimony to the survival of preindustrial craft, and so revivalists and Old-Time musicians deemed it truly authentic.

For many people who were not fans of Old-Time music, it was precisely this constant reference to a sense of rural past and preindustrial craft that made the music, and by extension the banjo, inauthentic, i.e., inauthentic for contemporary American life. How could this music address life in a postindustrial society? Although bluegrass could be accused of this as well, it was folk revivalists and Old-Time musicians who so self-consciously pursued antimodernism. Even if many revivalists and Old-Time musicians used their music as a form of conservative protest, it often degenerated into a nostalgia for a past that never existed.

Festivals have been a central, perhaps the central, performance events for both Old-Time and bluegrass music. Festivals are only partly about professional performance; the other important role of the festival is the encouragement of informal playing in parking lots and other areas away from the stage. Much of the lure of both bluegrass and Old-Time music is the participatory nature of the tradition. A standard repertory and a fairly standardized musical vocabulary (which tends to be limited and rather predictable) permits strangers to form instant musical ensembles.

In part, festivals (and fiddlers' conventions, etc.) are about creating community — musical and social. This is clear in Northern Old-Time festivals which have a fairly homogeneous crowd: white middle-class people seeking a musical alternative, and often a lifestyle alternative. Festivals in the South, especially bluegrass festivals, tend to attract a mixed crowd of working class and middle class, rural Southerner and urban visitor, conservative and liberal. Yet each creates a sense of community: the Southerners who grew up with the music renew their own social and familial past (and very often come as family groups), and the outsiders who adopt the music join with others to imaginatively create a sense of past and temporary community. The music, a self-consciously old-fashioned art, refers to the past, but not to just any past. It is, in the minds of Old-Time and bluegrass fans, a past held together by community (public or familial): it is a sentimental longing. Musicians create a sense of community by sharing in a highly coherent musical style and placing value on participation. It is revealing that they come together in festival situations, forming an actual community for a weekend. Conservative fans hold on to their old tunes in spite of a changing world while the children of the suburbs try to create, if for only a weekend here and there, social and artistic coherence and a sense of boundary and belonging.

I have not done a systematic count, but my informal noting of folk and bluegrass festival posters and pamphlets shows a marked preference for banjo iconography over any other instrument. The fiddle can be mistaken for a violin, the guitar is used in too many other kinds of music, the mandolin does not have a long history in this country, the dulcimer (either kind) is not very recognizable to the general public, but the five-string banjo can neither be mistaken nor forgotten. The damsel with the dulcimer has retreated before the boy with the banjo; the boy and the girl with the banjo no longer have to prove their right to the tradition. The banjo resonates with the sentimental ethos that had always nurtured it, a sentimental ethos that is a part of the generalized allure of bluegrass and Old-Time music. The "ol' banjo" of the rural South stands reinterpreted. Once plantation black, then mountain white, the five-string banjo now invites the children of late twentieth-century America (primarily the white children) onto the mountain porch of figure 34 to partake of the musical moment, to experience the not quite tamed wildness within, and to construct (if only for a weekend) a sense of authenticity — an authenticity that springs from the sentimental values of American culture.

Notes

1. Janelle Warren-Findley, in "Passports to Change: The Resettlement Administration's Folk Song Sheet Program, 1936–37," discusses various graphics used on the song sheets, including the Pollock drawing of figure 34. The article appears in *Prospects: An Annual of American Cultural Studies* v. 10 (1985), ed. Jack Salzman.

2. The argument for minstrel introduction is given in Robert B. Winans, "The Folk, the Stage, and the Five-String Banjo in the Nineteenth Century," *Journal of American Folklore* v. 89, n. 354 (1976): pp. 407–37. Arguing against Winans's conclusions and for Afro-American introduction are: Eugenia Cecelia Conway in her 1980 dissertation "The Afro-American Traditions of the Folk Banjo," and William Tallmadge, "The Folk Banjo and Clawhammer Performance Practice in the Upper South: A Study of Origins," in *The Appalachian Experience,* ed. Barry M. Buxton (Boone, N. C.: Appalachian Consortium Press), pp. 169–79.

3. Many young men from the Southern mountains served in the Union and Confederate armies during the Civil War and many would have been introduced to the banjo then; I have found photographs and references to banjoists performing on ship or at camp. See Webb, *Ring the Banjar!* pp. 11–12; Albert Bauer, *Stewart's Banjo and Guitar Journal* (February–March 1893): p. 7. Horace Weston, while in the Union Navy, received "fifty cents per month from each sailor of the crew for playing [the banjo] for their amusement" (*S. S. Stewart's Banjo and Guitar Journal,* June 1890, supplement section, "Death of Horace Weston").

4. Cecelia Conway discusses the traditions of duo banjos and banjo songs in her 1980 dissertation "The Afro-American Traditions of the Folk Banjo" and "The Banjo-Song Genre," in *Arts in Earnest,* ed. Patterson and Zug (Durham, N.C.: Duke University Press), pp. 135–46.

5. "Child" ballads are the old English and Scottish ballads included in the collection of Francis J. Child (1825–96) *English and Scottish Popular Ballads* New York: Dover Publications, 1965). Each ballad was given a number and all versions of a particular ballad share that number. Many folk song collectors have treated Child's collection as canon.

6. Louise Rand Bascom, "Ballads and Songs of Western North Carolina," *Journal of American Folklore* v. 22, n. 34 (April–June 1909): p. 238.

7. John C. Campbell, *The Southern Highlander and His Homeland* (New York: Russell Sage Foundation, 1921), p. 144.

8. In addition to secondary source material, I refer in this discussion to information gathered during interviews of banjo players done in southwestern Virginia and western North Carolina during the summer of 1985. An edited transcription of one of my interviews appears in "An Interview with Mrs. Bertie Dickens: Old-Time Banjo Player," *North Carolina Folklore Journal* v. 34, n. 1 (winter–spring 1987): pp. 61–65.

9. For photographs of a large collection of homemade banjos see John Rice Irwin, *Musical Instruments of the Southern Appalachian Mountains* (Norris, Tenn.: Museum of Appalachia Press, 1979). Irwin obviously privileges a primitivist aesthetic.

10. Clifford Kinney Rorrer, *Charlie Poole and the North Carolina Ramblers* (Eden, N.C., 1968), p. 2.

11. Some examples of early minstrel banjo tutors are: Elias Howe (Gumbo Chaff), *The Complete Preceptor for the Banjo* (1850), Phil Rice, *Correct Method for the Banjo: With or Without a Master* (1858, copies of both are in the special collections at Lincoln Center of the New York Public Library); Thomas F. Briggs, *Brigg's Banjo Instructor* (1855) and James Buckley, *Buckley's Guide for the Banjo* (1868, copies of both are in the Harris Collection at Brown University).

12. It can be argued that minstrel stroke style shares more with elevated banjo playing than with Southern clawhammer. Although the basic technique for striking the string was different, the use of the same favored tuning and the occasional playing in 6/8 time or with triplets evidences the direct lineage of minstrel stroke style to the elevated "classic" style of the late nineteenth century.

13. Henry D. Shapiro, *Appalachia on Our Mind: The Southern Mountains and Mountaineers in the American Consciousness, 1870–1920* (Chapel Hill: University of North Carolina Press, 1978); C. Vann Woodward, *Origins of the New South, 1877–1913* (Baton Rouge: Louisiana State University Press, 1951), chapter 15.

14. Shapiro, *Appalachia on Our Mind*, pp. 102–106.

15. These three films by D. W. Griffith are in the collection of the Library of Congress, Motion Picture, Broadcasting, and Recorded Sound Division.

16. Lears, *No Place of Grace*, chapter 2; Shapiro, *Appalachia on Our Mind*, chapter 9.

17. David E. Shi, *The Simple Life: Plain Living and High Thinking in American Culture* (New York: Oxford University Press, 1985), chapters 3 and 4.

18. Rebecca Harding Davis, "Qualla," *Lippincott's Magazine* v. 16 (16 November 1875): p. 577.

19. Maurice Thompson, "Hodson's Hide-Out," *The Century Magazine* v. 29, n. 5 (March 1885): p. 683.

20. William H. Turner, "The Demography of Black Appalachia: Past and Present," in *Blacks in Appalachia*, eds. William H. Turner and Edward J. Cabbell (Lexington: University of Kentucky Press, 1985), pp. 237–61.

21. See Edward J. Cabbell, "Black Invisibility and Racism in Appalachia: An Informal Survey," in *Blacks in Appalachia*, eds. Turner and Cabbell; Loyal Jones, "A Preliminary Look at the Welsh Component of Celtic Influence in Appalachia," in *The Appalachian Experience* ed. Barry M. Buxton (Boone, N. C.: Appalachian Consortium Press, 1983), pp. 26–33.

22. Josiah H. Combs, *Folk-Songs of the Southern United States* (Austin: University of Texas Press, 1967 edition), p. 11.

23. Turner, "The Demography of Black Appalachia," pp. 242–43.

24. James C. Klotter, "The Black South and White Appalachia," in *Blacks in Appalachia*, eds. Turner and Cabbell, p. 62.

25. Calvin S. Brown, Jr., "Dialectical Survivals in Tennessee," *Modern Language Notes* v. 4 (1889): pp. 409–12; William Taylor Thom, "Some Parallelisms between Shakespeare's English and the Negro-English of the United States," *Shakespeariana* v. 1, n. 2 (Dec. 1883): pp. 129–35.

26. William Goodell Frost, "Our Contemporary Ancestors in the Southern Mountains," *The Atlantic Monthly* v. 83, n. 497 (March 1899): p. 311.

27. Henderson Daingerfield Norman, "The English of the Mountaineer," *The Atlantic Monthly* v. 105, n. 2 (Feb. 1910): p. 276.

28. Dorothy Thomas, "That Traipsin' Woman," *Independent Woman* v. 13, n. 6 (1934): p. 169.

29. Catherine Marshall, *Christy* (New York: Avon Books, 1967), p. 51.

30. On American reactions to late nineteenth- and early twentieth-century immigration, see John Higham, *Strangers in the Land: Patterns of American Nativism 1860–1925* (New York: Atheneum, 1968); Barbara Miller Solomon, *Ancestors and Immigrants: A Changing New England Tradition* (New York: Wiley & Sons, 1956). On the growth of interest in things medieval and Anglo-Saxon, see William J. Courtenay, "The Virgin and the Dynamo: The Growth of Medieval Studies in North America 1870–1930," in *Medieval Studies in North America*, eds. Francis B. Gentry and Christopher Kleinhenz (Kalamazoo: Medieval Institute, 1982), pp. 5–22; Lears, *No Place of Grace*. Closely related to romantic Anglo-Saxonism was the contemporary interest in Teutonicism. The work of Francis Gummere, philologist and ballad scholar, provides a good example of turn-of-the-century Teutonicism (see *Founders of England* as an example). Many scholars before World War I pursued graduate studies in Germany, and the stamp of German romantic scholarship is very strong on this generation of American academics.

31. Graham Vulliamy, "Music and the Mass Culture Debate," in *Whose Music? A Sociology of Musical Languages*, eds. John Shepherd et al. (New Brunswick, N. J.: Transaction Books, 1977), pp. 179–97.

32. Julian Ralph, in his 1903 story "The Transformation of Em Durham," *Harper's Monthly Magazine* v. 107, n. 638: pp. 269–76, uses the ballad of "Lady Margaret" (Child 74) in the course of the story. Lucy Furman uses "Barbary Allen" (Child 84) in both "Hard-Hearted Barbary Allen," *The Century Magazine* v. 83, n. 5 (March 1912): pp. 739–44, and "Mothering on Perilous," *The Century Magazine* v. 81, n. 4 (Feb. 1911): pp. 561–65, as well as "Turkish Lady" (Child 53), and other ballads. Authors of nonfiction articles for popular magazines frequently mentioned ballad singing as part of their descriptions of mountain life. For example William Goodell Frost, *The Atlantic Monthly* v. 83, n. 497 (1899): p. 314.

33. Unsigned article, "Rescuing the Folk-Songs," *Literary Digest*, v. 54, n. 7 (Feb. 1917): p. 10.

34. Some examples: Charles Morrow Wilson, "Elizabethan America," *The Atlantic Monthly* (August 1929): p. 238, "We know a land of Elizabethan ways—a country of Spenserian speech, Shakespearian people, . . . We are speaking of the Southern highlands"; Unsigned, "Folk Singers," *Life* 20 (October 1947): p. 63, "In this backwater, living in cabins and on small farms, Americans like the ones shown on this and the following

pages still sing the songs and dance the dances that their forebears brought over from Elizabethan England." (The accompanying photograph is of an elderly white male banjo player.) John Kord Lagemann, "You'll be Comin' Round the Mountain," *Collier's* v. 121, n. 20 (15 May 1948): p. 85, "Tourists who go to the Great Smokies looking for hillbillies will find a proud people whose culture dates back to Shakespeare's day."

35. Pearsall, *Victorian Popular Music*, p. 218. On Appalachian students learning Morris and English sword dances see David E. Whisnant, *All That Is Native and Fine: The Politics of Culture in an American Region* (Chapel Hill: University of North Carolina Press, 1983), pp. 79–80, 200–202.

36. Thomas, "That Traipsin' Woman," p. 189.

37. Whisnant, *All That Is Native and Fine*, p. 47.

38. Combs, *Folk-Songs of the Southern United States*, p. 106.

39. Howard Brockway, "The Quest of the Lonesome Tunes," *The Art World* v. 2, n. 3 (June 1917): p. 230.

40. Lucy Furman, "Hard-Hearted Barbary Allen," *The Century Magazine* v. 83, n. 5 (March 1912): pp. 735–44.

41. Ellen Churchill Semple, "The Anglo-Saxons of the Kentucky Mountains," *The Bulletin of the American Geographical Society* v. 42, n. 8 (1910): p. 568 (reprint of 1901 article in the London *Geographical Journal*).

42. Catherine Marshall's *Christy* first went to print in October 1968. My copy, a paperback, is from the 14th printing of August 1969, and the book at that time had already sold 500,000 hardcover copies.

43. For examples, see John Fox, Jr., *The Little Shepherd of Kingdom Come* (New York: Charles Scribner's Sons, 1903); Louise Rand Bascom, "The Better Man," *Harper's Magazine* v. 132, n. 789 (1916): pp. 462–72; Elenor Risley, "Shady Cove," *Atlantic Monthly* v. 145 (February 1930): pp. 205–13.

44. Laura Spencer Portor, "In Search of Local Color," *Harper's Magazine* (September 1922): pp. 451–66.

45. Bruno Nettl, *The Study of Ethnomusicology: Twenty-nine Issues and Concepts* (Urbana: University of Illinois Press, 1983), chapter 24. See also Debora Kodish, *Good Friends and Bad Enemies: Robert Winslow Gordon and the Study of American Folksong* (Urbana: University of Illinois Press, 1986), especially p. 134. Benjamin's essay is in Walker Benjamin, *Illuminations* (New York: Schocken, 1968), 217–51.

46. Probably the most in-depth discussion of the history of Western concepts of authenticity (including Rousseau) is Lionel Trilling, *Sincerity and Authenticity* (Cambridge: Harvard University Press, 1972).

47. Robert Winslow Gordon, "Folk Songs of America: Banjo Tunes," *New York Times Magazine* (1 January 1928): pp. 10, 15.

48. Alice Payne Hackett and James Henry Burke, *80 Years of Best Sellers: 1895–1975* (New York: R. R. Bowker Company, 1977), p. 27.

49. Fox, *Little Shepherd of Kingdom Come*, p. 137.

50. Fox juxtaposes the 1890s collegiate banjo with the mountain banjo in his first novel, *A Mountain Europa* (New York: Harper and Brothers, 1894). The transfer of the banjo from southern black to southern white is in Louis Reed, "The Banjo String," *The Atlantic Monthly* v. 152, n. 2 (August 1933): pp. 175–85.

51. John Fox, Jr., "On Horseback to Kingdom Come," *Scribner's Magazine* v. 48 (August 1910): pp. 175–86.

52. Bascom, "The Better Man," pp. 462–72.

53. There were exceptions, for example the black string band The Mississippi Sheiks, who recorded on the Okeh label and were advertised in both the race and the old time (i.e., hillbilly) catalogues. See Tony Russell, *Blacks Whites and Blues* (New York: Stein and Day, 1970); Kip Lornell and J. Roderick Moore, "On Tour with a Black String Band in the 1930s: Howard Armstrong and Carl Martin Reminisce," *Goldenseal* v. 2, n. 4 (1976): pp. 7–13.

54. In addition to the general histories of Country music, see Clifford Kinney Rorrer, *Charlie Poole and the North Carolina Ramblers* and (same author) *Rambling Blues: The Life and Songs of Charlie Poole* (London: Old Time Music, 1982) for information on, and many photographs of, Poole and his changing band.

55. Many of my interviews with banjo players in Franklin County, Virginia, digressed into stories about Charlie Poole (Poole spent a lot of time in Franklin County). He is still a heroic figure for many, and his songs and banjo playing remain an important musical influence there.

56. On the cotton mill world that Charlie Poole came from see Jacquelyn Dowd Hall et al., *Like a Family: The Making of a Southern Cotton Mill World* (Chapel Hill: University of North Carolina Press, 1987), especially pp. 260–261.

57. Rorrer, *Charlie Poole and the North Carolina Ramblers*, p. 38. Poole recorded versions of Van Eps' "Infanta" (called "Sunset March") and "Dixie Medley" (called "Southern Medley").

58. Charles Wolfe, "Uncle Dave Macon," in *Stars of Country Music: Uncle Dave Macon to Johnny Rodriguez*, eds. Bill C. Malone and Judith McCulloh (Urbana: University of Illinois Press, 1975), pp. 40–63.

59. Charles Wolfe, "The Music of Grandpa Jones," *The Journal of Country Music* v. 8, n. 3 (1981): pp. 47–48, 65–82.

60. Bill Malone, on page 328 of *Country Music U.S.A.*, repeats this story, with the note that "neither [Charles] Wolfe or I know where it originated. It is just part of the large body of folklore that has circulated about Macon."

61. Robert Cantwell, *Bluegrass Breakdown* (Urbana: University of Illinois Press, 1984), chapter 11.

62. Pat J. Ahrens, *A History of the Musical Careers of Dewitt "Snuffy" Jenkins, Banjoist, and Homer "Pappy" Sherrill, Fiddler* (Columbia, S. C., 1970). This book contains the photographs to which I refer.

63. Plot summaries and miscellaneous information about "The Andy Griffith Show" are found in Richard Kelly, *The Andy Griffith Show* (Winston-Salem: John F. Blair, 1981).

64. Bill Davidson, "Thar's Gold in Them Thar Hillbilly Tunes," *Collier's* v. 128, n. 4 (28 July 1951): p. 45.

65. Malone, *Country Music U.S.A.*, p. 200.

66. For examples of writings on the folk music revival see: R. Serge Denisoff, *Great Day Coming: Folk Music and the American Left* (Urbana: University of Illinois Press, 1971); Jerome L. Rodnitzky, *Minstrels of the Dawn: The Folk-Protest Singer as a Cultural*

Hero; Robbie Lieberman, *My Song Is My Weapon: People's Songs, American Communism and the Politics of Culture, 1930–1950* (Urbana: University of Illinois Press, 1989); Robert Cantwell, "When We Were Good: The Folk Revival," in *Folk Roots, New Roots: Folklore in American Life*, eds. Jane S. Becker and Barbara Franco (Lexington, Mass: Museum of Our National Heritage, 1988); Oscar Brand, *The Ballad Mongers* (New York: Funk & Wagnalls, 1962); the folk revival magazine *Sing Out!*. For a different view of the folk revival, one that focuses on bluegrass and Old-Time music, see Neil V. Rosenberg, *Bluegrass: A History* (Urbana: University of Illinois Press, 1985).

67. Unsigned article, "Fiddling to Henry Ford," *Literary Digest*, v. 88, n. 1 (2 January 1926): pp. 33–34, 36, 38.

68. Michael Wallace, "Visiting the Past: History Museums in the United States," in *Presenting the Past: Essays on History and the Public*, eds. Susan Porter Benson, Stephen Brier, and Roy Rosenzweig (Philadelphia: Temple University Press, 1986): pp. 137–61.

69. Jean Thomas, the founder of the American Folk Song Festival, was an expert at media publicity. Perhaps this stems from her former occupation in Hollywood as a script girl. In addition to semifictional books that promoted folksong and her festival (for example the 1933 *The Traipsin' Woman*), she wrote articles for *Etude*, a music magazine, (Feb. 1944 and June 1948), had her festival written up in *Time* magazine (20 June 1938, 22 June 1942), and she promoted the career of singer and fiddler J. W. Day, whom she re-named "Jilson Setters of Lost Hope Hollow." The cover story for *Life* 20 October 1947 was Lunsford's Ashville, North Carolina folk festival. Eleanor Roosevelt's visit to the White Top Festival in 1933 drew national attention to that event. Folk music (including some banjo players) received additional media attention, as well as official sanction, when a special program was presented at the Roosevelt White House for the King and Queen of Britain. See *Folk Music in the Roosevelt White House*, a commemorative program published by the Smithsonian Institution.

70. David Whisnant gives a detailed analysis of the White Top Festival in *All That Is Native and Fine*, chapter 3.

71. On Bascom Lamar Lunsford and the Mountain Dance and Folk Festival, see Bill Finger, "Bascom Lamar Lunsford: The Limits of A Folk Hero," *Southern Exposure* v. 2, n. 1 (1974): pp. 27–37; David Whisnant, "Finding the Way between the Old and the New: The Mountain Dance and Folk Festival and Bascom Lamar Lunsford's Work as a Citizen," *Appalachian Journal* v. 7, n. 1–2 (1980): pp. 135–54; Loyal Jones, *Minstrel of the Appalachians: The Story of Bascom Lamar Lunsford* (Boone, N. C.: Appalachian Consortium Press, 1984). For a nonacademic, prerevival, account of Lunsford, see, Harold H. Martin, "Minstrel Man of the Appalachians," *Saturday Evening Post* v. 220, n. 47 (22 May 1948): pp. 30–31, 162, 164, and 167.

72. Jesse Lemisch, "I Dreamed I Saw MTV Last Night," *The Nation* (18 October 1986): pp. 374–76.

73. Warren I. Susman, *Culture as History: The Transformation of American Society in the Twentieth Century* (New York: Pantheon Books, 1973), chapter 9: "The Culture of the Thirties."

74. Thomas Hart Benton is a carefully chosen example. He, like many artists and intellectuals of the early twentieth century, was touched by radical politics, but eventually rejected Marxism and its guidelines for art. His work, too, is a glorification of the

Common Man. Benton was also an early performer and collector of American folk music. Charles Seeger spent musical evenings at the Benton household. See *Thomas Hart Benton: Chronicler of America's Folk Heritage,* especially the essays "Tom Benton's Folk Depictions" (by Archie Green) and "Thomas Hart Benton and American Folk Music" (by Alan C. Buecher).

75. Charles Seeger's reaction to the festival is mentioned in Whisnant, *All That Is Native and Fine,* p. 205. Pete Seeger's reaction to Lunsford's festival is in Jo Metcalf Schwartz, ed., *The Incomplete Folksinger* (New York: Simon and Schuster, 1972), p. 213.

76. Schwartz, *The Incomplete Folksinger,* p. 213.

77. D. K. Dunaway, "Charles Seeger and Carl Sands: The Composers' Collective Years," *Ethnomusicology* v. 24, n. 2 (spring/summer 1980): pp. 159–68; Richard A. Reuss, "Folk Music and Social Conscience: The Musical Odyssey of Charles Seeger," *Western Folklore* v. 38, n. 4 (1979): pp. 221–38.

78. David King Dunaway, *How Can I Keep From Singing: Pete Seeger* (New York: McGraw-Hill, 1981), p. 5.

79. Rosenberg, *Bluegrass: A History,* p. 13

80. Rosenberg in *Bluegrass: A History* discusses the analogy between baseball and bluegrass, pp. 20–21.

81. Thomas Adler's section, "Cultural/Contextual Aspects of the Competence," from his 1980 dissertation, "The Acquisition of a Traditional Competence: Folk-musical and Folk-cultural Learning Among Bluegrass Banjo Players," is the basis for much of the discussion on bluegrass players' concepts of the banjo. Analysis of Old-Time concepts of the banjo are largely based on my own ten years of playing Old-Time banjo and talking with Old-Time musicians, as well as some formal interviews.

82. Cantwell, *Bluegrass Breakdown,* p. 114.

83. Larry Sandberg, *Complete Banjo Repair* (New York: Oak Publications, 1979), p. 5.

84. Based on a conversation of May 1988 with Chuck Ogsbury, formerly of Ode and the creator of this advertisement. He stressed the work ethic (i.e., "meaningful" work) as an important aspect of the advertising message. He also said that though this advertising style communicated well with those already involved in the folk music revival, to increase sales and reach those outside of the philosophy of revivalists, he had to switch to an old style celebrity endorsement advertising campaign.

85. Frank Warner, "Frank Proffitt," *Sing Out!* v. 13, n. 4 (Oct.–Nov. 1963): p. 11.

Conclusion:
Sentimental Banjos

 GLEN ECHO PARK, an old amusement park just outside of Washington, D.C., hosted a bluegrass and Old-Time music festival on a bright Sunday in September. It was a fairly small, one-day affair; perhaps five hundred people gathered for a day of music and dance. The somewhat worn aspect of this turn-of-the-century entertainment establishment now implies an innocent past to today's visitors. The few rides that are left are silent, except for the merry-go-round with calliope, which has been started up for the day. But in the little amphitheater and in the "Spanish Ballroom" music is happening, a music that, like the ghostly amusement park, creates a sense of past. It is a protecting space set apart from the world.

An Old-Time music group performs on the stage with banjo, fiddle, guitar, and bass. Between musical numbers one member talks about the Southern mountain tradition to which they are trying to be faithful, but I notice that they have uncannily chosen many old minstrel theater songs to perform, pieces that have "gone into the tradition." I do not know if they realize their sources, and it is unlikely that the audience does. When the banjo player switches to an unfretted nylon-string banjo (more authentic to the old style gut-string sound of the Southern mountain tradition he tells us, but also, I realize, closer to the sound of an early nineteenth-century minstrel banjo), and the bass player plays the "bones" while the group performs *The Boatman's Dance* (originally written in dialect as *De Boatman's Dance*), I feel a bit unnerved. But the audience hears only the echoes from a Southern mountain past. Although the music is nostalgic, it is based on a selective memory. Perhaps that is the essence of nostalgia — selective memory.

All day long, especially as evening approaches, informal jam sessions appear in different corners of the park. The self-segregation of bluegrass and Old-Time musicians is clear; they cannot play together, especially the banjo players. The overpowering sound of the bluegrass banjoist drowns the subtleties of the Old-Time player, and the limitations of the Old-Time banjo style frustrate the bluegrass player. And so the musicians go to separate corners, the Old-Time musicians seeking sanctuary from the raucous tones of a neighboring bluegrass pick-up band. Singers gather around the bluegrass players to harmonize old country music standards. Clog dancers follow Old-Time musicians to their spaces, dragging their little plywood dancing platforms. The Old-Time player tunes his Fairbanks banjo, made for the Boston elite in the 1890s, to play the music of the poor-white South.

The only tenor banjoist in sight is a young man who plays Irish fiddle tunes. Irish tunes are popular with many Old-Time fiddlers, and often nearly impossible to play on the five-string banjo with clawhammer technique. But the tenor banjo works well, and it is now used in Ireland (so it must be authentic). Also, mandolin and fiddle players find it easy to learn, due to the similar tuning of strings. Dixieland revival banjoists do not come to this festival; their form of sentimental banjo music has its own separate protected performance spaces.

Old and young, male and female, Northerner and Southerner, working class and middle class, and bluegrass and Old-Time musicians all share the space and day. But John Jackson is the only black person. He is one of the performers.

John Jackson plays the banjo. An African-American banjo player is a rarity in the 1980s. The many banjo players present relish the occasion; perhaps they feel that they have tapped into some ancient root. Most banjo players in the 1980s know that the banjo originally came from Africa, but it seems a strangely distant and exotic past; however, John Jackson, although he prefers to play the guitar, now creates that connection to the banjo past for his audience. He is foremost recognized as a superb country blues guitar player; his banjo technique pales in comparison. Jackson can both up- and down-pick on the banjo, and sometimes he combines the two movements. His banjo learning was informal and his technique never formalized. Jackson grew up in rural Virginia and learned much of his music from commercial recordings. Although he is presented these days as a blues singer/guitarist, white country music has always been in his repertory. John Jackson is essentially an "old country guy" who wears denim overalls, grew up listening to the *Grand Ol' Opry,* and spends his time with other "old country guys," be they black or white.[1] Nowadays, as a winner of a National Endowment for the Arts folk artist award, he plays his country blues for a more upscale audience.

The performance of John Jackson reminds us of the cultural complexity of

American music; the role of commercial recording and the radio, the overlapping traditions of black and white rural Southerners, and the role of government agencies in preserving and institutionalizing certain traditions are all facets of the story behind John Jackson's career. It is important to his audience that he is an African-American—both his blues and his banjo playing seem to need this to be authentic. Yet, Jackson would not have enjoyed his late-in-life music career if not for the interest of the young white people of the folk music revival.

It is commonplace to say that American music developed its unique qualities through the interaction of different groups, especially through the combination of African and European elements. But all parties were not equal in power, and the interaction was and is politically and socially loaded. This is not merely a musicological polemic; the political and social implications of black-white musical interaction in the United States invest meaning into the very heart of the musical moment. We cannot understand the history of the banjo as an idea in American popular culture without situating it in its initial racial-political framework (acknowledging racial thinking as a political ideology). When Dan Emmett blacked his face in the 1840s to play the banjo (or when Elvis Presley sang rhythm and blues in the 1950s) he presented musical proof of black-white cultural interaction. American ideas of race gave meaning to Emmett's banjo playing, and the idea of the blackface banjo player eventually helped shape American ideas of race: the banjo became an active sign in American race ideology. In the nineteenth century, it was the banjo in the hands of a make-believe black man that had created meaning for the audience; at the festival in Glen Echo Park it was the banjo in the hands of a real black man that created a meaning, beyond the abstract sound, for the audience.

In this historical unpacking of various ideas of the banjo, I do not suggest that there was ever a resolution into consensus. Differing ideas did not passively give way one to the other to create a tidy chronology. They remained in conflict, within changing fields of semantic power. But one idea cut across many particularities, and the banjo has never been able to long escape its defining power: the sentimental idea, or perhaps it is better to say the ideas that belong to the sentimental side of American culture—pastoralism, primitivism or antimodernism, emotionalism, and nostalgia. Many of these concepts that originated with the African-American banjo clung like residue to new incarnations of the American banjo. The idea of the half-barbaric banjo was reformulated—but never fully rejected—when the Northern white "society lady," the youthful jazz man, or the Southern mountaineer played the banjo.

The banjo, in the United States in the late twentieth century, plays marginal musics, and it is protected within these boundaries. All of these types of music are part of twentieth-century American sentimental culture. Even the small group of musicians who continue to play the repertory inherited from the ragtime banjoists and the "classical" repertory from the most elevated of banjoists are playing a music that now refers to the past; and that banjo past is all the more precious for them because it is so obscure.

Will there be another modernizing idea of the banjo? The first such agenda came from early nineteenth-century minstrel performers like Joel Walker Sweeney, who simply added the fingerprint of the white man to the banjo and brought it into the popular theater. The truly modernizing agendas of the late nineteenth and early twentieth centuries, accompanied with an attempted escape from sentimental values, built upon a machine aesthetic. The first movement drew from the official values of Victorian America, and the second from the consumer and leisure values of the twentieth century, but both eras developed the banjo as a "musical mechanism." Metal machinery, in a sense, made the modern world, and banjo makers easily transformed the banjo into a machine-like object. But in the late twentieth century, postindustrial eyes view metal machines with gears and exposed nuts and bolts as rather old-fashioned. Can the banjo modernize in the age of computers, plastics, and superconductors? I do not know.[2]

Perhaps the banjo is not in need of a new modernizing agenda; it has always prospered within the sentimental ethos. Yet this role may be too constraining. The dichotomy of what I have been calling the "official" and "sentimental" values was a social construct that ordered and controlled the intellectual world. Within this metaphorical social structuring, the "official" and the "sentimental" values of American culture should not be thought of as overtly contradictory, but as ambivalently complementary. The "official" and the "sentimental" are like traditional American ideas of the "masculine" and the "feminine" or "the head" and "the heart." The one side questions the other—my head tells me yes, but my heart says no—and the first side usually wins. The official culture led Americans to accept all technological innovation as a rational reformer. The sentimental idiom—usually relegated to artistic expressions that lacked the threat of direct valual or political challenge—longed for the simplicity of an often mythical pastoral life and art; it was a backward glance incapable of setting a practical course for the future. The South as a region, African-Americans as a people, and "mountain whites" as a type have all been used by the dominant culture as representatives of the sentimental idiom. The banjo, because of its association with the South, African-Americans, and mountain whites, has never fully escaped that idiom. But the sentimental idiom, far from being debilitating in a strictly musical sense, has protected and sustained the banjo through the massive social and cultural changes of nineteenth- and twentieth-century America.

Notes

1. This description is based on informal conversations with Mike Seeger and Jeff Titon as well as John Jackson's discussion of his musical life while on stage at the Smithsonian Folklife Festival in July 1988.

2. Eddie Peabody, plectrum banjoist, developed and played an electric version of the four-string banjo called the "banjoline." It never became popular.

Bibliography

Archives and Special Collections:

Archive of Folk Culture, Library of Congress.
Ayer Collection, Archives Center, National Museum of American History, Smithsonian Institution.
Christine Dunlap Farnham Archives, John Hay Library, Brown University.
College Archives, Smith College.
Film Archives, Library of Congress.
Harris Collection, John Hay Library, Brown University.
Music Collection, New York Public Library at Lincoln Center.
Sam DeVincent Collection of American Music, Archives Center, National Museum of American History, Smithsonian Institution.
University Archives, John Hay Library, Brown University.
University Archives, Special Collections, Georgetown University.
Warshaw Collection, Archives Center, National Museum of American History, Smithsonian Institution.

Books, Articles, and Journals: *

Adler, Thomas
    1972   "The Physical Development of the Banjo." *New York Folklore Quarterly* v. 28, n. 3: pp. 187–208.
    1980   "The Acquisition of a Traditional Competence: Folk-musical and Folk-

---

*There are hundreds of banjo method books; only those cited in the text or in footnotes are included in the bibliography.

cultural Learning among Bluegrass Banjo Players." PhD dissertation, Indiana University.

Ahrens, Pat J.
    1970   *A History of the Musical Careers of Dewitt "Snuffy" Jenkins, Banjoist, and Homer "Pappy" Sherrill, Fiddler.* Columbia, S.C.: no publisher.

Austin, William W.
    1975   *"Susanna," "Jeanie," and "The Old Folks at Home": The Songs of Stephen C. Foster from His Time to Ours.* New York: MacMillan Publishing Co.; 2d ed. 1987 by University of Illinois Press.

Badger, R. Reid
    1989   "James Reese Europe and the Prehistory of Jazz." *American Music* v. 7, n. 1: pp. 48–67.

Baily, Jay
    1972   "Historical Origin and Stylistic Developments of the Five-String Banjo." *Journal of American Folklore* v. 85, n. 335: pp. 58–65.

Baker, Russell
    1982   *Growing Up.* New York: Congdon & Weed, Inc.

Bargainnier, Earl F.
    1977   "Tin Pan Alley and Dixie: The South in Popular Song." *Mississippi Quarterly* v. 30, n. 4: pp. 527–64.

Baroody, Elizabeth
    1976   "Banjo: The Sound of America." *Early American Life* v. 7, n. 2: pp. 56–57, 68.
    1981   "From Banjere to Banjo." *Country* (June): pp. 16–17.

Bascom, Louise Rand
    1909   "Ballads and Songs of Western North Carolina." *Journal of American Folklore* v. 22, n. 34: pp. 238–50.
    1916   "The Better Man." *Harper's Magazine* v. 132, n. 789: pp. 462–72.

Bickford, Zarh Myron
    1919   "The Banjo in the Orchestra." *Metronome* v. 35, n. 11: pp. 54, 56, 68.

Becker, Jane S., and Barbara Franco, eds.
    1988   *Folk Roots, New Roots: Folklore in American Life.* Lexington, Mass.: Museum of Our National Heritage.

Benjamin, Walter
    1968   *Illuminations.* New York: Schocken Books.

Berlin, Edward A.
    1980   *Ragtime: A Musical and Cultural History.* Berkeley: University of California Press.

Bikle, Lucy L. C.
    1928   *George W. Cable: His Life and Letters.* New York: Scribner's, reprinted 1967.

Bluestein, Gene
    1964   "America's Folk Instrument: Notes on the Five-String Banjo." *Western Folklore* v. 23, n. 4: pp. 241–48.

Brand, Oscar
    1962   *The Ballad Mongers.* New York: Funk & Wagnalls.

Brander, Matthews
    1915   "The Rise and Fall of Negro-Minstrelsy." *Scribner's Magazine* v. 57: pp.
           754–59.
Briggs, Thomas F.
    1855   *Briggs' Banjo Instructor.* Boston: Oliver Ditson and Co. In the Harris Collec-
           tion of Brown University.
Brockway, Howard
    1917   "The Quest of the Lonesome Tunes." *The Art World* v. 2, n. 3: p. 230.
Brown, Calvin S., Jr.
    1889   "Dialectical Survivals in Tennessee." *Modern Language Notes* v. 4: pp.
           409–12.
Brown, Janet
    1984   "The 'Coon-Singer' and the 'Coon Song': A Case Study of the Performer-
           Character Relationship." *Journal of American Culture* v. 7, n. 1–2: pp. 1–8.
Buckley, James
    1868   *Buckley's Guide for the Banjo.* Boston: Oliver Ditson and Co. In the Harris
           Collection of Brown University.
Buecher, Alan C.
    1984   "Thomas Hart Benton and American Folk Music." In *Thomas Hart Benton:
           Chronicler of America's Folk Heritage* (exhibition book, Linda Weintraub,
           Exhibition Curator: Bard College, Annandale-on-Hudson, N.Y.), pp. 69–
           77.
Cabbell, Edward J.
    1980   "Black Invisibility and Racism in Appalachia: An Informal Survey." *Appa-
           lachian Journal* v. 8, n. 1: pp. 48–54.
The Cadenza. "A music magazine devoted to the interests of banjo, mandolin and guitar
           players." Kansas City, Mo., 1894–1924.
Campbell, Edward D. C.
    1981   *The Celluloid South: Hollywood and the Southern Myth.* Knoxville: Univer-
           sity of Tennessee Press.
Campbell, John C.
    1921   *The Southern Highlander and His Homeland.* New York: Russell Sage
           Foundation.
Canby, Henry Seidel
    1947   *American Memoir.* Boston: Houghton Mifflin Co.
Cantwell, Robert
    1984   *Bluegrass Breakdown: The Making of the Old Southern Sound.* Urbana:
           University of Illinois Press.
Castle, Vernon
    1913   "Tango According to Castle." *Metropolitan* v. 38, n. 2: pp. 38–39.
Castle, Vernon, and Irene Castle
    1914   *Modern Dancing.* New York: Harper and Brothers.
Charters, Samuel B., and Leonard Kunstadt
    1962   *Jazz: A History of the New York Scene.* Garden City, N.Y.: Doubleday;
           reprinted 1981 by DaCapo Press.

Chase, Gilbert
    1987 *America's Music: From the Pilgrims to the Present*, rev. 3rd ed. Urbana: University of Illinois Press.
Clayton, Robert J.
    1978 *A Bibliography of the History and Playing Styles of the Five-String Banjo*. Washington: Library of Congress, Archive of Folksong.
Coben, Stanley
    1976 "The Assault on Victorianism in the Twentieth Century." In Daniel Walker Howe, ed., *Victorian America*. Philadelphia: University of Pennsylvania Press, pp. 160–81.
Cohen, Stu
    1983 "Banjo Makers and Manufacturers." *Mugwumps* v. 7, n. 2: pp. 10–13.
Combs, Josiah H.
    1916 "Old, Early and Elizabethan English in the Southern Mountains." *Dialect Notes* v. 4, n. 4: pp. 238–97.
    1925 *Folk-Songs Du Midi des Etats-Unis*, reprinted in 1967 as *Folk-Songs of the Southern United States*. Austin: University of Texas Press.
Condon, Eddie
    1947 *We Called It Music: A Generation of Jazz*. New York: Henry Holt and Co.
Converse, Frank B.
    1865 *New and Complete Method for the Banjo, with or without Master*. New York: St. Gordon & Son. In the Special Collections of the New York Public Library.
Conway, Eugenia Cecelia
    1980 "The Afro-American Traditions of the Folk Banjo." PhD dissertation, University of North Carolina.
Conway, Cecelia, and Tommy Thompson
    1974 "Talking Banjo." *Southern Exposure* v. 2, n. 1: pp. 63–66.
Coolen, Michael Theodore
    1984 "Senegambian Archetypes for the American Folk Banjo." *Western Folklore* v. 43, n. 2: pp. 117–32.
Courtenay, William J.
    1982 "The Virgin and the Dynamo: The Growth of Medieval Studies in North America 1870–1930." In Francis B. Gentry and Christopher Kleinhenz, eds., *Medieval Studies in North America*. Kalamazoo: Medieval Institute, pp. 5–22.
The Crescendo. The monthly publication of the American Guild of Mandolin, Guitar, and Banjo Players. Boston, 1908–1933.
Crichton, Kyle
    1938 "Thar's Gold in Them Hillbillies." *Collier's* v. 101, n. 18: p. 24.
Cunningham, Rodger
    1987 *Apples on the Flood: The Southern Mountain Experience*. Knoxville: University of Tennessee Press.
Daniel, Pete
    1986 *Standing at the Crossroads: Southern Life in the Twentieth Century*. New York: Hill and Wang.

Davidson, Bill
    1951   "Thar's Gold in Them Thar Hillbilly Tunes." *Collier's* v. 128, n. 4: pp. 34–35, 42–45.

Davis, J. Frank
    1925   "Tom Shows." *Scribner's* v. 77, n. 4: pp. 350–60.

Davis, Rebecca Harding
    1875   "Qualla." *Lippincott's Magazine* v. 16 (16 November): pp. 576–86.

Denisoff, R. Serge
    1971   *Great Day Coming: Folk Music and the American Left.* Urbana: University of Illinois Press.

Denning, Michael
    1987   *Mechanic Accents: Dime Novels and Working-Class Culture in America.* London: Verso.

Dennison, Sam
    1982   *Scandalize My Name: Black Imagery in American Popular Music.* New York: Garland Publishing, Inc.

DeSmaele, Gerard
    1981   "Banjo à cinq cordes: Histoire et informations pratiques à propos de la documentation." *Brussels Museum of Musical Instruments Bulletin* v. 9, n. 1/2.

Dobson, George C.
    1871   *Dobson Brothers' Modern Method for the Banjo.* Boston: White, Smith and Perry.
    1877   *Dobson's New System for the Banjo.* Boston: Oliver Ditson and Co.
    1890   *World's Banjo Guide.* Boston: White-Smith Music Publishing Co.

Douglas, Ann
    1977   *The Feminization of American Culture.* New York: Alfred A. Knopf.

Du Bois, W. E. Burghardt
    1961   *The Souls of Black Folk.* Greenwich, Conn.: Fawcett Publications, Inc. (Originally published in 1903.)

Dunaway, David King
    1980   "Charles Seeger and Carl Sands: The Composers' Collective Years." *Ethnomusicology* v. 24, n. 2: pp. 159–68.
    1981   *How Can I Keep From Singing: Pete Seeger.* New York: McGraw-Hill.

Edwards, Richard Henry
    1915   *Popular Amusements.* New York: Association Press; reprinted 1976 by Arno Press.

Epstein, Dena J.
    1975   "The Folk Banjo: A Documentary History." *Ethnomusicology* v. 19, n. 3: pp. 347–71.
    1977   *Sinful Tunes and Spirituals: Black Folk Music to the Civil War.* Urbana: University of Illinois Press.

Erb, J. Lawrence
    1917   "Music in the University." *Musical Quarterly* v. 3, n. 1: pp. 28–33.

Erenberg, Lewis A.
    1981   *Steppin' Out: New York Nightlife and the Transformation of American Culture, 1890–1930.* Chicago: University of Chicago Press.

Fass, Paula S.
    1977   *The Damned and the Beautiful: American Youth in the 1920s.* Oxford: Oxford University Press.
Ferber, Edna
    1935   *Show Boat.* New York: Modern Library.
Finger, Bill
    1974   "Bascom Lamar Lunsford: The Limits of a Folk Hero." *Southern Exposure* v. 2, n. 1: pp. 27–37.
Fischer, David Hackett
    1989   *Albion's Seed: Four British Folkways in America.* New York: Oxford University Press.
Folk Music in the Roosevelt White House
    1982   A Commemorative Program Presented by the Office of Folklife Programs at the National Museum of American History, January 31, 1982. (Original program 8 June 1939.)
Fox, John, Jr.
    1899   *A Mountain Europa.* New York: Harper and Brothers.
    1903   *The Little Shepherd of Kingdom Come.* New York: Charles Scribner's Sons.
    1910   "On Horseback to Kingdom Come." *Scribner's Magazine* v. 48 (August): pp. 175–86.
Fredrickson, George M.
    1971   *The Black Image in the White Mind.* New York: Harper and Row.
Frost, William Goodell
    1899   "Our Contemporary Ancestors in the Southern Mountains." *Atlantic Monthly* v. 83, n. 497: pp. 311–19.
Furman, Lucy
    1910–11   "Mothering on Perilous." *Century Magazine* v. 81: 296–302, 445–49, 561–65, 767–74, 853–59; v. 82: 57–64, 297–304, 391–96.
    1912   "Hard-Hearted Barbary Allen." *Century Magazine* v. 83, n. 5: pp. 739–44.
Gardner, Ella
    1929   *Public Dance Halls.* Washington, D.C.: U.S. Department of Labor.
Gatcomb's Musical Gazette, for banjo, mandolin, and guitar. Boston, 1887–99.
Genovese, Eugene D.
    1968   *In Red and Black.* Knoxville: University of Tennessee Press, reissued in 1984.
    1972   *Roll, Jordan, Roll: The World the Slaves Made.* New York: Vintage Books.
Gilbert, Douglas
    1940   *American Vaudeville.* New York: Whittlesey House.
Gillespie, Angus K.
    1976   "Pennsylvania Folk Festivals in the 1930s." *Pennsylvania Folklife* v. 21, n. 1: pp. 2–11.
Gordon, Robert Winslow
    1928   "Folk Songs of America: Banjo Tunes." *New York Times Magazine* (1 January): pp. 10, 15.

Gorn, Elliott J.
    1986   *The Manly Art: Bare-Knuckle Prize Fighting in America*. Ithaca: Cornell
           University Press.
Gossett, Thomas
    1985   *Uncle Tom's Cabin and American Culture*. Dallas: Southern Methodist
           University Press.
Gourlay, Ken A.
    1976   "Letter to the Editor." *Ethnomusicology* v. 20, n. 2: pp. 327–32.
Green, Archie
    1984   "Signifying Banjos." *JEMF Quarterly* v. 20, n. 73: pp. 19–32.
    1984   "Tom Benton's Folk Depictions." In *Thomas Hart Benton: Chronicler of
           America's Folk Heritage* (exhibition book, Linda Weintraub, Exhibition
           Curator: Bard College, Annandale-on-Hudson, N.Y.), pp. 32–67.
Hackett, Alice Payne, and James Henry Burke
    1977   *80 Years of Best Sellers: 1895–1975*. New York: R. R. Bowker Co.
Hall, Jacquelyn Dowd, et al.
    1987   *Like a Family: The Making of a Southern Cotton Mill World*. Chapel Hill:
           University of North Carolina Press.
Halttunen, Karen
    1982   *Confidence Men and Painted Women: A Study of Middle-Class Culture in
           America, 1830–1870*. New Haven: Yale University Press.
Hambly, Scott
    1977   "Mandolins in the United States since 1880: An Industrial and Sociocul-
           tural History of Form." PhD dissertation, University of Pennsylvania.
Harris, Joel Chandler
    1883   "Plantation Music." *The Critic* v. 3, n. 95: pp. 505–6.
Hasse, John Edward, ed.
    1985   *Ragtime: Its History, Composers, and Music*. New York: Schirmer Books.
Hawthorne, Julian
    1890   "Millicent and Rosalind." *Lippincott's* v. 44, n. 23 (January): pp. 5–45.
Higham, John
    1968   *Strangers in the Land: Patterns of American Nativism 1860–1925*. New York:
           Atheneum.
Hopkins, J. S.
    1914   *The Tango and Other Up-to-Date Dances*. Chicago: Scalfield Publishing Co.
Hopper, James
    1910   "Banjo Nell." *Collier's* v. 49, n. 23: pp. 15–17, 26–27.
Horowitz, Helen Lefkowitz
    1984   *Alma Mater: Design and Experience in the Women's Colleges from Their
           Nineteenth-Century Beginnings to the 1930s*. New York: Alfred A. Knopf.
Howard, Norman
    1957   "A History of the Banjo." Unpublished manuscript in the Special Collec-
           tions of the New York Public Library, Lincoln Center.
    1959   "The Banjo and Its Players; Collected from Various Sources." Unpublished
           manuscript in the Special Collections of the New York Public Library,
           Lincoln Center.

Howe, Daniel Walker, ed.
    1976 *Victorian America.* Philadelphia: University of Pennsylvania Press.
Howe, Elias (Gumbo Chaff)
    1850 *The Complete Preceptor for the Banjo.* Boston: Oliver Ditson and Co.
Humphrey, Grace
    1918 "Banjos for the Boys!" *Everybody's Magazine* v. 39 (October): pp. 59, 90.
Igoe, Lynn Moody, with James Igoe
    1981 *250 Years of Afro-American Art: An Annotated Bibliography.* New York: R.
           R. Bowker Co.
Irwin, John Rice
    1979 *Musical Instruments of the Southern Appalachian Mountains.* Norris, Tenn.:
           Museum of Appalachia Press.
Jackson, Bruce, ed.
    1967 *The Negro and His Folklore in Nineteenth-Century Periodicals.* Austin: Univer-
           sity of Texas Press.
Jervis, Simon
    1974 *High Victorian Design.* Ottawa: National Gallery of Canada.
Johnson, Claudia D.
    1976 "That Guilty Third Tier: Prostitution in Nineteenth-Century American
           Theaters." In Daniel Walker Howe, ed., *Victorian America.* Philadelphia:
           University of Pennsylvania Press, pp. 111–20.
Johnson, Robert
    1969 "Stewart Banjos." *Relics* v. 5, n. 4: pp. 10–12, 24.
Jones, Loyal
    1973 "The Minstrel of the Appalachians: Bascom Lamar Lunsford at 91." *J.E.M.F.
           Quarterly* v. 9, n. 1: pp. 2–8.
    1983 "A Preliminary Look at the Welsh Component of Celtic Influence in
           Appalachia." In Barry M. Buxton, ed., *The Appalachian Experience.* Boone,
           N.C.: Appalachian Consortium Press, pp. 26–33.
    1984 *Minstrel of the Appalachians: The Story of Bascom Lamar Lunsford.* Boone,
           N.C.: Appalachian Consortium Press.
Kasson, John F.
    1978 *Amusing the Million: Coney Island at the Turn of the Century.* New York: Hill
           and Wang.
Kaufman, Elias
    1973 "S. S. Stewart Banjos." *Mugwumps* v. 3, n. 3–6 (a series of articles).
Kaufman, Elias, and Madeleine Kaufman, eds.
           The 5-Stringer: Newsletter of the American Banjo Fraternity, 1980–90.
Kelly, Richard
    1981 *The Andy Griffith Show.* Winston-Salem, N.C.: John F. Blair.
Kimball, Robert, and William Bolcom
    1973 *Reminiscing with Sissle and Blake.* New York: Viking Press.
Kirby, Jack Temple
    1978 *Media-Made Dixie: The South in the American Imagination.* Baton Rouge:
           Louisiana State University Press.

Klotter, James C.
 1985 "The Black South and White Appalachia." In William H. Turner and Edward J. Cabbell, eds., *Blacks in Appalachia*. Lexington: University of Kentucky Press.
Kodish, Debora
 1986 *Good Friends and Bad Enemies: Robert Winslow Gordon and the Study of American Folksong*. Urbana: University of Illinois Press.
Kouwenhoven, John A.
 1948 *Made in America: The Arts in Modern Civilization*. New York: Doubleday & Co., Inc.
Krehbiel, Henry Edwards
 1914 *Afro-American Folksongs: A Study in Racial and National Music*. New York: G. Schirmer.
Krick, George C.
 1938 "The Banjo." *Etude* v. 56, n. 3: pp. 192, 198.
 1941 "Teacher or Salesman?" *Etude* v. 58, n. 4: p. 279.
 1941 "The Mandolin and Banjo." *Etude* v. 58, n. 6: pp. 421–22.
 1941 "The Future of the Fretted Instruments." *Etude* v. 58, n. 11: pp. 791, 793.
 1942 "Will the Banjo Stage a Comeback?" *Etude* v. 60, n. 7: pp. 493–95.
LaDelle, Frederic
 1913 *How to Enter Vaudeville*. Jackson, Mich.: Frederick LaDelle Co.
Ladner, Robert, Jr.
 1968 "Behold, the Noble Banjo!" *Music Journal* v. 26, n. 5: pp. 23, 49.
Lagemann, John Kord
 1948 "You'll Be Comin' Round the Mountain." *Collier's* v. 121, n. 20: pp. 85–90.
Lears, Jackson
 1981 *No Place of Grace: Antimodernism and the Transformation of American Culture, 1880–1920* New York: Pantheon Books.
Lemisch, Jesse
 1986 "I Dreamed I Saw MTV Last Night." *The Nation* (18 October): pp. 374–76.
Leonard, Neil
 1962 *Jazz and the White Americans: The Acceptance of a New Art Form*. Chicago: University of Chicago Press.
Levine, Lawrence W.
 1977 *Black Culture and Black Consciousness*. Oxford: Oxford University Press.
 1984 "William Shakespeare and the American People: A Study in Cultural Transformation." *American Historical Review* v. 89, n. 1: pp. 34–66.
 1988 *Highbrow/Lowbrow: The Emergence of Cultural Hierarchy in America*. Cambridge: Harvard University Press.
Libin, Laurence
 1985 *American Musical Instruments in the Metropolitan Museum of Art*. New York: Metropolitan Museum of Art.
Lieberman, Robbie
 1989 *My Song Is My Weapon: People's Songs, American Communism and the Politics of Culture, 1930–1950*. Urbana: University of Illinois Press.

Linn, Karen
     1987   "An Interview with Mrs. Bertie Dickens: Old-Time Banjo Player." *North Carolina Folklore Journal* v. 34, n. 1: pp. 61–65.
Logan, Olive
     1879   "The Ancestry of Brudder Bones." *Harper's* v. 63, n. 347: pp. 687–98.
Lornell, Kip
     1974   "Pre-Blues Banjo and Fiddle." *Living Blues* v. 18: pp. 25–27.
Lornell, Kip, and J. Roderick Moore
     1976   "Clarence Tross: Hardy County Banjoist." *Goldenseal* v. 3, n. 3: pp. 7–13.
     1976   "On Tour with a Black String Band in the 1930s: Howard Armstrong and Carl Martin Reminisce." *Goldenseal* v. 2, n. 4: pp. 9–12, 46–52.
Lund, Ralph Eugene
     1928   "Trouping with Uncle Tom." *Century Magazine* v. 115, n. 3: pp. 329–37.
Malone, Bill C., and Judith McCulloh, eds.
     1975   *Stars of Country Music: Uncle Dave Macon to Johnny Rodriguez.* Urbana: University of Illinois Press.
     1979   *Southern Music, American Music.* Lexington: University of Kentucky Press.
     1985   *Country Music U.S.A.,* rev. ed. Austin: University of Texas Press.
Marshall, Catherine
     1967   *Christy.* New York: Avon Books.
Martin, Harold H.
     1948   "Minstrel Man of the Appalachians." *Saturday Evening Post* v. 220, n. 47: pp. 30–31, 162, 164, 167.
May, Larry
     1980   *Screening Out the Past: The Birth of Mass Culture and the Motion Picture Industry.* Chicago: University of Chicago Press.
McBride, Ray, and Randy Stearn
     1973   "Banjos and Dulcimers." In Eliot Wigginton, ed., *Foxfire 3.* Garden City, N.Y.: Anchor Books.
McCabe, Elizabeth Maddox
     1965   "The Banjo: Made in America." *Music Journal* v. 23, n. 5: pp. 30–31.
McCardell, Roy L.
     1905   "Opper, Outcault and Company." *Everybody's Magazine* v. 12, n. 6: pp. 763–72.
McGill, Josephine
     1917   "Following Music in a Mountain Land." *Musical Quarterly* v. 3, n. 3: pp. 364–84.
McGohan, Henry Morton
     1942   "Original American Folk Music." *Etude* v. 60, n. 8: p. 527.
McKay, Claude
     1929   *Banjo.* New York: Harper and Brothers; reprinted 1957 by Harcourt Brace Jovanovich, Inc.
McNeil, W. K., ed.
     1989   *Appalachian Images in Folk and Popular Culture.* Ann Arbor, Mich.: UMI Research Press.

Mercier, John Denis
    1984 "The Evolution of the Black Image in White Consciousness, 1876–1954: A Popular Culture Perspective." PhD dissertation, University of Pennsylvania.
Miles, Emma Bell
    1904 "Some Real American Music." *Harper's Monthly Magazine* v. 109, n. 649: pp. 118–23.
    1905 *The Spirit of the Mountains,* a facsimile edition by the University of Tennessee Press, printed in 1975.
    1930 *Strains from a Dulcimore.* Atlanta: The Bozart Press.
Mouvet, Maurice [Monsieur Maurice]
    1914 *The Tango and Other Dances* [title page missing from Library of Congress copy].
Nathan, Hans
    1962 *Dan Emmett and the Rise of Early Negro Minstrelsy.* Norman: University of Oklahoma Press.
National Bureau for the Advancement of Music
    1929 *Fretted Instrument Orchestras.* New York: National Bureau for the Advancement of Music. (A Guide to Procedure on Organizing and Maintaining Ensembles of Banjos, Mandolins, Guitars and Other Plectrum Instruments.)
Nettl, Bruno
    1983 *The Study of Ethnomusicology: Twenty-nine Issues and Concepts.* Urbana: University of Illinois Press.
Newcomb, Horace
    1980 "Appalachia on Television: Region as Symbol in American Popular Culture." *Appalachian Journal* v. 7, n. 1–2: pp. 155–64.
Norman, Henderson Daingerfield
    1910 "The English of the Mountaineer." *Atlantic Monthly* v. 105, n. 2: pp. 276–78.
Odell, George C. D.
    1927–49 *Annals of the New York Stage.* 15 vols. New York: Columbia University Press; reprinted 1970 by AMS Press.
Odell, Scott
    1971 "Folk Instruments." *Arts in Virginia* v. 12, n. 1: pp. 31–37.
    1980 "Banjo." *New Groves Dictionary of Music and Musicians* v. 2. London: Macmillan Publishers Ltd.
Paskman, Daily
    1928 *Gentlemen, Be Seated! A Parade of the Old Time Minstrels.* New York: Clarkson N. Potter, Inc.
Patterson, Daniel W., and Charles G. Zug eds.
    1990 *Arts in Earnest: North Carolina Folklife.* Durham, N.C.: Duke University Press.
Pearsall, Ronald
    1973 *Victorian Popular Music.* Newton Abbot, U.K.: David & Charle.
Peiss, Kathy
    1986 *Cheap Amusements: Working Women and Leisure in Turn-of-the-Century New York.* Philadelphia: Temple University Press.

Portor, Laura Spencer
    1922   "In Search of Local Color." *Harper's Magazine* (September): pp. 451–
           66.
Post, Charles N.
    1903   "The Origin and Growth of the Guitar, Mandolin and Banjo Industry in
           America." *Music Trades* v. 26, n. 24: p. 77.
Ralph, Julian
    1903   "The Transformation of Em Durham." *Harper's Monthly Magazine* v. 107,
           n. 638: pp. 269–76.
Rasof, Henry
    1982   *The Folk, Country, and Bluegrass Musician's Catalogue.* New York: St. Martin's
           Press.
Reed, Louis
    1933   "The Banjo String." *Atlantic Monthly* v. 152, n. 2: pp. 175–85.
Reuss, Richard A.
    1979   "Folk Music and Social Conscience: The Musical Odyssey of Charles Seeger."
           Western Folklore v. 38, n. 4: pp. 221–38.
Rice, Phil.
    1858   *Correct Method for the Banjo: With or without a Master.* Boston: Oliver
           Ditson and Co. In the Special Collections of the New York Public
           Library, Lincoln Center.
Riis, Thomas L.
    1986   "The Music and Musicians in Nineteenth-Century Productions of *Uncle
           Tom's Cabin.*" *American Music* v. 4, n. 3: pp. 268–86.
Risley, Eleanor
    1930   "Shady Cove." *Atlantic Monthly* v. 145 (February): pp. 205–13.
Rorabaugh, W. J.
    1979   *The Alcoholic Republic.* New York: Oxford University Press.
Rorrer, Clifford Kinney
    1968   *Charlie Poole and the North Carolina Ramblers.* Eden, N.C.: no publisher
           (Tar Heel Printing, Inc.).
    1982   *Rambling Blues: The Life and Songs of Charlie Poole.* London: Old Time
           Music.
Rosenberg, Neil V.
    1985   *Bluegrass: A History.* Urbana: University of Illinois Press.
Rotundo, Anthony
    1982   "Manhood in America: The Northern Middle Class, 1770–1920." PhD
           dissertation, Brandeis University.
Rowlett, Darrell
    1969   "The Banjo: Born in Dixie." *Music Journal* v. 27, n. 4: p. 76.
Russell, Tony
    1970   *Blacks Whites and Blues.* New York: Stein and Day.
Sandberg, Larry
    1979   *Complete Banjo Repair.* New York: Oak Publications.
Sanders, Arthur H.
    1960   "The Banjo Story." *Hobbies* v. 6, n. 5: pp. 33, 47.

Saxton, Alexander
  1975 "Blackface Minstrelsy and Jacksonian Ideology." *American Quarterly* v. 27, n. 1: pp. 3–28.
Schauffler, Robert Haven
  1923 "Jazz May Be Lowbrow, But—." *Collier's* v. 72 (August 25): pp. 10, 20.
Schreyer, Lowell H.
  1985 "The Banjo in Ragtime." In John Edward Hasse, ed., *Ragtime: Its History, Composers, and Music.* New York: Schirmer Books.
Schuller, Gunther
  1968 *Early Jazz: Its Roots and Musical Development.* New York: Oxford University Press.
Seeger, Pete
  1962 *How to Play the 5-String Banjo,* rev. 3rd ed. Published by the author in Beacon, N.Y.
  1972 *The Incomplete Folksinger,* Jo Metcalf Schwartz, ed. New York: Simon and Schuster.
Semple, Ellen Churchill
  1910 "The Anglo-Saxons of the Kentucky Mountains." *Bulletin of the American Geographic Society* v. 42, n. 8: pp. 561–94.
Shapiro, Henry D.
  1978 *Appalachia on Our Mind: The Southern Mountains and Mountaineers in the American Consciousness, 1870–1920.* Chapel Hill: University of North Carolina Press.
Shapiro, Nat, and Nat Hentoff
  1966 *Hear Me Talkin' to Ya.* New York: Dover Publications.
Sharpe, A. P.
  1966 *A Complete Guide to Instruments of the Banjo Family.* London: Clifford Essex Music Co.
Shearin, Hubert G.
  1911 "British Ballads in the Cumberland Mountains." *Sewanee Review* v. 19, n. 3: pp. 313–27.
Shelton, Robert
  1964 "Banjo Bars Plunk Along Here Hoping to Re-create Happy Days." *New York Times,* 3 January.
Shepherd, John, et al.
  1977 *Whose Music? A Sociology of Musical Language.* New Brunswick, N.J.: Transaction Books.
Shi, David E.
  1985 *The Simple Life: Plain Living and High Thinking in American Culture.* New York: Oxford University Press.
Shrubsall, Wayne
  1975 "Ralph Stanley's Banjo Style." *Sing Out!* v. 23, n. 6: pp. 7–8.
  1987 "Banjo as Icon." *Journal of Popular Culture* v. 20, n. 4: pp. 31–54.
Smith, L. Allen
  1983 *A Catalogue of Pre-Revival Appalachian Dulcimers.* Columbia: University of Missouri Press.

Smulyan, Susan Renee
     1985 "'And Now a Word from Our Sponsors . . .': Commercialization of Ameri-
           can Broadcast Radio, 1920–1934." PhD dissertation, Yale University.
Solomon, Barbara Miller
     1956 Ancestors and Immigrants: A Changing New England Tradition. New York:
           John Wiley & Sons, Inc.
Southern, Eileen
     1983 The Music of Black Americans: A History, 2d ed. New York: W. W. Norton
           & Co.
Spaulding, Walter Raymond
     1935 Music at Harvard. New York: Coward-McCann, Inc.
Spitzer, Marian
     1925 "The Lay of the Last Minstrels." Saturday Evening Post v. 197, n. 36: pp.
           12–13, 117.
Stewart's Banjo and Guitar Journal. Philadelphia, 1883–98.
Stewart, Samuel Swain
     1881 Noted Banjo Players. Philadelphia: Stewart, Banjo and Music Depot.
     1886 The Banjo Philosophically. Philadelphia: S. S. Stewart.
     1888 The Banjo: A Dissertation. Philadelphia: S. S. Stewart.
Stringer, Arthur
     1920 "The Drums of Dusk." Hearst's Magazine v. 38, n. 1: pp. 11–13, 72.
Stuckey, Sterling
     1987 Slave Culture: Nationalist Theory and the Foundations of Black America. New
           York: Oxford University Press.
Susman, Warren I.
     1973 Culture as History: The Transformation of American Society in the Twentieth
           Century. New York: Pantheon Books.
Tallmadge, William
     1983 "The Folk Banjo and Clawhammer Performance Practice in the Upper
           South: A Study of Origins." In Barry M. Buxton, ed., The Appalachian
           Experience. Boone, N.C.: Appalachian Consortium Press, pp. 169–79.
Taylor, Julie M.
     1976 "Tango: Theme of Class and Nation." Ethnomusicology v. 20, n. 2: pp.
           273–91.
Taylor, Wesley, and Mitch Whitmore
     1979 "Leonard Webb Makes a Gourd Banjo." Foxfire v. 13, n. 1: pp. 12–
           38.
Taylor, William R.
     1979 Cavalier and Yankee: The Old South and American National Character.
           Cambridge: Harvard University Press.
Thom, William Taylor
     1883 "Some Parallelisms between Shakespeare's English and the Negro-English
           of the United States." Shakespeariana v. 1, n. 2: pp. 129–35.
Thomas, Dorothy
     1934 "That Traipsin' Woman." Independent Woman v. 13, n. 6: pp. 169, 188–89.

Thomas, Jean

    1933   *The Traipsin' Woman.* New York: E. P. Dutton and Co., Inc.

    1944   "How Music Ended a Famous Feud." *Etude* v. 62, n. 2: pp. 96–98.

    1948   "Romeo and Juliet of the Mountains." *Etude* v. 66, n. 6: pp. 345–46, 390.

Thompson, Maurice

    1885   "Hodson's Hide-Out." *Century Magazine* v. 29, n. 5: pp. 678–85.

Tirro, Frank

    1977   *Jazz: A History.* New York: W. W. Norton & Co.

Titon, Jeff Todd

    1977   *Early Downhome Blues: A Musical and Cultural Analysis.* Urbana: University of Illinois Press.

Toll, Robert C.

    1974   *Blacking Up: The Minstrel Show in Nineteenth-Century America.* New York: Oxford University Press.

Trilling, Lionel

    1972   *Sincerity and Authenticity.* Cambridge: Harvard University Press.

Tsumura, Akira

    1984   *Banjos: The Tsumura Collection.* Tokyo: Kodansha International Ltd.

Turner, George Kibbe

    1913   "The Puzzle of the Underworld." *McClures* v. 41 (July): pp. 99–111.

Turner, William H., and Edward J. Cabbell, eds.

    1985   *Blacks in Appalachia.* Lexington: University of Kentucky Press.

Unsigned Articles:

    1888   "How to Build a Banjo." *The Boy's Own Paper* (15 December), reprinted in *Mugwumps* v. 3, n. 2 (March 1972): pp. 23–25.

    1890   "Banjoist Weston Gone." *Morning Journal* (New York), 26 May.

    1903   "The Father of the Banjo." *Music Trade Review* v. 37, n. 13: 33.

    1904   "The Banjo Not Decadent." *Music Trade Review* v. 38, n. 2: 41–42.

    1917   "Rescuing the Folk-Songs." *Literary Digest* v. 54, n. 7: p. 10.

    1917   "Hunting the Lonesome Tune in the Wilds of Kentucky." *Current Opinion* (February): pp. 100–101.

    1919   "Passing of the Minstrels." *Literary Digest* v. 62 (16 August): pp. 28–29.

    1926   "Fiddling to Henry Ford." *Literary Digest* v. 88, n. 1: pp. 33–34, 36, 38.

    1931   "Death of 'Uncle Tom'." *Outlook* v. 157, n. 3: pp. 89–90.

    1932   "Interest Widens in Songs of Folk Origin in the Southern Mountains." *The Musician* v. 37, n. 3: p. 17.

    1936   "Folk-Lore Is Preserved in a Festival." *Literary Digest* v. 122, n. 5: pp. 21–22.

    1941   "Folk Songs in the White House." *Time* v. 37, n. 9: p. 57.

    1942   "Singin' Gatherin'." *Time* v. 39, n. 25: p. 44.

    1943   "Minstrel Shows." *Life* v. 15, n. 1: pp. 80–84.

    1943   "Gentlemen, Be Seated." *Time* v. 42, n. 13: pp. 48, 50.

    1946   "Whoop-and-Holler Opera." *Collier's* v. 117, n. 4: pp. 18, 85.

    1947   "Folk Singers: Mountain People Remember the Old American Music." *Life* v. 23, n. 16: pp. 63–66.

    1948   "Dat Yam Rag." *New Yorker* v. 24, n. 31: pp. 23–24.

1950 "Is It Fair?" *NEA Journal* v. 39, n. 7: p. 485.

1955 "Plinkety-Plunk." *Time* v. 66, n. 5: pp. 30–31.

1955 "Strummin' Up a Banjo Boom." *Life* v. 39, n. 7: 105–6, 108.

1956 "Country Musicians Fiddle Up Roaring Business." *Life* v. 41, n. 21: pp. 137–44, 146.

1956 "Banjo Jam at Yale." *Life* v. 41, n. 22: pp. 193–94.

1960 "Like from Halls of Ivy." *Time* v. 76, n. 2: pp. 56, 61.

1960 "Folk Frenzy." *Time* v. 76, n. 2: p. 81.

1969 "Cadwell's Banjo." *New Yorker* v. 45 (12 April): pp. 39–41.

Walker, Kent

1931 *Staging the Amateur Minstrel Show.* Walker H. Baker Co.

Wallace, Michael

1986 "Visiting the Past: History Museums in the United States." In Susan Porter Benson, Stephen Brier, and Roy Rosenzweig, eds., *Presenting the Past: Essays on History and the Public.* Philadelphia: Temple University Press.

Waller, Altina L.

1988 *Feud: Hatfields, McCoys, and Social Change in Appalachia, 1860–1900.* Chapel Hill: University of North Carolina Press.

Walsh, Jim

1948–49 "Sylvester Louis Ossman, 'The Banjo King'." *Hobbies* v. 53, n. 7: pp. 32–33, 8: pp. 36–37, 9: pp. 31–32, 11: pp. 31–32.

1956 "Fred Van Eps." *Hobbies* v. 60, n. 11: pp. 31–33, 12: pp. 32–36; v. 61, n. 1: pp. 30–35, 2: pp. 29–35.

Warner, Frank

1963 "Frank Proffitt." *Sing Out!* v. 13, n. 4: p. 11.

Warren-Findley, Janelle

1985 "Passports to Change: The Resettlement Administration's Folk Song Sheet Program, 1936–1937." In Jack Salzman, ed., *Prospects: An Annual of American Cultural Studies* v. 10. N.Y.: Cambridge University Press.

Webb, Robert Lloyd

1976 "Banjos on Their Saddle Horns." *American History Illustrated* v. 11, n. 2: pp. 11–20.

1984 *Ring the Banjar! The Banjo in America from Folklore to Factory.* Cambridge: MIT Museum. Published in conjunction with exhibition of the same name, 12 April–29 September 1984, in the MIT Museum Compton Gallery, Cambridge, Mass.

Weissman, Dick

1976 "67 Tunings for the Five-String Banjo." In Larry Sandberg and Dick Weissman, eds., *The Folkmusic Sourcebook.* New York: Alfred A. Knopf, pp. 219–22.

Whisnant, David E.

1979 *Folk Festival Issues.* Los Angeles: J.E.M.F./UCLA

1980 "Finding the Way between the Old and the New: The Mountain Dance and Folk Festival and Bascom Lamar Lunsford's Work as a Citizen." *Appalachian Journal* v. 7, n. 1–2: pp. 135–54.

1983   *All That Is Native and Fine: The Politics of Culture in an American Region.*
        Chapel Hill: University of North Carolina Press.

Williams, Herman K.
1980   *The First Forty Years of the Old Fiddlers Convention: Galax, Virginia.* Published
        by the local Moose Lodge; includes lists of winners and reprints of local
        newspaper accounts.

Williams, Lillian Walker
1904   "In the Kentucky Mountains: Colonial Customs That Are Still Existing in
        That Famous Section of the Country." *New England Magazine* v. 30, n. 1:
        pp. 37–45.

Wilson, Charles Morrow
1929   "Elizabethan America." *Atlantic Monthly* v. 144 (August): pp. 238–44.

Winans, Robert B.
1976   "The Folk, the Stage, and the Five-String Banjo in the Nineteenth Century."
        Journal of American Folklore v. 89, n. 354: pp. 407–37.
1979   "The Black Banjo-Playing Tradition in Virginia and West Virginia." *Journal
        of the Virginia Folklore Society* v. 1: pp. 7–30.

Wodehouse, P. G.
1934   *Thank You, Jeeves.* London: H. Jenkins.

Wolfe, Charles
1981   "The Music of Grandpa Jones." *Journal of Country Music* v. 8, n. 3: pp.
        47–48, 65–82.
1983   "Take Me Back to Renfro Valley." *Journal of Country Music* v. 9, n. 3: pp.
        9–27.

Woodrow, Frank M.
1895–96 *Woodrow and Acker's Standard Directory of Banjo, Guitar and Mandolin
        Artists, Teachers and Composers of the United States and Canada,* vv. 1 and 2.
        Newton, Iowa: Frank M. Woodard and Daniel Acker.

Woodward, A.
1949   "Joel Sweeney and the First Banjo." *Los Angeles County Museum Quarterly*
        v. 2, n. 3: pp. 7–11.

Woodward, C. Vann
1951   *Origins of the New South, 1877–1913.* Baton Rouge: Louisiana State Univer-
        sity Press.
1974   *The Strange Career of Jim Crow,* 3rd rev. ed. New York: Oxford University
        Press.

Zolotow, Maurice
1944   "Hillbilly Boom." *Saturday Evening Post* v. 216, n. 33: pp. 22–23, 36, 38.

Index

Books in the Series
Music in American Life

Only a Miner: Studies in Recorded Coal-Mining Songs
Archie Green

Great Day Coming: Folk Music and the American Left
R. Serge Denisoff

John Philip Sousa: A Descriptive Catalog of His Works
Paul E. Bierley

The Hell-Bound Train: A Cowboy Songbook
Glenn Ohrlin

Oh, Didn't He Ramble: The Life Story of Lee Collins
as Told to Mary Collins
Edited by Frank J. Gillis and John W. Miner

American Labor Songs of the Nineteenth Century
Philip S. Foner

Stars of Country Music: Uncle Dave Macon to Johnny Rodriguez
Edited by Bill C. Malone and Judith McCulloh

Git Along, Little Dogies: Songs and Songmakers of the American West
John I. White

A Texas-Mexican *Cancionero*: Folksongs of the Lower Border
Americo Paredes

San Antonio Rose: The Life and Music of Bob Wills
Charles R. Townsend

Early Downhome Blues: A Musical and Cultural Analysis
Jeff Todd Titon

An Ives Celebration: Papers and Panels of the Charles Ives
Centennial Festival-Conference
Edited by H. Wiley Hitchcock and Vivian Perlis

Sinful Tunes and Spirituals: Black Folk Music to the Civil War
Dena J. Epstein

Joe Scott, the Woodsman-Songmaker
Edward D. Ives

Jimmie Rodgers: The Life and Times of America's Blue Yodeler
Nolan Porterfield

Early American Music Engraving and Printing: A History
of Music Publishing in America from 1787 to 1825
with Commentary on Earlier and Later Practices
Richard J. Wolfe

Sing a Sad Song: The Life of Hank Williams
Roger M. Williams

Long Steel Rail: The Railroad in American Folksong
Norm Cohen

Resources of American Music History: A Directory of Source Materials
from Colonial Times to World War II
D. W. Krummel, Jean Geil, Doris J. Dyen, and Deane L. Root

Tenement Songs: The Popular Music of the Jewish Immigrants
Mark Slobin
Ozark Folksongs
Vance Randolph; edited and abridged by Norm Cohen

Oscar Sonneck and American Music
Edited by William Lichtenwanger

Bluegrass Breakdown: The Making of the Old Southern Sound
Robert Cantwell

Bluegrass: A History
Neil V. Rosenberg

Music at the White House: A History of the American Spirit
Elise K. Kirk

Red River Blues: The Blues Tradition in the Southeast
Bruce Bastin

Good Friends and Bad Enemies: Robert Winslow Gordon
and the Study of American Folksong
Debora Kodish

Fiddlin' Georgia Crazy: Fiddlin' John Carson, His Real World,
and the World of His Songs
Gene Wiggins

America's Music: From the Pilgrims to the Present,
Revised Third Edition
Gilbert Chase

Secular Music in Colonial Annapolis: The Tuesday Club, 1745-56
John Barry Talley

Bibliographical Handbook of American Music
D. W. Krummel

Goin' to Kansas City
Nathan W. Pearson, Jr.

"Susanna," "Jeanie," and "The Old Folks at Home": The Songs of
Stephen C. Foster from His Time to Ours
Second Edition
William W. Austin

Songprints: The Musical Experience of Five Shoshone Women
Judith Vander

"Happy in the Service of the Lord": Afro-American Gospel
Quartets in Memphis
Kip Lornell

Paul Hindemith in the United States
Luther Noss

"My Song Is My Weapon": People's Songs, American Communism,
and the Politics of Culture
Robbie Lieberman

Chosen Voices: The Story of the American Cantorate
Mark Slobin

Theodore Thomas: America's Conductor and Builder
of Orchestras, 1835-1905
Ezra Schabas

"The Whorehouse Bells Were Ringing" and
Other Songs Cowboys Sing
Guy Logsdon

Crazeology: The Autobiography of a Chicago Jazzman
Bud Freeman, as Told to Robert Wolf

Discoursing Sweet Music: Town Bands and Community Life in
Turn-of-the-Century Pennsylvania
Kenneth Kreitner

Mormonism and Music: A History
Michael Hicks

Voices of the Jazz Age: Profiles of Eight Vintage Jazzmen
Chip Deffaa

Pickin' on Peachtree: A History of Country Music in Atlanta, Georgia
Wayne W. Daniel

Bitter Music: Collected Journals, Essays, Introductions, and Librettos
Harry Partch; edited by Thomas McGeary